ZEN ODYSSEY

ZEN ODYSSEY

*The Story of Sokei-an, Ruth Fuller Sasaki,
and the Birth of Zen in America*

Janica Anderson and
Steven Zahavi Schwartz

Forewords by Sean Murphy and Joan Watts

Wisdom Publications
199 Elm Street
Somerville, MA 02144 USA
wisdompubs.org

Library of Congress Cataloging-in-Publication Data

Names: Anderson, Janica, author. | Schwartz, Steven Z., author.
Title: Zen odyssey / Janica Anderson and Steven Zahavi Schwartz.
Description: Somerville, MA : Wisdom Publications, 2018. | Includes bibliographical
  references. |
Identifiers: LCCN 2017023336 (print) | LCCN 2017045140 (ebook) | ISBN 9781614292746
  (ebook) | ISBN 1614292744 (ebook) | ISBN 9781614292586 (pbk. : alk. paper) | ISBN
  1614292582 (pbk. : alk. paper)
Subjects: LCSH: Sasaki, Ruth Fuller, 1892-1967. | Sasaki, Shigetsu, 1882-1945. | Zen
  Buddhists—Japan—Biography. | Zen Buddhists—United States—Biography. | Zen priests—
  Japan—Biography. | Zen priests—United States—Biography. | Zen Buddhism—United
  States—History.
Classification: LCC BQ843 (ebook) | LCC BQ843 .A354 2018 (print) | DDC 294.3/927092
  [B] —dc23
LC record available at https://lccn.loc.gov/2017023336

ISBN 978-1-61429-258-6   ebook ISBN 978-1-61429-274-6

22 21 20 19 18   5 4 3 2 1

Cover design by Philip Pascuzzo. Interior design by Tony Lulek. Set in Sabon Lt Std 10.5/16.

Wisdom Publications' books are printed on acid-free paper and meet the guidelines for permanence and durability of the Production Guidelines for Book Longevity of the Council on Library Resources.

♻ This book was produced with environmental mindfulness.
For more information, please visit wisdompubs.org/wisdom-environment.

Printed in the United States of America.

Please visit fscus.org.

Contents

FOREWORD
by Sean Murphy

Although it's not as widely known as it ought to be, the first American known to experience satori, one of the first to ordain as a monastic in the Japanese Zen tradition, and the first to become abbot of a Japanese temple was a woman: Ruth Fuller Everett (later Fuller Sasaki). The first acknowledged Zen master to live and teach in America and "bury his bones" here was Sokei-an Sasaki. In a remarkable case of—what? synchronicity? karma?— the two met and became, first, collaborators and, later, husband and wife.

This important book of Zen "firsts" provides, for the first time, the full story of these key figures in the unfolding of Zen in America, in a colorfully readable and engaging narrative of East meeting West—a meeting that, as of this writing, has blossomed into a marriage in its own right.

If not for these two pioneers, and their partnership, Zen might never have taken root in the West—a feat that, in Sokei-an's words, was "like holding a lotus to a rock." As one of the many who have walked in their footsteps in the years since, I owe them a great debt of gratitude. That gratitude extends now to the existence of this fine book. Nine bows to Janica Anderson and Steven

Zahavi Schwartz for their excellent work in bringing these Zen pioneers to the eyes of a new generation.

Sean Murphy, author of *One Bird, One Stone:*
108 Contemporary Zen Stories

FOREWORD

by Joan Watts

Ruth Fuller (Everett) Sasaki was a study in contrasts and contradictions.

I knew her as Granny Ruth. During the era of this story, I was a young child, and Granny lived in a brownstone on the east side of Manhattan in what would be considered high style. When she traveled to see us in Evanston, Illinois, her visits always brought much excitement for me and my sister, Anne. She'd arrive, having taken the Pullman sleeper from New York to Chicago, and would be deposited by taxi on our doorstep wearing hat, gloves, furs, and sensible shoes, and with a full set of Mark Cross luggage. Her hugs and kisses were punctuated by her signature scent of violets and freshly powered cheeks. She always brought gifts that would delight us. When we visited her in New York City, we'd be treated to trips to FAO Schwarz, museums, ice cream parlors, the ballet, and the Rockettes at Radio City Music Hall.

We'd also amuse ourselves in her amazing five-story home. Once inside, off the hustle and bustle of city streets, the ambiance was quiet and elegant. I remember spending hours exploring the various rooms. The first floor had an entry and dining room, main kitchen, and an elevator, which we loved to ride instead of mounting the sweeping stairway to upper floors.

There, for us, the mysterious began. On the second floor was the meditation hall (*zendo*) of the Buddhist Society of America, where people came and went, sitting in the darkened hall for hours. We'd hear occasional chanting, gongs reverberating, and clappers clapping. The scent of incense hung heavily in the air. A large library opposite the zendo had a grand piano, shelves to the ceiling with hundreds of volumes including Zen texts in Chinese and Japanese, chintz-covered sofas on either side of a large fireplace, and Asian art objects including a beautifully painted Japanese screen. There was even a kitchenette where tea was made for students and guests. Behind that was an incredible laundry room with a floor-to-ceiling dryer where freshly washed clothes were hung to dry.

The third floor had two large suites. One was Granny Ruth's bedroom, with large oak beds made of sixteenth-century English choir stalls, Granny's vanity, a wall of closets, and a bathroom. The other suite was Sokei-an's room and their combined study. There was a beautiful carved red-and-gold lacquer bed from Beijing where Sokei-an slept. His bathroom was decorated with a pine forest motif, and it was stocked with his favorite pine-tar soap.

The fourth floor was a guest apartment with a living room and small kitchen, two bedrooms, and an outdoor patio with huge ceramic foo dogs. The fifth floor was the servants' apartment, occupied by Lawrence the butler, a gracious man, and Kitty the cook, Lawrence's pretty wife. Several other servants lived "out."

Sokei-an Sasaki was a wonderfully peaceful man. Everything he did was carefully executed or quietly spoken. I sensed Granny and Sokei-an were very devoted, that she would move heaven and earth for him, that he was indebted to her for her help. Together they continued his mission to translate medieval Chinese Zen texts.

I remember Sokei-an giving lectures in the zendo. I remember him eating a breakfast of applesauce with cinnamon, served by Lawrence in the main dining room, with Chaka, his beautiful cat, sitting by his side. I remember students coming and going from the zendo and library, quietly discussing their studies and the war. I remember Sokei-an's internment, Granny's despair and fear, and his release from prison and his illness.

What I remember most was his death. My mother brought me with her to New York on the overnight train—me with my favorite teddy bear. I remember the hush and sadness permeating the entire household. I remember attending services in the zendo honoring those who died in the bombing of Hiroshima and Nagasaki. I remember that after his death I slept in his bed during visits. I remember pondering his death mask, beautiful and peaceful, which hung over the fireplace in the room that was now only Granny's study. I played with the index cards, colored pens, pencils, and paper clips on her desk; Chaka wandered through rooms and basked in the sunlight on a windowsill.

After Granny Ruth returned to Japan, determined to finish the translation work that was Sokei-an's mission and to continue her studies, I lived at her small subtemple, Ryosen-an, for a year in the late 1950s. I watched the construction of the library and zendo and the creation of the gardens. A large pine tree was carefully balled and moved to make room for the zendo.

Ruth was in her element, directing household staff and scholars, and entertaining guests from around the world, serving up delicious Japanese and American meals for appreciative guests, knees akimbo as they sat on the dining room tatami. She made amazing apple pies. After dinner she would smoke her Benson & Hedges cigarettes and regale guests with stories of past travels, including trips she made on the Orient Express across Europe, Russia, and

China, during which she was served Beluga caviar in a large bowl of crushed ice.

The simple Japanese-style home had no running hot water, no bathroom plumbing (farmers collected the waste for their fields), no central heating—it was a damp, raw cold in the winters with only braziers to warm one's cold hands and feet. She slept on a futon on the tatami under heavy quilts. Her room was also her study, where she sat on a *zabuton* at her desk, with countless index cards of Chinese characters, their meaning carefully noted; dictionaries; volumes of Chinese Zen texts; and a typewriter. At the end of the day, she would invite visitors and scholars to join her for a martini with *rakyo*, her favorite pickled onion with just a touch of sweetness. She tolerated the hot, humid summers and monsoons. She still maintained some of her creature comforts— tweed suits, cashmere sweater sets, silk blouses, and Rubinstein cosmetics, which she periodically ordered from Bergdorf Good- man. In the summer she wore thin cotton dresses. She always wore her pearl earrings.

During this time she was officially ordained a priest at the head temple in Daitoku-ji and was named abbess of Ryosen-an, a remarkable feat for a foreigner, let alone a woman.

Granny Ruth was without a doubt a driven woman, exceptional in her abilities to take on challenges. She accomplished most of what she wanted in life, but not without ruffling some feathers and making a few enemies along the way. There were those who doubted her loving relationship with Sokei-an, who were jealous of her abilities, and who condemned her wealth. However, her contribution to the understanding of Rinzai Zen is unequivocal. In many ways, I considered her an intellectually pure student and practitioner of the subject, while my father, Alan Watts, also a scholar and a driving force for the interest in Buddhism in the

United States, was primarily a popularizer of the subject. Her writings and translations will undoubtedly endure for generations to come.

My sister, Anne Watts, my half-brother, Michael Gamer, and I are indebted to Janica Anderson for her years of research into the lives of Ruth and Sokei-an. This book has been a tremendous effort on her part and will certainly be appreciated, not only by our family for generations to come but also by those students of Zen who will, as a result of this book, turn to Ruth's writings and translations in collaboration with Sokei-an and others in order to pursue the subject on deeper levels.

Joan Watts
Livingston, Montana

COMING HOME TO A STRANGE HOUSE
Nanzen-ji temple, Kyoto, Japan, April–August 1932

No one like her had ever been inside the *zendo* before, this shadowy world of silence and precision. The monks were walking in before her, slowly but deliberately, with not a motion wasted, taking their positions for the evening meditation. Ruth carefully followed Eizan, the senior monk assigned to assist her, observing each detail of his entry into the hall, bowing where he bowed, pausing where he paused, finding the place set for her on a *zafu* in the back of the hall as silently as possible. It was very important to observe the protocol exactly—especially to not disrupt the practice of the others.

She understood that each meditator, as still as a statue, was focused exclusively on his own personal inner practice, as she herself had been focused, separately, over the past month of intensive training since arriving in Japan. One morning she had experienced an unusual moment in her meditation, and not long after the monks had invited her to join them in the zendo—for a single night. And now, for the first time ever, someone like her—no, not someone *like* her, only *she herself*, Ruth Fuller Everett—was entering the inner world reserved for the monks.

A single dim electric light cast shadows of the monks against the *shoji* screen that divided the hall. The thin glow and the shadows on the screen awakened something in her—something alien, unnamable, a whispered hint of some ancient mystery, but also somehow deeply familiar. The whole thing was utterly strange. And yet she felt she had come home.

This arrival, this entry into the hidden world of Zen, was entirely unexpected. But it was why Ruth had come to Japan. It had been a difficult process, but it was the sort of challenge she was built for. Really, all it took was undying determination. And, as her mother had never tired of reminding her, she had plenty of that. She could sit still for hours, days if necessary, if that was the path to—what? Enlightenment? *Satori, kensho*—many of the texts Ruth had immersed herself in treated *that* experience as central. An interesting psychological experience indeed.

Nanshinken Roshi sometimes dropped hints. If he would talk about it at all—which he mostly wouldn't—he might call it a breakthrough, a glimpse of seeing into things as they are. But it was barely an insinuation, made in the midst of drinking tea or preparing winter squash. She found it difficult to reconcile this seemingly offhand attitude with the military-like discipline that made his temple sparkle. His manner was a combination of hard and soft that was unlike anything in her experience. Either way, he seemed allergic to explanations: "Work hard. Work harder. Practice with strong effort and perhaps something will happen."

Well, something did happen—after only a month in Japan. She had been doing her *zazen* in the little house across from the temple—not in the absurd, bright green upholstered Morris chair her hosts had graciously provided, which would kick out into a full recliner with horrifying speed if you happened to hit the pearl buttons a certain way, but properly, on a zafu and *zabuton* set on the floor. She sat alone, apart from the monks in their zendo, which was still forbidden to her. When the glimpse of a deeper reality arrived—not unbidden, but after giving up on layers of preconceptions, waiting, giving up on waiting, returning to the koan, becoming exasperated with the koan—she felt it merited communicating.

She did her best to explain this interesting experience to her interpreter, who wrote it down in Japanese. The next morning Ruth had the note taken to Nanshinken.

She hadn't been back in the little house for long when Roshi clattered at the back door and came running in, wearing his white under-kimono, excitedly waving the note. "This is what I've been waiting for, this is what I've been waiting for!" he said in Japanese that Ruth, even at that rudimentary stage in her learning, understood directly.

Later that day the interpreter came to explain the situation. "Roshi asked the monks to let you sit in the zendo. They will not allow it—they are absolutely opposed. It is against the regulations of Nanzen-ji for a woman to sit, and they will not allow it."

It was late April. On the first of May, the summer *osesshin*, the intensive practice period, was about to begin. Preparations were in full swing, with monks getting the temple ready for hundreds of visitors in addition to the forty-seven monks who would squeeze into the *sodo*. Ruth was satisfied expecting to continue her own practice outside, in the little house Nanshinken had built as his personal temple. She had made her breakthrough; it didn't matter so much which building she sat in. Anyway, there was no room in the sodo, which had been built to seat thirty-six. Those who would not fit in the sodo would be placed in the *hondo*, the main temple building. Except for Ruth, who was not invited inside.

The first two days of the osesshin were devoted to services and to feeding all of the temple supporters, some two thousand people. The place was crowded with lay visitors, students, and local dignitaries bringing offerings and partaking of ceremonial meals. In the midst of all this, one of the senior monks, who spoke some English, crossed the road to visit Ruth. "The monks are asking you to sit one night with them. Please come at seven o'clock and sit until half past nine." So. What changed? Did Nanshinken persuade them to let her in?

It was still rather cold for the first of May, and she had no special clothes—the fashion of the day favored very tight skirts, which would not be acceptable. Her assistant Kato-san figured out something for her to wear: Ruth had a dark Chinese silk robe that they agreed would be suitable, with a black velvet coat to keep her warm.

Convincing Warren this trip to Japan was necessary had been an ordeal, but not really more so than the day-to-day negotiations of their contentious household. A more traditional, submissive wife would not even have considered the undertaking in the first place—or at least would have approached her spouse more gingerly, to ask permission. But most of the women in Ruth's circles pursued studies and activities to make themselves interesting, sometimes to promote important social causes. They had gotten the vote, after all—and not by asking permission of their husbands.

But however serious these personal pursuits, Ruth felt that ultimately they were not as important as her project—her mission—clearly was. It was not simply for her own sake that she was compelled to move forward. She considered herself a scientist, a researcher who might discover a cure for the malaise she witnessed in the world all around her—or perhaps not discover something new so much as receive, translate, convey an ancient, well-known solution back to her own land, as Bodhidharma (known as Daruma to the Japanese) had carried the Buddha's awakening from India to China fifteen centuries ago. She saw a way to replenish a grave deficit in her own culture. Ruth did not ask permission; it was her right. In fact, if she were qualified, which she presumed she was, it was her responsibility.

They had taken a three-month, first-class trip through Japan, Korea, and China—purely for pleasure—two years earlier, in 1930. Much of the world was reeling from the hard times everywhere, but the Everett fortunes were barely touched.

The trip had been a family sightseeing tour with twelve-year-old Eleanor and her governess. Warren had been taken with the geishas, who bowed and kneeled before him with sake and *shamisen* music, and with the cormorant fishing, still being practiced though already with a hint of anachronism. They had all been enraptured by the beautiful music of pigeons in Peking flying in flocks of fifty or more with whistles tied to their tails, and bemused by the noisome "honey carts" with their casks of human manure slowing progress on the roads. Ruth had managed in varying ways to satisfy her deep and ever-growing interest in Buddhism, which Warren tolerated—how could he do otherwise?—or rather indulged, as he would put it. He did not, could not, really recognize the depth of her seriousness. Strangely, or perhaps not so strangely, Nanshinken was the one who could see that right away.

Was it a good marriage? Warren was a good man. Marrying him had maintained her position in that class of people for whom the Depression was something one merely read about in the morning paper. He was twenty years her senior, and he exercised his will with the authority of someone accustomed to being in charge. He was a bully as a lawyer, and at home. But she had nerves of steel and could withstand his outbursts.

In 1923, Warren had sent them to Nyack, New York, for their safety; he was prosecuting Al Capone's henchmen and worried about kidnappings. It was in Nyack where she first became acquainted with yoga and Indian philosophy, at Pierre Bernard's retreat. Warren's worldly precautions were not without positive consequences.

He was getting more difficult, though. Any little thing might set him off. Politics. A tennis partner stood him up. A package did not arrive on time. Eleanor, still a child in so many ways at thirteen, tearful and terrified by his shouts as he instructed her on driving the Packard convertible. One of his clerks misfiled a brief—it could be recovered, with some effort, but it cost the clerk his job, poor fellow. And Ruth had to hear about it for days afterward.

Even if Warren's anger was not always justified, there was a pattern. Of course it was all to do with being crippled from polio. For the crime of being imperfect he had been bullied relentlessly as a boy. So he made sure he could beat anyone. It was usually some violation of his high standards that set him off—some perceived violation, at least. That was something she and Warren did have in common. Not the outbursts, but the standards. She was a stickler for details. If something was out of place, it had to be made right, even if she would not dream of berating and cursing the way Warren did so readily.

Nanshinken was exemplary in that regard. Everything here at his temple was just so, and accomplished through respect and devotion, because of his commanding yet somehow gentle presence. Of course the monks applied themselves with unfailing self-discipline. And sometimes he did shout at them.

Perhaps that sense of order and discipline was one of the reasons she felt at home in this zendo—even at ease, though of course *ease* was not the right word. Nothing about it was at all easy. And yet . . . So often people think of order as being restrictive, tying up their hands—as if they knew some better way to do things. But she could see through that. It was just laziness. Really, when everything was taken care of correctly, that's what made the real work possible. And what was that work, precisely? This. Sitting here, in this precisely composed place. Striving to penetrate the koan.

Nanshinken was different; he really was full of ease, taking visible, noticeable delight in the midst of the military rigor. And he was not in the least concerned that his robes were five sizes too large—practically a tent over him, a man of small physique. That disregard for his vestments was one of the things that endeared him to Ruth. And actually, even if the robes were a misfit for his body physically, they were a true fit for his being. He had the *nyoi*, the ceremonial baton, that Hakuin himself had used, passed down through eight generations of Dharma transmission to Nanshinken Roshi, the living embodiment of the Buddha's enlightenment in the present. Could the robes possibly be that old as well? They certainly had belonged to Dokutan Sosan Roshi, Nanshinken's teacher, who inherited them from his teacher Tankai Gensho Roshi. Three generations, maybe more, of sweating Zen masters. Good enough for them, good enough for him. Nothing to waste a moment of precious attention on.

The first trip to Japan had been exciting and enjoyable, and educational in its own way. She had planned it, made all the arrangements, written to family friends and especially Warren's business contacts—with associates all over the world, meeting with the likes of Chiang Kai-shek's ministers, one might imagine he worked

for the Department of State. Of course their American friends had
warned them of all manner of hazards and hostilities, but the
whole thing had come off smooth as clockwork, delightful and
diverting as much as anything.

It had been her idea. They had been to Europe several times;
she had spent the previous ten years or more—really since Eleanor
came, and then certainly after the miscarriage—deeply immersed
in her studies of Buddhism and Indian philosophy, going so far
as to learn Sanskrit and Pali to read sutras in the original. Her
studies always had to be late at night, since Warren dominated
the dinner table with his own discourses and insisted on reserv-
ing the evening for family time or entertaining guests. The tour,
of course, had to be a family trip, which meant in a way it was
more Warren's trip. Not that he begrudged the visits to temples
and receptions with Zen priests—not in the least. Rather, he put
them in the same category as the special invitations they received
to see the Imperial Palace in Kyoto and the Forbidden City—
though perhaps not quite as special as those—a rare privilege but
well deserved by someone of his stature. However, he found the
exoticism of a three-hour meal of raw fish served by geishas or a
day spent watching the cormorant fishing more noteworthy than
conversations about meditation.

In fact, the introduction that had been most crucial for Ruth
barely registered with Warren. Toward the end of their stay, their
Chicago friend William McGinnis, who had lived in Kyoto for
many years—and who was interested in Buddhism, and had even
published a book called *Introduction to Mahayana Buddhism*—
brought her to meet Dr. Daisetz Teitaro Suzuki and his wife,
Beatrice Lane Suzuki. Ruth already knew this D. T. Suzuki by
reputation, having found some of his early writings on Zen in
English, and was intrigued. As her study of Buddhism had deep-

ened over the years, through the texts of both Theravada and Mahayana persuasions, she felt a growing sense of disappointment that the original insight of the Buddha had become cluttered, encumbered with precepts and details that had little to do with its essence; it was not until she came to Zen that she found the simple, eloquent truth reestablished.

All her life Ruth had been determined to go deeper into things, under the veils of this commonplace life that occupied most everyone—that occupied her most of the time. But she had always seen beyond, sensed and known there was something beneath the surface. In her twenties when she first encountered writings from the East, she felt an immediate recognition, a flash of discovery. The Buddha's awakening was not merely a story: It was approachable, available. It was practical. And Ruth was a highly practical person.

At forty years old, in many ways Ruth was already an expert on the subject of Buddhism. But as much as she studied and understood, her knowledge was still from the outside; without practical training from within the living source, it would remain so. This is what tugged at her. With Dr. Suzuki that afternoon, she felt she was finally meeting someone who could receive her full intention, and it came naturally to say to him, "I consider that the core of Buddhism is meditation. The Zen school calls itself the meditation school. If you would be so kind as to instruct me in this method of meditation that the Zen school teaches, I am convinced that with faithful practice, it will eventually lead me to the fulfillment of the Buddha's Buddhism for myself."

Over the next few days, Dr. Suzuki showed Ruth the basics of sitting practice and how to handle her mind in meditation. He gave her a copy of his book *Essays on Zen Buddhism: First Series*. "All this is very well," he said, "but if you really want to learn Zen meditation, you should come back to Japan for a more extended stay. You would find more benefit in three or four months of practice here than in years of working on your own."

Ruth, on her second trip to Japan, 1930.
Courtesy of the estate of Ruth Fuller Sasaki.

The Suzukis took Ruth to Empuku-ji temple in Yawata, just outside of Kyoto, where they had helped Kozuki Tesshu Roshi establish a small dormitory and meditation cave for foreigners to practice zazen. She could envision herself coming back to this place, meditating in this cave. But that was not to be: soon after the visit, Kozuki Roshi was killed in an automobile accident. His successor was not interested in training foreigners.

A year and a half later, after Ruth had spent sixteen days alone on the *Asama Maru* crossing the Pacific from Seattle, Mr. Ikeda was there to meet her at the dock in Yokohama. A business associate of Warren's, he had been their guide in Japan when they traveled as a family. She was relieved to see him. Not that she had really doubted he would come, but you can never be entirely certain. They exchanged their greetings, friendly and cordial, not particularly formal—after all, they had previously traveled in each other's company for several weeks.

After seeing to the entry paperwork and her valises and steamer trunks, Ikeda brought her to a waiting area. There was Dr. Suzuki. He greeted her a bit stiffly and immediately apologized: "Please forgive me. I'm very sorry, but Daitoku-ji temple will not have you."

During Ruth's months away, as she corresponded with Dr. Suzuki, he had arranged for her to stay at Koto-in, a subtemple of Daitoku-ji, where Ueda Gizan Roshi had some rooms set aside. It had sounded definite. But now that was off, and with no explanation, just this slightly awkward apology from Dr. Suzuki. What could she do? She had come all this way. Of course nothing was certain. But still. She had to have a real Zen master. As much as she respected Dr. Suzuki, it would not be enough simply to stay with him and his American wife. "Please do not worry," Dr. Suzuki said. "I will see if Nanshinken Roshi will take you."

Mrs. Suzuki had already arranged for Kato-san to keep house for Ruth, and for a young Japanese man, an English student of hers named Oguri-san, to act as interpreter and secretary.

After some searching they were able to find a beautiful house on the Kamo River in Kyoto, and Ruth moved in there.

On a cold but bright afternoon at the beginning of April, an American woman, accompanied by a Japanese gentleman wearing traditional ceremonial dress, paused as they crossed the bridge over Lake Biwa Canal to gaze at the cherry trees along the bank, which were beginning to scatter their pale pink petals onto the breeze-ruffled waters. After an unspoken moment they turned and headed up the long avenue lined with *sugi*, the graceful and stately Japanese cedar trees that delineate the path to the outer gate of Nanzen-ji temple.

As they entered the grounds, two monks, still wearing their heavy winter robes, stopped as they passed the visitors and bowed deep and low. Clearly the gentleman, at least, was familiar to them. The visitors bowed in return, then paused for a moment at a stone bridge that arched over a lotus pool where the plants were still brown and withered from winter frosts. What if the answer is no?

They passed through a low gateway in the first wall, then turned to the left to take the road to the main temple.

Where the sunlight filtered between the giant sugi, tiny new maple leaves made dancing shadows on the wide dirt path. The man and woman climbed the broad steps of the great gray Mountain Gate and passed under its wide, curving roofs. Before them the open doors of the large red-lacquered building revealed an inner darkness that even at a distance was relieved by the golden gleam of huge figures on the high altar; but rather than enter, they again turned to the left.

Long, sloping roofs of a group of buildings were visible over the top of a white wall that stretched back into pine woods to the north and up a slope to the east. In the middle of the wall the main doors of a tile-roofed gate were wide open, as if in expectation of their coming. The gravel paths beyond the gate showed marks of being freshly swept with a twig brush; stone blocks at the entry-way of the main building within the enclosure were not yet quite dry from a recent washing.

The paper shoji doors of the building were pushed aside, but the place appeared deserted. On the entrance stone the gentleman stepped out of his immaculate *geta* sandals with their white leather straps and, standing on the shining boards of the veranda, he clapped his hands and called out sharply, "Tadaima!"

Immediately the sound of bare feet running accompanied the sight of two young monks, heads newly shaven, wearing their best blue robes, who kneeled in welcome on the pale *tatami* of the inner room. The lady, struggling to untie the knots of her shoelaces, could not return their salutations with anything approximating grace. The monks waited with a calm, natural dignity, not showing the least annoyance at her predicament, until the cumbersome Western shoes had been arranged in order by the side of the white-strapped getas.

Then they made a hand gesture that, if the lady had been at home, would have meant *Go away!* but in Japan was a cordial invitation to follow. They led the way down tatami-covered corridors, along verandas bordering peaceful old gardens, and then into a medium-size room, the reception room, which had been prepared for their coming.

Here again the shoji had been thrust wide open to the sunshine and the gardens. Two cushions were arranged in the seats of honor near the *tokonoma*, which displayed a black-and-white painting of Kannon, the Buddhist goddess of mercy, and a simple arrangement of pine branches. In one corner of the room was a painted screen with a pattern obliterated by time, except for some faint golden glimmers. Another cushion was placed opposite the first two, with a large, thin book covered with purple and silver brocade alongside it.

After a few moments composing herself, the woman stole a glance around the room. She saw in the opposite corner an item of furniture that seemed absurdly out of place: a Morris chair, upholstered in bright green velour, its red mahogany arms dotted with pearl buttons. What was this beautiful monstrosity doing in a Japanese Zen Buddhist temple?

Again they heard the soft, quick pattering of feet in the corridor. In the open doorway stood a short, thin, elderly man; his head and face were closely shaven. He was wearing a long, coarse, dun-colored robe that seemed to have been made for someone several sizes larger than he was and appeared at least as old as the wizened man inside it. Around his neck a sort of bib of old brocaded stuff hung almost to his waist. On his feet were white wool tabi socks. He bowed, but not so low as the lady and gentleman, who hid their faces completely as they bowed their heads to the floor three times in strict ceremonial fashion. With a short, quick gesture the priest motioned them to take their places on the cushions facing him.

Once all were seated, he and the gentleman exchanged greetings in curt, terse-phrased Japanese.

The two young monks reappeared, with red lacquer cups of tea poised high on red lacquer stands and plates of thin, dry rice cakes. The guests sipped the tea and set their cups down. With a penetrating gaze, the old priest scrutinized the lady's face. He turned to speak to the scholar, and the lady in turn scrutinized the face of the priest: a rugged face, weathered by seventy years, but at the same time young and bright. The lips were thin and straight; the chin firm, slightly protruding. On each side of the mouth were deep lines running down from the nostrils—lines she would come to recognize as belonging to the face of practically every longtime practitioner of Zen—but it was the eyes of the priest that intrigued her most. They had such life showing in them, such vitality as the lady had never seen before, and which she would see only again in another man who had also accomplished what this priest had accomplished. A kind face, but a face of energy and of will.

After some exchange of words the scholar turned to the lady and, in her own language, told her that the roshi had agreed to accept her as a pupil.

Then Kono Mukai, Nanshinken Roshi, master of this grand and ancient temple complex and of the entire Nanzen-ji branch of Rinzai temples, addressed Ruth directly. With Dr. Suzuki as interpreter, he said, "Of course you can't sit in the zendo. And you can't do much in your own house, where you have servants and other distractions. I have a personal temple here, across the road, which I built some years ago and where I will live when I retire. Nobody lives in it—you're welcome to have it. I would like you to come to the house every day and do nothing but zazen all day long. If you come at nine in the morning I will give you the key. You can bring a *bento* for lunch. You are to sit zazen there all day long, and at five or six o'clock you can bring the key to me and go home. Please do not bring any books with you."

That's all she was to do. Nanshinken didn't talk about her coming to him for *sanzen*, the face-to-face, being-to-being meeting between master and student that is central to Rinzai Zen. He said, "Now I will give you a koan." He brought out his *Mumonkan* (*The Gateless Gate*) and read the first koan, in Japanese. Dr. Suzuki translated: "A monk asked Joshu, 'Does a dog have buddha nature?' Joshu replied, '*Mu!*'"

Ruth asked, "Why do you give me a koan? You don't know whether I'm ready."

Nanshinken replied, "I think you're ready. Anyway, you begin

with this." He showed her how he sat and how he breathed, and
how to handle the koan.

Six days a week she did as he said. At nine in the morning she
went to his *inryo* to get the key for the little house. He usually
insisted on having her join him for tea. Then she would take the
key and go across the road. And she would sit. She had a couple of
zabutons—he said she must sit *seiza*, ladies' fashion, kneeling. Her
assistant Kato-san, whose husband had been a priest at Nanzen-ji
before he died, suggested she sit with a couple of little cushions
under her. That was the way she practiced.

She was to do nothing except sit and breathe, and when her legs
got tired, she could walk up and down in the garden; that was all.
Once in a while Roshi would send a monk over with some food
or to clean the yard. At those times the monk would stop and talk
with Ruth. But otherwise, for six days a week that first month, she
did nothing except sit and breathe.

At her house on the Kamo, Ruth followed practically the same
regime. She got up at five every morning. From five until seven she
did zazen. Then she got dressed, had breakfast, and at half past
eight left for Nanzen-ji, usually taking a taxi in the morning for the
three or four miles from the house to the temple. She was there all
day—she would have tea and a bento lunch of sandwiches, soup,
or something she could fix on a *hibachi* herself. At night she would
walk home, for the exercise. Then after taking her bath she would
go sit again until midnight. She allowed herself five hours of sleep
a night.

After a month of this routine, wrestling with her koan, something broke open in her mind, and the monks invited her inside
their temple.

That first night in the zendo—the one night she was allowed to be there—she sat with fortitude and vigor, not expecting anything. In awe at simply being present in this mysterious, foreign place, she found the hours passed easily.

At the end of the evening Eizan came up to her as she got off the *tan*, the sitting platform, and said, "You sat very well tonight." He repeated, "You sat very well—will you come tomorrow night?" Of course she was delighted.

The second night Ruth went again at seven o'clock. Soon after she situated herself on the zafu, the old roshi came in and stood in the doorway. He quickly scanned the room, and with dark eyes blazing he began shouting, sharply, louder than she could have imagined. The force of his angry voice, barking and bellowing—this small-bodied giant—was enough to make Ruth tremble.

At the time she didn't know what he said. She found out later: he said everybody's morning sanzen had been terrible, and therefore there would be no sanzen that night. There would be no walking, no breaks. They would sit straight through. Ruth, as everyone, had to sit two and a half hours without moving. The pain was excruciating. To keep from fainting, all she could do was watch where the reflection of the weak electric light hit the black stone floor. As long as she could see that, she wasn't falling off the *tan*.

Nobody moved all night, until they stopped at nine thirty. They had to lift Ruth off the *tan* because she couldn't move. Her legs were completely paralyzed. Eizan came again and said, "You sat very well tonight—would you come again tomorrow?" So she went the third day.

The third night she was allowed to have sanzen with Roshi. He said Ruth was to sit at the end of the line, because he would give her a little longer sanzen than anybody else.

She was reasonably comfortable the third night, and she had her first sanzen, with Eizan acting as an interpreter. At the end of the third night Eizan said to Ruth, "All the monks now invite you to come and sit every night with them. You sit like Kannon and are a great inspiration to them, so please come." From that point forth she went every night.

Some time later, while Ruth was visiting another temple, a student of the roshi there challenged her: "You must have had a great problem. Why else would someone like you begin Zen practice?"

She found the very question rude. She responded as directly as she felt it merited. "No, there was no great problem."

It was as she had presented it to Dr. Suzuki when she first met him: her whole trip, this project, this adventure, was based on the simple question of whether it might be possible for a Westerner, one raised in the culture of duality, of *I think, therefore I am*, to realize any benefit by following this method of training in all its particulars. It was not at all a stretch to suppose that one might benefit in some way—that was directly evident, or it would not have been worth the bother of getting herself here, despite her husband's protests, in spite of the implausibility of it all. Why couldn't she just find a teacher at home in America? Because there wasn't one. And even if there had been, how could it be possible to truly enter the practice with her entire being at home, somehow continuing to live her regular life? Dr. Suzuki had said as much.

Shakyamuni Buddha expressed simple, direct truths: that all people suffer, and that there is a way out within this lifetime. So yes, suffering, *dukkha*, a problem, a great problem—a universal one, shared by every human, by every being with buddha nature, experienced by each according to the particulars of one's individual conditions. And the solution—a universal one, available to any human, not just Japanese or Chinese or Indian—the Buddhadharma, this practical, precise method of getting to the root of reality.

She had in common with the historical Buddha that she came from a background of privilege and that her personal sufferings— her domineering mother, her challenging marriage, her daughter's difficult birth and subsequent health problems, her miscarriage— were not truly overwhelming, were not really the compelling subject of her ruminations, were not the main force pushing her into practice.

There may have been an inkling of a further possibility, though she was careful not to make much of it: all those accounts of people—aristocrats, warriors, common people, women, anyone— who had broken through the veil, overcome their preconceptions and stepped into a world of profound immediacy. She would rarely admit even to herself that this was what she was doing, that it was of more than superficial interest to her. For now, she confined her purpose to simply experiencing any results whatsoever, without trying to chase after more, without imagining that there was something to be chased after. That other stuff was better left to the realm of fable and fantasy, a distraction, not a respectable goal. Her sensible attitude was as much as anything what qualified her to sit with the monks.

The next time they had osesshin, in June, the monks said, "We now would like you to sit with us all day long, not only the night." They had Ruth stay continuously at the temple, at Senko-an, Nanzen-ji's private hermitage house where she'd been going for zazen.

At four o'clock in the morning they began with sutra chanting, syllables intoned from the gut, meant to emerge as physical sound from the throat without so much as tickling the mind with their meaning. From that they went into the sodo for a short period of zazen. They came back after a quickly eaten breakfast for a longer period of zazen, and sanzen with Roshi if he was admitting them—if he was not yet impatient with their inept responses. In the afternoon, when there was a break of an hour or two, Ruth would go and lie down. Then she would come back in the middle of the afternoon to sit again.

Around four in the afternoon there was sutra chanting again, and then supper, and back into the zendo until ten or eleven at night.

Ruth found this routine strangely beautiful. Difficult, physically arduous, but somehow lovely. The first day of sitting—from four in the morning straight through—her legs were knotted in pain by evening, with another two hours of seiza to go before it was done. But she was feeling a profound spaciousness. Something beyond explanation.

Roshi came back with her that night to the little house where she was staying for the sesshin. He had one of the monks start the fire, and he himself went out to make sure it was burning brightly and the water was hot. He waited until she'd taken her bath, then he massaged her shoulders. He left, and she slept there and got up again at four in the morning.

Practice with strong effort and perhaps something will happen. But what was it that happened? How could she describe the experience? Could it be possible to reach such an experience in America? As Roshi had said from the start, it would not really be possible in her house on the Kamo, with people bustling around and everything else. It was possible at Senko-an—her weeks of zazen there were the beginning of this unlocking. When any aspiring student—even a very experienced one, even an ordained monk—would arrive at a temple, he would find the gates shut. It was not until after a week, two weeks, of heroic, continuous zazen outside the gates, day and night without pause, that the gates would open and he would be admitted within. Of course it was not the literal gate that was most important.

Zazen in the little house had opened the gates. That was the beginning of practice. Within the sodo there was a palpable difference. The stillness was electric. Simply stepping into the full silence brought her into sharper awareness, as if on the polished deck of a dark boat floating on a mirror-calm pond, unmoored and yet not drifting. And during osesshin, the sitting interspersed with walking meditation, zigzagging slowly along the *rokas*, the covered passageways, and the bowing and chanting—intoning syllables in a Japanized Chinese-Sanskrit that was beyond the immediate comprehension of anyone here, which was partly the point—all of this activated a physical awareness in the world of sound and motion, vibration of vocal cords and chest, entering another dimension. She saw subtleties of color with her physical eyes that had been hidden before. With her physical ears she heard previously unknown subtleties of sound. Her entire being was sensitized, attuned, aware of a unity of all life.

She still felt like an ordinary person—not an adventurer, nor a scholar or artist. Over time, leading up to this, she had felt a hunger, a yearning to understand the *why* of existence, to find her place in the great universe. Before entering the zendo she had a sense of herself—of most people—as being only half-conscious, half-awake to what life really is. She felt she had begun to penetrate that. But through it and within it, she still felt like an ordinary person.

She recognized the simple humanness of Nanshinken, of these monks—extraordinary though they were, it was their effort and persistence that seemed heroic and unusual. Their beings were human. But her husband and daughter, her neighbors in America—they too were just as heroic in their way, just as deserving of her honor and compassion. Her time in this sanctuary had awakened a simple tenderness toward people—the monks, her family and neighbors, everyone—that she had not really been aware of lacking before. No one was a stranger.

Ruth came to know Nanshinken as a simple and devout man, utterly free of pretension in spite of his important position at the head of one of the primary Rinzai temples in Japan, whose tastes showed his country origins. His clothes were always old. Even when he was dressed up for a ceremony his *kesa* showed no particular refinement.

He was purely a monk's man; he lived for training his monks. When he would give *teisho*, Dharma lectures, the monks would enter in a row, silhouetted against the shoji screens. In the early morning the light would illuminate the shoji, and Ruth would see their outlines—first the monks themselves coming in, then the head monk who carried Roshi's book, then Roshi, followed by the boy who carried Roshi's *tikka*.

Nanshinken would come in and stand at the side of his seat before going to make his *raihai* to the Buddha. That Ruth would never forget—his hands as he came in, the shape of his head and his slight body in the voluminous kesa. And the way he entered the hondo. His bowing was like a child's. No fuss, no arrangement of robes. He came in and put his hands together like a child and made his raihai. Sweet, simple devotion. She always felt a twinge in her heart.

Not long after he'd become roshi of Nanzen-ji, Nanshinken was invited to give a sermon at a temple in the country. He went in his ordinary clothes, and he went alone, without an attendant monk.

He stepped off the third-class train car and there was nobody to meet him. Farther down the platform he saw flags flying and lots of people. So he trudged to the temple, and when he got there, people were waiting. They all asked, "Where were you, where were you?"

"I was on the train."

"We didn't see you." They had all been at the first-class carriages, expecting to see somebody in grand robes with an attendant. He decided then that, to make an impression upon the country people, he must wear a gaudy kesa, so he bought something in red with gold.

He told Ruth that he did not know who his parents were. He was born in 1864, in Aichi Prefecture. He had been brought up in a farming family, but he believed he had been left with that family as a baby. He thought he came from a very good family, because he remembered, as a child, a beautiful veiled lady who he assumed was his real mother coming to visit him from time to time. As he was speaking about this he would look at his hands and say, "These are not a farmer's hands; these are a gentleman's hands." He did that many times.

The emotion was visible in his face when he spoke about this lady with the veil, while gazing at his own delicate hands now lined with the passage of so many years, a whole lifetime between. Who was this mysterious woman? He never knew anything.

Though he was raised in the farmer's family, he did receive some education. Perhaps someone had made some provision for his training. He became a novice monk at age nine and entered Shogen-ji monastery, near Gifu, at seventeen. He was also sent to Hanazono University for two years and later studied with a famous Confucian scholar. When he first became an adult monk, he didn't progress quickly. He was at Kokeizan Eiho-ji, a big Nanzen-ji branch temple, also in the countryside of Gifu—it took him three years before he was able to pass the Mu koan. One day he took a little Kannon statue out—his solution to the koan was to throw Kannon in the river. When he came back, the monks ran to him and said, "Roshi wants to see you." So he went into the roshi's room and the roshi said, "Well?"

After that, Nanshinken passed forty-odd koans in forty-odd sanzens. The roshi had made every effort to hold back Nanshinken's satori, as teachers often do if they think someone is going to be exceptional. In 1903, at thirty-nine, he became head monk of Nanzen-ji, and six years later they made him roshi and *kancho*, chief abbot in charge of the whole Nanzen-ji branch of temples. He was very strict. He was strict in his own life and strict with his monks.

He didn't want the monks to read. There was nothing in books that served his training method. When he would secretly slip into the kitchen at Senko-an, his private refuge, he would sometimes read the paper. But he was not at all intellectual.

Neither was he an artist in the usual sense. Through his mastery of Zen he became a master of *zenga* painting and calligraphy, eventually becoming renowned for his Daruma scrolls. These brush paintings, produced since Hakuin's day—quick cartoon-sketch portraits of Bodhidharma, often with a verse in loose, spontaneous calligraphy—reveal the moment-to-moment awakening that defines Zen.

Nanshinken produced them with a quickness and immediacy that could seem almost offhand if you didn't know better. Since Hakuin, that's been a central element of zenga—it's not about the brushstrokes on the paper, it's the years of training and realization that make the brush move with an effortless breath in the moment, with no planning or preparation apart from all the self-refinement. For Nanshinken the paintings were a lighthearted pastime, an expression of ease within the rigor of his Zen. He was fully present in their creation—and then more or less indifferent to them. He had no interest in art as an object, unless perhaps as a gift object, a token of appreciation for a temple supporter's donation or some other occasion.

He especially enjoyed painting a version depicting a female Daruma, known as Onna Daruma, Lady Daruma, which refers to the story of a warrior—or perhaps Daruma himself, the usually austere and rigorous bringer of Buddhism from India to China—in a liaison with a beautiful courtesan. When the warrior comes into his tent, he sees her with a red cloak of his thrown over her head, and exclaims, "Oh, Lady Daruma!" Nanshinken gave Ruth one of these Onna Daruma paintings, but he did not want her to know the story behind it. He certainly would not want her to think it was Daruma himself—with a courtesan! That would not be proper. Ruth's secretary Oguri-san later translated the story for her, amused by Nanshinken's reluctance to reveal the meaning.

One hot summer night, Nanshinken walked with Ruth and Oguri-san across the bridge, around the Shimogamo district, where there were several restaurants. One was brightly lit, and on the second floor the shoji had all been thrown open. From the street below, the three onlookers could hear laughter and shamisen music. They could see the geishas serving, standing up and walking around, bowing and smiling their coy geisha smiles. The old roshi stood there looking up and said, "Mmm, I wonder what a geisha party is like. I've never been at one."

He never drank sake. He wouldn't allow anybody who drank to be a priest in Nanzen-ji.

Nanshinken liked doing samu work with the monks, or on his own. He had a vegetable garden in the back of the little Senko-an hermitage, and he would go out there to work, as a break from the sodo. In the vacation times of summer, he would come down to the house, and he and Ruth would have vegetarian food together.

If somebody banged on the door at six in the morning, it would be Nanshinken, wearing a lightweight cloth wrap and an old straw hat. When he got bored at the sodo he'd stay over for two or three days. They fixed him up in a room, and he would work in the garden and run around the house in his *fundoshi* loincloth.

He wasn't interested in talking much to Ruth—he had no interest in intellectual conversation. He read the paper and chatted with Kato-san—gossiping would be the more accurate term, which Ruth disapproved of but tolerated because she was completely devoted to him. Nanshinken was devoted to her as well: she surmised that she was one of the joys of his old age.

He loved her tomato sandwiches. One day at Senko-an they were cleaning the altar that he had taught her to arrange, and Nanshinken said that when they died, their *ihai*, their mortuary tablets, would go on the altar together. He said, "If you die first I will put cake and tea in front of your ihai. But if I die first, you put coffee and tomato sandwiches in front of mine."

The monks were all completely devoted to Nanshinken as well. They were frightened of him too, because he could really use a stick, as small as he was. One night a big country boy went in for sanzen. After a few minutes the others heard a big clatter, and the doors burst open. Nanshinken had thrown off his robe and came out in his white under-kimono, with his stick—Hakuin's nyoi. Somehow he'd gotten ahold of the collar of this great big fellow, who was a foot and a half taller than he, and was pushing the boy ahead, kneeing him in the behind and hitting him. Ruth imagined the boy had given a foolish answer that was too much for Roshi's patience.

In the sodo the stick was rarely used. The only time it was used violently was when they had to drive out some young boys who didn't want to go for sanzen. In the zendo, Ruth was never hit but once, and that was a joke. She knew it was a joke—a grin spread over the whole room, and it was done.

During sanzen Nanshinken never talked much. His sanzen was always short. And many times he wouldn't even let the monks come in. If he didn't like the way sanzen was going he just shut it down—he wouldn't have any more. He'd get bored and slam the door so nobody else could come in. They never knew when he would lose his temper. He'd just slam the door and that was it. The good students, who really wanted to have sanzen, had to hustle to get the front seats, because with so many people they would never get their turn otherwise. Nanshinken used to have sanzen five times a day during osesshin time.

He didn't eat sodo meals. He had his own kitchen and was an excellent cook. Everyone hated to be *onji* for Nanshinken, because he was so strict. When a pair of boys, two onji—he always had two—would be appointed, they had to be under his jurisdiction about cooking. It was very onerous.

He was a sodo roshi through and through. He kept the grounds of Nanzen-ji immaculate. Everything was run like a military camp—everything exact and strict, absolutely tight. There was no easiness. And yet the feeling was wonderful.

At Ruth's final osesshin before returning to America, Nanshinken insisted that she come join him for his special supper every night, a simple meal of *kaboro*, daikon stewed in soy and water. She didn't mind that in itself; what bothered her was that he would call Eizan up and begin to gossip—in the midst of osesshin, when she and all the monks were steeped in the most profound silence! She fumed silently—there was nothing she could do but eat the boiled kaboro.

The last time Ruth had sanzen with Nanshinken during that first spring and summer in Japan was a very hot night in late summer. Nanshinken was giving sanzen in his *yozashike*, his private outer room, because it was too hot in his ordinary sanzen room. He sat there with all the screens open to the garden—such a hot night, and he had on the same big old robe.

That night he told her, full of concern and sweetness, "You must go back to America. There you may teach people how to sit."

Nanshinken got angry at Ruth one time that same summer.

She had been invited to give the monks a talk at the farewell tea party they had for everybody at the close of the summer osesshin. She had some time in advance to think about it and wrote out in English what she wanted to say. She had Oguri-san translate it into Japanese, and then she read it to the group in Japanese. It was very short. She said there was one thing she had felt living there in the sodo that she wanted to speak about: that everybody was concerned, and correctly, with their own enlightenment; that they must never forget Shakyamuni had gotten his enlightenment only to help all sentient beings; and that in their eagerness to get their own enlightenment, they must never forget they were working for the benefit not of themselves alone but of everybody. Then she presented each with something none of them had—a Japanese-language copy of the *Dhammapada*.

When she finished the speech, she proceeded to send the books around to everybody in the great big circle. But it didn't go down well. They felt she had stepped out of line by trying to correct their behavior and presuming to bring them books when Roshi forbade them.

Though in the end it didn't damage her good relations with Nanshinken, he was angry that she had criticized the attitude of the sodo. She respected him deeply, but even so, it was true—what she said in her speech was absolutely true.

Then she was gone. Summer was over. Ruth returned to the United States, bereft. She felt a gaping emptiness. Not the spaciousness of the Zen experience—though maybe that was somehow lurking in the background—but just a flat, hollow feeling. How could she go back to normal life after what she had experienced? She suspected she would never recover the sense of completeness she had found in these months at Nanzen-ji. Could she return to the temple? She would return.

DYNAMITE IS VERY QUICK

California–Oregon–Washington–New York, 1905–1919

Shigetsu. Before he became Sokei-an he was called Shigetsu, which means "pointing to the moon." As a child, he was Yeita, the name his parents gave him, and then from the moment of his first satori, kensho, when the gates of Zen opened to him, he became Shigetsu—until his *inka*, when his teacher recognized that his mastery was equal to if not greater than his own, authorized him to teach, and gave him the name Sokei-an, after the Sixth Patriarch. But here, in this river of the American West, he was still Shigetsu. Pointing to the moon.

And sitting on this cold rock in the river, the moon reflected in the flowing water—the same moon, the different moon, appearing, breaking up, returning, dissolving, emerging distorted and fragmented, then forming again—in his vision, his mind. Not *his* mind, just *mind*. He would come every night to sit zazen instead of sleeping, or rather, he would eventually drift off to sleep while sitting zazen all night, after a long day of clambering among giant tree stumps, carefully setting charges of dynamite, retreating just in time. Dynamite is very quick. It is good training for a Buddhist.

Who ever sees the moon? Everyone looks at the pointing finger. He saw the moon. This water in the river—this other mirror, not

hidden at all—reflected the moon imperfectly, not as plainly as
the water in the lotus pond at Ryomo-an in Japan where he had
walked, around and around, circling the pond for many hours,
all night with his koan: *Before mother and father, what was your
face?* The koan was always with him, day and night. *Before this
life, before your ancestors were conceived, what was your original
being?* But not in some previous time: right *now!* For months he
had turned it around and around, this koan of the Sixth Zen Patriarch, which became his koan, bringing a new answer every morning to his teacher Sokatsu. And every morning Sokatsu would
ring the bell: *Out!* Until the night of walking around the pond,
when the world opened up and he brought his teacher the right
answer, by being in it. He had seen the moon. He had seen his
original face.

He was still in it, that other place, which was also this place.
The shining trance. The present world. He remained in it, would
clarify it further as the years went on, but would never depart
from it. People often think it is far away, the state of shining
presence—perhaps it is far off in some fairytale land. But it is not
far away. It is right here. He could show it to people, by being in
it—this would become his main way of teaching. *Show me your
original face.* Anyone with a sufficiently clear mind and a basic
understanding, free of distracting concepts, could witness it and
be changed by it. *Dharmakaya*, the absolute state.

Ryomokyo. Abandoning the concepts of subjective and objective.
Concepts that had teased him, harassed him in his youth, both
abstract and concrete. "What is it I see that is real? What is real,
what is true? What makes something beautiful? Is beauty real? Do
others see it as I see it?

Ryomokyo-kai. Society for abandonment of the concepts of

Sokatsu Shaku.
Courtesy of the First Zen Institute of America.

subjective and objective. It was exactly what he needed. Sokatsu
Shaku, who would become his teacher, revived this lay society that
Sokatsu's teacher, Soyen Shaku, had allowed to fall away. Soyen's
teacher Imakita Kosen had begun Ryomokyo-kai: Buddhism had
needed a new breath of life in modern Japan. Soyen had neglected
it, not so interested in training laypeople, but Sokatsu plunged
into the project as a true believer. He himself had begun his training as a lay student, and before long he would turn his back on
the temple establishment for good. He found supporters in the
university and government and, with his teacher's blessing, built
the small temple he called Ryomo-an, "the Hermitage Beyond
Subjectivity and Objectivity."

When the youth who was then still Yeita stepped through the gates of Ryomo-an, he did not know quite what to expect, apart from something that might drive away the torments of his confusion. He kneeled before Sokatsu, this imposing being in robes, bowing his forehead down to the floor. When he sat up, a pair of eyes gazed fully into his being with a look that cut through everything. These deep, unfathomable eyes penetrated, completely unforeseen, beyond walls of noisy resistance.Everything dissolved. For the first time Yeita could remember, there was peaceful silence. There was no problem. Sokatsu had peered into his very soul. That was all.

Yeita immediately began intensive meditation training, observing his jittery mind in motion. Attempting to let the train of thoughts—incessant thoughts, many cars long—pass him without being carried along or run over. Sokatsu gave him his first koan: *Before father and mother, what were you?* He was assigned to stand at the temple gate and greet guests.

After a few weeks, Sokatsu asked him, "How long have you been studying sculpture?"

"About six years."

"Carve me a Buddha!"

Yeita spent two weeks carving a Buddha statue. He worked carefully, intent on every detail being correct, the face an expression of calm concentration and perhaps something more, something that conveyed wise understanding. When he determined that his work was satisfactory—he allowed himself to think it might even be just right—he brought the carving to his teacher, hopeful for a positive reception. Even a bit proud of his work. Maybe he was still a student in Zen, but he was becoming, was already, a real artist.

Sokatsu took the offered carving and, with hardly a glance at it, flung it out through the open window into the pond. It made a thin, weak "plip" as it hit the water. Sokatsu rang the bell.

Yeita sat stunned for a moment, then quickly bowed and backed out of the meeting room. He had misunderstood the instruction: Sokatsu had said nothing about a wooden statue. The Buddha he was to carve was himself.

In 1905 Yeita finished his university studies, stepped out of Ryomo-an with the his eyes peeled open, and was drafted into the army to work in a transportation unit in Manchuria, where the Japanese were fighting the Russians. He drove a truck loaded with dynamite.

Sokei-an at Ryomo-an with students and Zen Master Sokatsu Shaku,
circa 1902. Sokei-an is at far right, bottom.
Courtesy of the First Zen Institute of America.

He was under live fire. The truck might be hit by a shell and explode at any time. Every day he awoke expecting to be dead before evening. Dynamite is very quick. It is good training for a Buddhist.

The dynamite work in Oregon was with a Japanese contractor, a friend, but Shigetsu had been living and working with the Americans around Medford for a few months, finding them open and big-hearted. Everybody worked hard and respected him for working hard, without regard to his ancestry, even if his English was still awkward.

He had never heard of a cuspidor before. These Americans had a custom of spitting frequently, outdoors or in, and inside every building and household, in train cars, in restaurants, were these vessels for receiving it. Shigetsu was acquainted with the pleasures of tobacco smoking, but the habit of chewing it, which produced prodigious spitting, remained foreign to him. Still, his teacher had admonished him that he must become familiar with American customs, and he accepted this one without judgment or presuming superiority.

In Medford he had a job cleaning the cuspidors in a bar. When he finished for the morning he would walk around and meet people, talk to them in their shops, politely interrupt their activities to greet them and learn a little bit about their lives. He did so to practice his English but also to find out how they made their way in this vast, wide-open land. Daily life is the real koan.

Things had been worse in San Francisco, where the people shunned him for not being white. There the trolleys passed him without stopping—or would stop for a white passenger and then roll away before he could step on. Cinemas were the same. Hoping to improve his English by watching a movie on occasion, he was turned away: "You people have your own theaters."

The churches were the worst. Sometimes he could sneak into a movie theater, but never a church. He imagined it could be worthwhile to hear what the ministers considered important for living an upstanding life, but the doors were closed to him: "You people have your own churches." The newspapers were full of lies and libels about "the Yellow Peril." Laws forbade anyone of Japanese ancestry from becoming a citizen or marrying a non-Japanese person. In 1913 a California law would prohibit Japanese people from purchasing land. There were sometimes beatings, riots, lynchings.

As hard as it was for him, it was worse for his wife Tomeko. She quickly determined that confining herself to the few square blocks of Japantown was the only way to bear the daily insult of residing in this city of bigotry and violence. Even so, she was upset all the time, especially after their son, Shintaro, was born. She longed to return to Japan. Though there had been—was still—some affection between them, affection had never been the basis of their union and would not be enough to hold it together. They had married out of devotion for their teacher Sokatsu, because he was not willing to travel with an unmarried woman in the group. To avoid the taint of scandal. To not cast doubt on the possibility of entering America.

Anyway, Shigetsu had already broken with the group—been cast out, in fact, in one of Sokatsu's sharp rejections—over the strawberry-farming fiasco. There was a piece of land, a worked-over, barren scrap of dirt east of San Francisco, across the bay in the hills above Hayward. The senior student of the group, Shigetsu's Dharma brother Goto Zuigan, who knew some English, had seen an advertisement in the newspaper. Sokatsu sent Goto to have a look and, not knowing the first thing about farming, they bought the place, with some absurd idea of growing strawberries.

They thought it was a good idea—to support the group while solidifying the beginnings of a Zen center for lay practice in the San Francisco area.

There was an old farmhouse, a falling-down barn, an emaciated cow, and ten acres of dead dirt. The ex-farmer who sold them the failed land—it was dirt cheap, at least—slipped away as quickly as he could, glad to be rid of the burden, looking over his shoulder half-expecting them to chase after him when they discovered there was no way on earth they could get decent fruit out of that poor excuse for soil.

They needed fertilizer. Mostly they needed farmers, which they certainly were not. They were city people, university students, poets, philosophers—he was an artist—this group of Sokatsu's who came to America to plant seeds of Zen. Shigetsu saw through it quickly, saw the futility, and did not hold his tongue. So Sokatsu sent him packing after a few brief, contentious weeks, back to San Francisco.

He found his way to the Art Institute, where an artist named Richard Partington took him in, gave him a place, and was willing to treat him as a person when no one else in the city looked him in the eye. Even the other art students kept their distance; they accepted his presence in the studio, but his paintings were never selected for the group exhibitions, and when it came time to gather works for a show in Paris, he was not even considered. He did not tell them that his sculpture teacher Takamura Koun had lived in Paris, had studied and worked in the studio of Rodin—in fact was the most renowned modern sculptor in Japan.

Or that he himself had developed mastery of traditional temple carving by the time he was seventeen. But no matter. At least there was Partington, who recognized his skill and who accepted him without judgment as a fellow human being, and Shigetsu showed his appreciation by carving his teacher a set of wooden doors for his house in San Francisco.

Takamura Koun, Sokei-an's sculpture teacher, and his students, circa 1900. Sokei-an is leaning against a tree staring off to the left. Courtesy of the First Zen Institute of America.

It took two years for the rest of Sokatsu's group to give up farming. In 1908 they came back to the city. The dust settled from the farming incident; Sokatsu readmitted his rebellious disciple. The whole group worked together again to revive the project of a lay Zen center in the city. First they set up in a small building on Sutter Street, in the heart of Japantown. It seemed to be going well. After several months they moved a few blocks away to Geary Street, with fifty Japanese students and a few Americans coming for zazen, sanzen meetings with Sokatsu, weekly teisho lectures, and somewhat abbreviated though still intensive sesshins, one in the summer and one for Rohatsu, ending on the eighth of December, the Buddha's Enlightenment Day.

They kept it up for two years, but the time wasn't right. Sokatsu, who had said the future of Buddhism is in North America, determined that America was not quite ready, as it had been not quite ready when his own teacher Soyen Shaku had first visited Chicago in 1893, or when Soyen came to San Francisco in 1905 for a few months with his student Nyogen Senzaki, Sokatsu's Dharma brother.

Sokatsu had personal reasons to return to Japan as well. His teacher Soyen had summoned him. The unmarried woman who was Sokatsu's unacknowledged consort, Eichoku, who had come with them to America, had returned to Japan nearly two years earlier.

Without Sokatsu and the daily ongoing conduit to the deep truth that he provided, the mirror to Shigetsu's own awakening, the young disciple was in danger of slipping into the trance of emptiness that swallowed many otherwise capable Zen students. But Sokatsu entrusted him to stay. He would get to know America better, and when the time was right he would share the Buddha's great wisdom with those who might be open to it. There were not many people in Japan who were truly open to it, who saw Buddhism as something more than a set of rites for funerals. Perhaps this new land was indeed where the future lay for Buddhism.

The San Francisco branch of Ryomo-an disbanded; the rest of the group returned to Japan with Sokatsu in 1910. Tome, Tomeko, wanted to go back with them, but Shigetsu felt an affinity for America. His English was improving. In spite of the hassles and prejudice, he was learning to appreciate America, Americans. He thought he might be able to introduce them to Buddhism. He was not yet certain how that could be done, but he, a true man of Zen, was comfortable with uncertainty, with preparing the ground for the seed and allowing it to grow when the time was right—even if it took a hundred years.

Art, which had been his calling and life's highest purpose before he entered Zen, would become a job, and exchanging one medium for another was a practical matter. In America, though he had studied painting and sculpture, he dropped both in favor of writing, casually rejecting the more cumbersome media as impractical; he would have needed a studio, canvas, paints, brushes, clay, plaster—none of which he could afford. He would have needed to hire beautiful models.

He always had his precious carving tools near at hand, and he would turn to them on occasions throughout his life; even in the dismal barracks of the internment camp near the end, they would continue to bring a form of solace. But here, in his early, hopeful years in America, he went first from carving to painting, selling all of his student works for a little income, then became a writer of tales about America that he sold to Japanese newspapers and magazines for a little more income. In between he found a dozen other ways to earn money.

In February 1911, Shigetsu decided to walk north. He walked through the Cascade Range, crossing the Oregon border in the snow. He and his wife made an agreement that he would stay with the family during the winter and then could roam around the rest of the year on his own, working where he could, practicing zazen, doing his best to carry out Sokatsu's instruction to familiarize himself with this country—the responsibility rested on his shoulders.

In Medford he found no prejudice. The people in this little working town in southern Oregon had no pretensions of being more important than anyone else. If you could work, you earned their respect as a fellow worker. That was enough. He wore overalls all day, as did many of them. They respected his capacity for physical work. He was big for an Asian man, even big compared to many of these Americans, standing nearly six feet tall, and physically powerful. He could do the work, whether setting charges of dynamite to clear a field of stumps or cleaning cuspidors or washing butter plates in some Wild West hotel or loading woodchips into the incinerator at the sawmill.

Not that they were always at peace with each other. He left the job at the bar because of a dispute with the barman. The owner sided with Shigetsu and fired the barman, but what was the point in continuing to work where he had caused a conflict?

For a few weeks he worked as a taxi dancer, escorting lonely girls around the roller-skating rink. The boys didn't seem to mind. In this small town where everyone knew each other, they were often shy with each other when left to their own devices. The girls were happy to be invited for a turn around the rink with him, not at all concerned that he was different, a foreigner. He was a good dancer, agile, confident, graceful. Anyway, it was just dancing, nothing else, no unspoken expectation of something more intimate. He met each partner with a direct, relaxed presence that let them forget their loneliness for a few minutes. His geisha aunts had trained him well. He enjoyed this job, but the music on the automated organ was limited and repetitive, and after a little while it grated on him too much, so he quit. That's when he found the dynamite work.

Shigetsu sat on his flat rock in the Rogue River, nightly grappling with the next set of koans, with a little dog at his feet to keep snakes away. Without his teacher. No one to ring the bell, no one to verify his accomplishment—no one to tell him that all the answers to the next forty-four koans he thought he had mastered were wrong. He had not mastered them at all. Sitting on his ancient, unshakable rock in the Rogue River, they came to him one by one, the answers—then all at once. But his insight was not yet complete. He could not get there alone.

He might be cut off from his teacher, but not from nature, the source itself. He set the koans aside and focused on direct sensory experience. He opened his ears. All sounds were welcome. The rushing stream, the barking dog, the clicking turtle, the hooting owl, the crack of a rifle, the rattling train. All phenomena are mutable. Everything is in a state of change. No separation between mind, perception, phenomena. The five shadows of consciousness are the fundamental delusion of sentient beings. But emptiness is also illusion. The sharp whistle of the train across the valley roused him from his sitting sleep-trance every morning, as the sky was showing its first hint of light.

Tomeko was finding San Francisco unbearable. After Shigetsu had worked and traveled through the Pacific Northwest on his own, he moved them all to Seattle, which Tomeko found much more hospitable. It was here, in 1912, that their second child—a daughter, Seiko—was born. For a time, they lived among Coast Salish Indians on an island in Puget Sound; this was the only place in America where Tome felt comfortably welcome.

Here was a place where the people looked more like her. Like the Japanese at home on another group of islands far away, the Salish ate fish and shellfish, seaweed, the fruits of the forest. They were an ancient coastal people who followed the rhythms of the sea and the seasons. Now they had been pushed to the edges of what had once been entirely their world, by these rude white Americans who cut down whole forests and had no reverence.

Tome did not share her husband's fantasy that Americans could grasp Buddhism. They just wanted to take everything for themselves. If anything, the Americans should learn from these ancient

Tomeko, Sokei-an, and children while living on an island off Seattle,
Washington, circa 1912.
Courtesy of the First Zen Institute of America.

people, the Salish, reverence and respect and generosity. But they
were too caught up in their own bullying ways to notice what they
were destroying.

He worked on railroad gangs, with Japanese crews. Northern
Pacific, Great Northern Railway. After the Chinese Exclusion
Act in 1882, Japanese workers came to fill in the gaps—and
then after 1907 they too were cut off, mostly, except for the
picture brides that these lonely old men sent for to keep them
company in their rustic shacks far from civilization, many of
them city girls who left behind families and homes in Japan that,
though poor, already had electricity, to confront this grim fron-
tier where they had to labor over a smoky wood fire and eat
potatoes instead of rice. By 1910 most of the main rail lines

were finished, but there were branch lines being added, trestles, bridges, tunnels, repairs. The work was not hard to come by. He worked for Union Pacific in Utah as a paymaster, which took him all over the Salt Lake region.

Each spring he went walking, covering hundreds of miles. Up and down the Cascades, along the coast, along the Columbia River, Hood River, Deschutes River. Up the Yakima on the Washington side. Out along the winding Snake, through dry lands, across Idaho, Montana, to Missoula, once all the way to Billings—though he took the train back to Seattle.

Once he met a tramp. "Where is your country?" he asked. The tramp replied, "My country? The earth under my feet is my country."

Along the banks of the Columbia there was an old man who had originally come west looking for gold. "I was headed for the Klondike, '98 or thereabouts. Here is as far as I got. I'd done a good bit of digging already. Now I'm an old man." He had set up a homestead in a hollow where the frost never hardened, and grew potatoes, trading them once a year to a little steamboat that came up the river with commodities he needed.

"And why is it you live this way?"

"I'm an old man. No one ever asked why I want to be alone." Silence. "I've forgotten how to speak human words." He had been absorbed in the breath of the mountains, unreachable. Even if he has attained limitless understanding, Shigetsu thought, how does this benefit human beings?

There were Japanese men and families—sugar beet farmers, fishermen, cannery workers, mill workers, railroad laborers, shopkeepers, dry cleaners, restaurant owners—scattered throughout the west. Shigetsu visited them, collecting their stories, selling them subscriptions to the *Great Northern News*. In this way they reached out across a gulf of desperate loneliness to the homeland they had left behind, often in poverty, and to others of their countrymen who like them had settled in rough corners of this vast new country.

Sometimes Shigetsu traveled in the raiment of a Salish Indian. He had lived among them and felt kinship. He wanted to experience America and Americans another way, where people saw him another way. No one suspected his origins were from a different tribe. He was a convincing actor. More and more he saw himself as American and not really Japanese.

Americans could be big-hearted and generous, but their minds were brittle, unstable. When confronted with contradictions and experiences that confounded their prejudices, they tended to react angrily, impatiently, unable to see beyond their expectations. This would be the biggest challenge in planting his Zen seeds in this new land.

He had begun writing for Japanese newspapers, publishing books of poems, a volume of prose sketches called *A Vagabond in America*. His stories were all secretly Buddhist stories, but if the Buddhism had not been secret, no one would read them. They were stories about people he met on the train, in bars, while working on the railroad, while walking across the Northwest. His column in the paper was called Nonsense. He was an entertainer.

Shigetsu found skilled work around Seattle as a woodcarver. He did not see one medium as inferior or superior; he simply preferred what was available and practical.

When he first approached a prospective employer, the studio head asked if he was any good.

"Not so good—but if you hire me you'll see what I can do."

"This is a place of business, not a training school. Don't waste my time."

A friend counseled him: Here you have to be direct. Humility won't get you anywhere in America. You have to promote yourself. "Tell them you are the best, you worked for the most important temples in Japan to carve the most intricate and prominent ornaments on their beams, you did your work perfectly—then demand seventy-five dollars a week!"

Was it possible to teach these people Buddhism? You had to spell things out: *this is how it is*. But you can't teach Zen by talking about it. It's something that happens to you. There's no gate; it does not let you in. And then, with great effort and a buddha to meet you eye to eye, it does.

He stood on a wooden bridge on a little island in Puget Sound. The wind was moving. The trees were moving. Mind was moving. Then the movement was only the sound of the universe roaring. He leaned on the railing of this little wooden bridge and forgot himself. He heard the universe through the ears of the universe. It was a perfect mirror of sound—no beginning, no end, consciousness reflecting itself.

Each spring it was with relief and high spirits that he took leave from his family. He and his wife were not constantly at odds, but the tranquility of their home left something to be desired.

He treasured the moments with his son, Shintaro, and daughter Seiko. But when Tomeko became pregnant again in 1916, they agreed it would be best for her to return to Japan with the children. Her family was there. His mother was ill; Tomeko could help look after her. It was not perfect, but it would be better for all of them. He would send them his earnings.

So they left. He brought them to the ship in port, helped them with their trunks, and walked back down the ramp alone. Perhaps he would never see them again, would never meet his new baby. His chest felt tight, his heart a heavy lump sinking lower and lower, pulling down at his throat with ragged tethers that threatened to snap.

He remained in Seattle for a week, utterly alone. Everywhere he looked—there, behind that tree—he saw his young son peering out at him, that small round face, those questioning, uncertain eyes hesitant to meet his own. But of course it was only a shadow. It was much harder than he expected. He thought he was stronger than that. He thought he could bear his loneliness. It was more than he could stand.

After another week, the sadness was too much. He packed his few things, bought a ticket, and took a train to New York.

He had experienced kensho, the first gate. It was still with him; he had never left it.

Was enlightenment a remedy for loneliness? Was Buddhism, founded on the noble truth of suffering, effective at relieving the most basic of sorrows—longing for your departed child, for your dead father, for the mother you did not even meet until you'd been cast out of your childhood home? Shigetsu's first profound satori at the lotus pond, breaking through the turmoil in his own mind, had scoured him of the delusion that he was separate from the universe, that there was any meaningful boundary between himself and other beings. For days he half-floated, ecstatic, seeing his own face when he looked at another person approaching him. There was no possibility of loneliness.

But now, ten years later, after deepening his zazen and seeing into the koan of daily life—after watching his wife and children depart, perhaps never to meet them again—he saw that it was not always so. The loneliness, the longing could pull at him as easily as ever—it was not erased. It could arise, by necessity would arise, when the conditions invited it. The difference was that he did not demand of it or of the universe an explanation; perhaps he would not be buried by it, perhaps he now understood how to dance with it, as a capricious but not unjust partner. But to truly be reconciled to it, with it, he would need to go further in his practice. And without his teacher, there was only so much he could do.

Maybe east was the wrong direction. Maybe he should have gone back to Japan, to be near his children, to be with Sokatsu. But as much as he contemplated that, he needed to be here. Sokatsu needed him to be here. He arrived in New York.

He found his way to the Great Northern Hotel on Fifty-Seventh and Sixth Avenue, which advertised rooms for two dollars a night, with discounts for those arriving from the West. The next morning he inquired at the Yamanaka furniture company. They sent him to a small shop run by a Mr. Mogi, who gave him night work carving ivory and wood, painting boxes. There was a sailor who slept there, who spent long hours talking with him as he worked— about the lonely life of a merchant seaman, about women and money and the world and not belonging to any country.

One morning Shigetsu came into a mirror-lined hall and saw a wooden box. It was exactly his size. Though it had no markings, he knew it had been delivered for him. He would be killed and buried in this box. He spent weeks suspicious of everyone, avoiding situations where he might be trapped. He guarded his every move. And then the delusion evaporated, the episode passed.

He lived in a rooming house in Washington Square, another on East Fifteenth Street, and other rooms and studios. He was painting and writing, working at the carving shop at night, spending the day walking to every end of this crowded island, perching on a rock or a bench in Central Park or Battery Park doing zazen. Before long he began meeting people.

Between his writing and carving, he was earning two hundred dollars a month, which after sending most of it back to his wife in Japan was still enough for eating the American food he enjoyed and dressing fashionably in city clothes that fit him.

Sokei-an in Greenwich Village, circa 1916.
Courtesy of the First Zen Institute of America.

Elizabeth Sharp, who became his girlfriend, saw him as high-strung. Sometimes his fingers would tremble. But with a paint-brush in his hand the trembling ceased completely.

He became a regular at Petrillo's in Greenwich Village, holding forth in the back room for a rapt audience of other writers and artists, endlessly reciting his poetry or comic monologues about bumbling monks in compromised situations, or the Analects of Confucius, which he learned as a child from his father the scholar, or koans retold in the voice of a ghost or a drunk or a dog. *Does a dog have Buddha nature? Woof!* He was seen dancing in the moonlight under Washington Square Arch.

Women found him charming. So did the men he encountered in these bohemian circles. He was like no one they had met. The same could probably be said for many of them: Max Bodenheim, king of the Greenwich Village bohemians, who collaborated with him in translating poems of Li Po for *The Little Magazine*— embellishing too much, crowding the purity of the original Chinese, in Shigetsu's opinion. The "Vagabond Poet" Harry Kemp, who thought of Shigetsu as a young Japanese poet though they were the same age, and who fondly appreciated his wit and dignity. Aleister Crowley the occultist, whose egotism repulsed Shigetsu. Katherine Ruth Heyman, a prominent classical pianist and composer, an intimate of Ezra Pound, who published a treatise called *The Relation of Ultramodern to Archaic Music.* Paul Swan, a painter, sculptor, dancer, actor, who invited Shigetsu to dance with him onstage. John Barrymore and the Hungarian photographer Nickolas Muray fencing in the backyard of the Bamboo Forest and Tao Tea Garden on MacDougal Street.

Certainly he did not seem typical for a Japanese man. They had all met plenty of poets and performers, but no one who was also a true Zen man, though he kept that in the background, mostly. His girlfriend Elizabeth Sharp, a fashionable beauty from a Southern family, a writer of pulp fiction and editor of women's magazines, managed to solve the first six koans—which had taken him months—more or less immediately. This annoyed him to no end. But mostly he kept the intensity of his practice to himself. He did not presume to call himself a Zen teacher at this point, certainly not a master, though he saw that he would become both.

He never touched alcohol. This was not so much out of his commitment to the Buddhist training precepts—certainly there were great masters who were fond of the fiery water of wisdom. Overly fond, in his opinion. Even Soyen Shaku, Sokatsu's teacher, whom he revered practically as a saint. But alcohol disgusted him. His father had been an alcoholic and had died from it, at least in part. Both father and son suffered from high blood pressure, but the sake couldn't have helped, and Shigetsu avoided it like poison. When others in the room at Petrillo's verged on overdoing the booze, somehow his stern presence, even disguised as an exuberant raconteur, reined them in.

His writings became popular in Japan, published in the magazine *Chuokoron* and books of prose sketches entitled *Night Talks about America*—the allusion to Zen Master Hakuin's famous *Idle Talk on a Night Boat* would be lost on most readers, but no matter—and *America and Americans Seen from the View of Money and Women*. And his first volume of poetry, called *Kyoshu*, which means "homesickness."

He had served in the Japanese army in Manchuria and was not, in all circumstances, opposed to war. When the United States entered the war in 1917, he found his way to a U.S. Army recruitment office and tried to enlist. "I was a soldier in the Japanese Army. Our countries are allies. I have lived in America for more than ten years." He was refused.

He loved America. He loved the sense of freedom and possibility, though he saw many people trapped in the constraints of

their expectations and delusions. He loved New York. He loved
the Pacific Northwest, his decade of rough tramping through its
mountains and river valleys. In the west he had been close to
nature. In New York he was close to people. To pass through
the dusty turmoil of the world you must know the main road.
Those who lived close to nature—the Salish, the tramps, the her-
mit potato farmer in the Columbia River Valley—knew that they
were not separate from nature. The people of the city often forgot
this basic truth.

But really so did most of these Americans, who separated their
heads from their bodies, their minds from their experience of the
immediate world. To dispense healing medicine you must first
investigate the source of the illness. There is the Zen master who
secludes himself in the wilderness, dissolving into dharmakaya,
pure consciousness, and the one who stands in the midst of a busy
intersection of the crowded city with crap on his face. *Sentient
beings are numberless, I vow to save them all.* Sometimes it is the
same person.

In 1919 there were still more than seventy thousand horses in
Manhattan. Only two years earlier, in March 1917, when Shigetsu
was just finding his footing in the city, the horse population had
been well over a hundred thousand. But electric streetcar lines and
the internal combustion engine were gradually, and then quickly,
replacing them.

City horses were driven—literally, relentlessly—to the point of
exhaustion, were overcrowded in filthy stables that often resembled the tenements of their human counterparts, and rarely survived more than three or four years before collapsing, often in
their harnesses. Each year in the early twentieth century, fifteen
thousand of them died on the city streets; their carcasses were

hauled to designated offal docks to be transported to rendering plants outside the city.

For Shigetsu, their presence was a matter-of-fact aspect of the urban tangle—not overlooked, but no more remarkable than any other ingredient of this frothy soup of human, machine, and beast. Until one day it wasn't.

There in front of him on dusty, noisy Sixth Avenue on a sweltering August afternoon lay a horse on the pavement, dead, twisted in its traces. The wagon was still upright but turned at an awkward angle. The wagoner and another man, his assistant or a bystander, were shouting at each other, standing there, gesturing. Other people were walking past, not stopping, barely registering that this beast had collapsed. Vehicles were trying to pass in the street; a truck stopped, unable to continue. The driver got out, shouting at the wagoner. Everybody shouting, flies buzzing around the dead animal. Shigetsu, who welcomed all sounds into his ears, heard none of it. Something had happened. Nothing was left in his mind. He stood, stunned, watching, not seeing, not hearing. That horse had been alive and now was a corpse, still, dead, an empty heap on the hot pavement. Breath and then no breath. What was the difference?

It was evening by the time he found himself in his room, the light fading. He packed his bags. The next morning he would book a train for Seattle. From there he would sail to Japan to return to his teacher.

HALF-AWAKE IN AMERICA
Hinsdale, Illinois, 1932

In the United States life was empty. Not the Zen kind of empty; here it was a flat emptiness, full of chatter and gossip. Not that her time in Japan had been free from gossip—across the road from the zendo, in the little house, Nanshinken would visit and chat with her housekeeper. Ruth did not approve of gossip of any sort, but of course she could not say anything against her beloved teacher.

In the United States the gossip grated on her, tugged at her fortitude. She would have no part of it. She must find a way to maintain her practice and not succumb to the pettiness.

She gave talks to groups of people interested in Buddhism. She found that she had both more and less to say than before. Giving talks was a way to keep her from feeling that returning to America was entirely pointless. It was a way to cast about for the possibility of finding a teacher in this land. She was not hopeful.

She described her experience. But when questioned, when invited to explain more precisely, to reach beyond the names of people and the atmospheric details, she encountered a familiar barrier. She would suggest that it must be experienced. This was unsatisfactory.

This mysterious state. What is it? What is. Arrives with intense effort but not that kind of effort. Flees if chased. Defies explanation. As subtle as a brushstroke in water. We do not deal in metaphor: Bring me the thing itself. Show me your original face!

Everything with her marriage was strained. Warren's health was failing; he was becoming more and more of an invalid, barely able to walk even with assistance. What he expected of Ruth was unrealistic, based on an image of what was proper for a wife of her station. Had he forgotten whom he married? He needed a caregiver and a sounding board. That was not who she was or what she was becoming. They had been married fifteen years but had never reconciled their differences, and as his condition deteriorated so did his already limited ability to recognize her.

For years she had accommodated him, establishing a well-run household with efficiency and not a little elegance. In 1926 they had built a house in Hinsdale just outside of Chicago, which Ruth had designed along with the architect Benjamin Marshall. They called it Swan House—the eaves featured carvings of swans—a stately house modeled after English country retreats, with a slate roof and European-style lead gutters, a wine cellar, a carriage house, brick pavers from Madison Street in Chicago. Ruth designed the landscaped gardens, with a large Buddha by a small pond; for outdoor parties, they hung up Chinese lanterns.

Inside Swan House, they decorated with treasures from their travels, most notably the contents of fifty-eight packing crates sent back from their family trip to Asia in 1930: silks, fine linens and embroideries, jades and jewels, paintings and porcelains, lacquerware and lanterns; deep blue paving tiles, glazed to match those that crown the Temple of Heaven, for flooring; a pair of three-foot porcelain lions to guard her door; fine, gold-leaf papers to cover her walls; drapes and upholstery of imperial gold and red satin; three magnificent Tang dynasty burial figurines posed upon the window sill; a Siberian tiger skin sprawled across the floor; a giant cinnabar lacquered *kang* for her bed; her desk a grand marvel of satin-smooth teak; ashtrays of jade or quartz; in a wall niche, ornamented with more cinnabar lacquer, a timeworn, exquisite Tibetan Buddha. Warren, a devoted Anglophile, had his rooms furnished in an English style.

Swan House, Hinsdale.
Courtesy of Ann Grube.

For years Ruth had been patiently fielding Warren's outbursts—which were more frequent and inconsolable as arteriosclerosis advanced to his head. She had carved a small, secluded nightly space for herself and her studies, for her necessary but already eroding practice of zazen. It was becoming impossible to squeeze herself into that cramped space.

Over the years they had graciously entertained hundreds of guests—business associates, visiting dignitaries. Though her appreciation for every guest was not uniform, she truly excelled at this and

took pride in the hospitality she provided. It was not this aspect of
their life together that wore down her patience; in fact, it was one of
the few remaining sources of satisfaction for her in America. On her
own, in her own way, she would maintain this gracious attention to
guests throughout her life, inspiring enthusiastic regard, even some
small renown, among the steady stream of visitors she received.

Ruth's brother David, Warren, Eleanor, and Ruth at Swan House.
Courtesy of Anne Watts.

She and Warren had traveled together as amicable companions,
with Eleanor in tow, to Europe numerous times, and to Asia, supporting each other's diverging interests. The break had come with
her own separate trip to Japan, her months at Nanzen-ji, though
this was a symptom, not a cause, of their impending dissolution.
Her absence, her independence, was intolerable to Warren. And
for Ruth, back in the States after finding her true home in the
zendo, Warren was becoming unbearable.

And Eleanor was beside herself: She felt ignored. All these small abandonments—her mother's remoteness, her father's growing dependence. She felt burdened and lonely. She threatened to run away.

Nanshinken's matter-of-fact statement when Ruth first arrived in Kyoto—that she would find it difficult to do anything, meaning meditate, in a bustling household with "servants and other distractions"—was even more accurate here, where the distractions were persistent and displayed absolutely no regard for her training. At least in Kyoto, even away from the temple, people respected her purpose. In Japan, if a robed monk walks down a crowded boulevard, no one will disturb his concentration. How likely would this be in America? There was respect for scholarly pursuits, to a point—women who took their studies beyond mere self-improvement were looked at suspiciously, as if their ambitions somehow undermined all propriety—but no accommodation for a proven method of direct engagement with reality, which alone had the potential to pierce through the shallow, hollow, petty squabbles and delusions of domestic existence that formed the vast proportion of most people's lives.

All she wanted, really, was to immerse completely in the profound waters of true Zen practice, as she had entered in Japan. As much as she admired the sentiment that a serious student should be constantly grappling with the koan, through all activities night and day—even among crowds, even in dreams—she could not sustain it here. In spite of her dedication, without a context that supported contemplative pursuits, she experienced an erosion of attention. For one thing, there was no teacher to guide her through sanzen. And no matter how stubborn her devotion, in practical terms she was a beginner, in no position to bully her way

through the clamor—as she supposed Warren would attempt if in
her situation.

On Sundays, Warren's sister Mary and Mary's husband, Gus-
tavus, continued coming for dinner. After dinner the men smoked
cigars and the women played mahjong—the set was housed in
an exquisite teakwood box. Eleanor loved to play. It was one of
the few diversions that brought her fully into a feeling of family; even when they took trips together, these seemed carefully
choreographed, with each of them separately seeking particular
entertainments. Overall she felt a distance from her parents, and
now her father was falling apart before her eyes.

The main job of her upbringing for the past seven years had
been consigned to a governess, whom at least she trusted and
was fond of—a comfort and a blessing compared to the cold
and unforgiving nanny who had caused her great humiliation in
her earlier years. She would never forget a Valentine's party her
parents gave; the nanny costumed her as Cupid, with nothing to
cover her five-year-old body but a wide red ribbon strung from
shoulder to hip, and paraded her among the guests at the cocktail
hour, equipped with a tiny golden bow and arrow. Whose delightful idea was that?

As Eleanor grew older, she became ill with asthma—so ill that
for two springs her mother sent her with a nurse to the dry desert
air of California. They stayed at a dude ranch, where she learned
to ride a horse and fell in love with the wranglers. She learned to
measure distances to be traveled by seeing through the crystalline
air on starlit nights. More than anything she was captivated by
the effects of light: the shifting hues at dawn and dusk that seemed
to make of the mountains living things, solid but ever-changing,
subtle and immense. She felt their embrace as a physical force,

majestic and protective. They evoked a sense of peaceful security and radiant joy—evidence of profound dimensions of life beyond the stuffy, constricting rooms of Hinsdale.

The Roof Presses Down
Tokyo, 1920–1921

Does a horse have Buddha nature?

Sentient beings are numberless: I vow to save them all.

Sokatsu Shaku sat in the meeting room of Ryomo-an just as before, stately, radiant. The master on his Dharma throne. There was no indication of any disruption. Shigetsu bowed and gave his solution to the next koan. The bell rang. *Out!*

Japan had changed. There was a clamor to expand, a claim for more land. He felt it too. The person once named Yeita Sasaki, now for more than a dozen years known by his Buddhist name Shigetsu, had changed.

He was fifteen when his father died, and there was not enough money to clothe him properly. So the gangly youth had been forced to wear his father's robes, which draped over him like rumpled sacks. His father, a Shinto priest from an illustrious samurai family, had been a large man, standing six feet three inches tall; Yeita, though growing, had not reached this height. The clothes bore the Sasaki family insignia, which was widely recognized. When Yeita wore these robes in public, he would occasionally encounter some feudal servant of the Sasakis or another family, who would bow deeply before him—to the robe, not to the uncomfortable sixteen-year-old boy wearing it. This absurd reverence for the trappings of authority nauseated him.

When he returned to Japan, Shigetsu felt the weight of generations squeezing the breath out of him. His house was too small, too crowded. This island was a cramped temple with a low roof pressing down on his head. Too little air. He struggled to move freely. In his dreams now he wandered through the vast spaces of Montana, the forests of Oregon. Or else the vigor and clamor of the streets of New York—streetcars, people shouting and gesturing, dying horses.

As a boy, he had been a dreamer. His father told him Chinese bedtime stories. He loved reading fairy tales. He filled his waking hours with daydreams and stories of his own invention. As a youth, he tried tracing the contours of the dream world, keeping a notebook and pencil near his bed to record what he could. At first he was unable to recall details. His mind was chaotic—it didn't obey his control. Eventually he trained himself to memorize the dreams so exactly that he could note down all the details in his book. That was the beginning of his meditation.

Had he lost the distinction between fantasy and reality? He would write as much as ten pages at a time, trying to keep track of each passing thought. At a certain point he came to see the flow of thoughts as something separate from himself—endless, unstoppable. He realized that trying to follow this stream would never free him from the tangles of thoughts arising unbidden. So he gave up. That was the first glimmer.

As a young child Yeita had believed the stories his father told him, until he encountered evidence that exposed them as fantasy. By the age of five, he saw through the fairy tales. It came to his mind that God is universal vast space, infinite time and infinite power. Not some magical being who listens to the words and pleadings that emerge from a human throat.

Yeita would ask his father, "What is in the deepest part of the shrine?" His father would tell him that place was inhabited by God. One day, the boy snuck inside to find out for himself.

A festival was going and every priest was busy in the shrine, so he had a chance to slip out from the big room given over to the ceremonies and go into the deepest part to see God. He thought of himself as a mouse. He saw candlelight at the end of the hall, its long flames fluttering toward the high ceiling. There was a screen hanging down, dividing the human world from God. His heart was fluttering just like the candle's fire.

He hesitated. Many times he hesitated to roll up the screen. He bowed, and again bowed, like the priest, and recited the ritual phrase his father always intoned. Then he crept in.

There, inside the deepest part of the shrine, it was very dark. He could not see anything, although a faint light behind the screen shone at his back. He searched out the square box on the square pedestal and found a round white thing lying on the box. He gazed into it. His eye made out some form: a startled face. A round mirror with his own startled face in the darkness.

Years later, he confessed this adventure to his father. "Yes," said the elder Sasaki, "I know there is the mirror. But I have not been there yet."

Now Shigetsu recognized dreams and spontaneous thoughts alike as *rupa-skandha*, the mental shadow of phenomena arising and dissolving. Is it real? It is not solid. If you investigate rupa-skandha, you will observe that there is nothing solid in the material world. You will see patterns—the universe is orderly. One thing leads to another. Mind is orderly.

Do you know what to expect? There are patterns, there are maps of the patterns. Is this the same as knowing the future? The future is a prediction, an expectation. A fantasy. A source of disappointment. For many Zen students, disappointment is the beginning of practice.

Yeita's father, Tsunamichi Sasaki, the descendent of a samurai family that had guarded Takamatsu Castle on the small island of Shikoku since its founding in 1588, was a Confucian scholar and a master of Classical Chinese and ancient Japanese, as well as a Shinto priest. Every evening he would sit with his only son and teach him the Shinto hymns and scriptures, Chinese poetry, and calligraphy. His shrine, Konpira, was dedicated to the *kami* of the sea and was a favorite of sailors. What was his belief? In any case, it was not identical to the belief of the sailors.

When Yeita was fifteen, his father had a severe stroke. Another Shinto priest instructed Yeita to go up to his father's shrine and bring back holy water to sprinkle on his father's face—this would keep him alive, the priest said. But when Yeita entered the shrine, he felt numb. He tried to pray, but he was unable to muster any feeling. Where was the kami? He could not feel any presence. The water was simply water, and he did not bring any back.

When the priest asked why he did not bring the water, Yeita said, "No use." Until that day he had felt close to the kami, but now, when he most needed it, there was nothing. And soon after that his father died.

Two days later, a letter arrived. It was a notice of appointment: Tsunamichi Sasaki was to be posted to the Grand Shrine of Ise— the most important Shinto site in the country. A great honor. The message was read at the funeral to his dead body.

The people of Goi village begged Yeita to go to the Shinto university and become a priest to take the place of his father. But if he had ever had such an inclination, it was gone.

He walked out among the pine trees under the bleak winter sky, wondering where was his father now. "His soul is scattered all over, like heat or light." And then, with attention somewhere aloft, Yeita stumbled over a tree root. He stopped where he was. His toe throbbed. "If my father is everywhere," he thought, "he will be in this pine tree root, on the tip of my tongue, on the tip of this bruised toe."

When he returned to Japan, Shigetsu's entire attention was focused on his practice. The hundred koans he had solved in Oregon—he had been wrong about every single one. Without his teacher. Now he was with his teacher again, untangling, sharpening.

The first set of koans, the *hosshin* koans, opens the realm of dharmakaya, true nature—seeing the true nature of oneself and the universe. The pure light in each instant of thought. True nature is not about feeling good or bad. True nature is not good or evil. There is a sense of recognition when you get there. Before you were born, your original face. The first kensho is a glimpse into this realm. Most people, even those who catch the first glimpse, never progress beyond it. The Zen student must make dharmakaya the constant dwelling place.

When there is no longer any barrier between the eye and one's true nature, when the realm of dharmakaya is immediate and present beyond the slightest doubt, the next set of koans, the *kikan* koans, are for sharpening discernment, distinctions, differentiation—observing phenomena from an awakened perspective. These koans are for untangling. These are the ones Shigetsu wound and unwound on the rock in the Rogue River in Southern

Oregon, in secluded pockets of Battery Park and Central Park, certain he had mastered all of them. Each time he brought his response to Sokatsu now, the reaction was quick and sharp: *Out!* The bell rang. Shigetsu bowed and retreated.

For months this was the pattern, as it had been at the beginning of his training. How long? A year? Two years? Constant effort. And then, in the rainy cold season, one after another, the barriers dissolved. What was the difference? Nothing that could be spoken or visible to a visitor, but something as obvious to Sokatsu as chickens roosting in a tree on a snowy morning.

It is a fight. They are martial artists, bowing into the ring, master and student. Be quick! The student has one chance. A single strike: *Not right!* The bell rings. *Out!* The fight is over.

The student is defeated. Train harder! Your head is on fire—the whole world is on fire! What *samadhi* will save you?

In the Japan of Shigetsu's childhood, before trains connected every village and remote outpost, people walked everywhere. There were horses in Japan, but they had been for warfare mostly, or in some places for farming. If you wanted to get somewhere, unless you were a samurai or noble, you walked.

After his father died, Yeita spent a year walking through the mountains of Nagano Prefecture, a wide region of snowy peaks across central Honshu known as the Japanese Alps. There was not enough money. He went with his mother to live with her family in Kamakura. It was decided that he would apprentice to a carpenter there. He quickly showed aptitude for carving, so for the next two years the master carpenter trained him to carve temple ornaments—the dragons, elephant heads, birds, and other figures that adorned the roof beams and finials of Japanese temples.

In the mountains, there were dozens of Buddhist temples being restored. Some had been damaged in the violent *haibutsu kishaku* destruction of the early Meiji era; some were simply in need of maintenance after a period of neglect. In any case, there were plentiful opportunities for this sort of work. After his apprenticeship, Yeita, as he was still called, set out with his carving tools and spent a whole year walking from village to village. He would stay in a place for a month or two, working on the temple carvings, and then walk a few days until he came to another village where his skills could be useful.

He always loved to walk. The rhythm of the mountain paths calmed his turbulent thoughts. Many of the temples and monasteries in Japan are built on high ridges or at the edges of cliffs. The exertion, the view in winter over shimmering, snow-covered valleys, the profound silence of the monasteries—all of this sharpened the air. His eyes became clearer. He learned to extend his hearing outward, to accept sounds as they occurred.

In his early wood-carving apprenticeship, he had been nervous about hitting his own hand instead of the wood. He was striking the blow from his elbow. His teacher admonished him to use his brain. Study what you are doing. Observe what is needed to strike gracefully and effortlessly. Keep the mind steady and relaxed. He learned to use his brain, then his heart, then nature. "Use it all—mind, brain, and heart—but use it relaxed. Tension kills function. It fills the brain, and you become like a squeezed lemon. Hold your mind and heart very lightly, and keep your strength in your nature."

Readiness is his entire being. This time he lands a blow. There is a pause, the slightest nod from the teacher. Acknowledgment. Sanzen is over, but this time the bell signals success.

When it arrives: profoundly familiar and utterly unexpected. Simply known, and then directly demonstrated and acknowledged.

The third set of koans, the *gonsen* koans, are for penetrating insight through words and phrases. Zen is the sect of wordless enlightenment—how can words be a tool of emancipation? Nevertheless, this is the practice.

Beyond the specific gonsen koans, *jakugo*, capping phrases—which a rational interpretation mistakes for nonsense—are traditionally given by a Rinzai student when completing a koan. These help confirm successful understanding.

As a teacher, Sokei-an would often refer students to *Alice in Wonderland* as an appropriate source for jakugo. This sort of nonsense is the opposite of misunderstanding. It is the opposite of meaningless. If you read it from an awakened state, you recognize the validity of its expression immediately. So it is with the gonsen koans.

When Shigetsu returned to Japan from his years in America, he was an awkward giant in an ill-fitting suit of unspoken expectations, hemmed in by delicate walls, his arms punching through the shoji screens. The suit, which in his youth had been too big, was now tight and constricting. Only with his teacher Sokatsu did he feel spaciousness. Not necessarily ease, but that was not the point. The point was to complete his training.

His wife had changed. She would fly into unprovoked rages. He had seen her upset before, but this was new. This was not the greeting he had hoped for. Her time in America had left her bitter, perhaps something more—something had shaken loose in her. She was no longer a student of Sokatsu. She spoke ill of him; she snarled and spat at the mention of his name. In fact she had left Zen entirely, drifting into the Jodo Shinshu sect—Pure Land Buddhism, which mapped a path to salvation simply by accepting the power of a savior, Amida Buddha. To Shigetsu, this sounded too much like the missionary priests he had scoffed at as a child—still scoffed at, considered simpleminded, misleading, misrepresenting the subtlety of the Buddha's true teaching. To Shigetsu, this made his wife even more of a stranger. True penetration of the jewel of wisdom required intense and single-minded effort. No one was going to just come along and give it to you. He could imagine his wife drifting even further, entirely abandoning the treasure they had shared, drifting into ever shallower waters until perhaps she would run aground. In America, there had been friction between them. But now she was unreachable. Their alliance had crumbled to dust.

Even worse, his children hardly acknowledged him. For the two oldest, born in America, it had been three years since they had seen him. Three years of absence, infected by poisonous slurs against America, which he now considered his true home. Poisonous slurs against him. Tomeko turning against him—if that was how things stood now, it was something he could endure. But his children?

Their third child, a daughter named Shihoko, born in Japan soon after Tomeko returned and now three years old, had never met him. If eventually she would become a devoted daughter, it would be in spite of these unfortunate circumstances.

As a boy he spent many hours immersed in the world directly around him—watching the flowing stream, listening to birds—in a blissful reverie. He was present with nature. But at the same time, nothing fully penetrated his senses in a way that brought him beyond himself. One afternoon, when he was thirteen or fourteen, he was walking alone along a country road. He met a

boy about his age, who looked about like he did. They looked
at each other. It was simple. There was a feeling of communion.
They did not speak. He felt he was not alone.

A little while later he met a Zen monk. He looked at the monk
and smiled and looked at him again. He tried to search the monk's
mind. He felt, "This person is not thinking anything at all." He
smiled again. The monk did not smile back.

It was his first contact with a Zen master. Later he went to
Ryomo-an and met Zen Master Sokatsu Shaku, who looked at
him with his great eyes, and that was all.

*We practice mindlessness meditation. The mind that is yours is a
trap. Lose that mind!*

Mindlessness is the opposite of not paying attention.

The koan penetrated every thought—day and night, in the active
state and the dream state, through intensive meditation without
pause, the koan was with him.

Following the gonsen koans, the student arrives at the "difficult
to pass through" koans—the *nanto* koans, which are likened to
crossing eight arduous mountain passes. These nanto koans and
the final set, the *goi* koans, would occupy Shigetsu the rest of his
time in Japan. And then he would be finished with his Zen. When
he finished, he would continue to meditate.

Sokatsu was a fierce master. Lineage holder through seven generations of Hakuin Ekaku's Rinzai line, further back through Linji,
through the Sixth Zen Patriarch Huineng, through Bodhidharma
who carried Buddhism from India to China, the unbroken line
to the Buddha himself—directly, person-to-person, face-to-face,
eye-to-eye, being-to-being. This is the eye of Buddha staring at

you. The same undying light. Guarding the gate. This is the master you must overcome. Benevolent? Harsh? It is simple. In this place there is no mercy, no forgiveness. Another chance—*now!*

Sokatsu, after receiving full Dharma transmission from Soyen Shaku at age twenty-nine, traveled barefoot through Burma, Siam, Ceylon, and India for two years, with only his robes and begging bowl. When he returned, he was expected to succeed Soyen as chief abbot and head monk of Kencho-ji and Engaku-ji, the two preeminent Rinzai temples in Japan.

But Soyen decided Sokatsu was still too young, so he had Sokatsu revive the lay training center that Kosen Roshi had started. This was where Sokatsu remained. For the rest of his life he devoted himself entirely to training lay Zen students.

There was more to it than that.

Among Sokatsu Shaku's disciples was a wealthy doctor, a widower with a daughter. The daughter, Eichoku, was in her late teens when her father brought her to Sokatsu, with the idea of Sokatsu taking her on as a student. And then quite suddenly the doctor died.

The doctor had left his substantial estate to his daughter Eichoku, and he had appointed Sokatsu as her guardian.

In 1912 Soyen retired from Engaku-ji. Nobody thought there would be the slightest problem about Sokatsu, his chosen successor and a brilliant prodigy, being elected the new roshi and kancho. But the day before the election, the major newspapers in Tokyo broke a story of this man—this priest of Engaku-ji—who had misled his ward, who was living with her and squandering her fortune.

So it was not to be—Sokatsu lost the election. He shook the

dust of temples off his feet. For the rest of his life, he had nothing to do with the temple establishment—the greatest Zen master of his age, turning his back on the institution and its authorities. It worked both ways: for the rest of his life, in spite of his abilities and accomplishments, the temple establishment scorned him and thereafter shunned his students—never recognized their legitimacy, never credited their attainments—because of his indiscretions.

He continued to live with Eichoku until his death at eighty-four. In fact they were entirely devoted to each other. She never expressed any hint of disappointment—in spite of how he used her wealth, he treated her with the utmost kindness.

He never would marry her, though his students often urged him to take off his *koromo* and become a real lay teacher. But he refused. He always shaved his head and always wore his koromo in public.

Eichoku took the role of his onji, waiting upon him with the utmost formality, and he in turn addressed her with the utmost formality.

She was a fine *koto* player. Sokatsu encouraged her to study koto and was very proud of her playing. Every so often a teacher would hold a recital, and Eichoku would play. Sokatsu never missed a recital, sitting right up in the front row, but with a scarf over his head and down over his face.

In order to travel to America with Eichoku, Sokatsu felt he needed a married couple in the group—so it was for her sake that Sokatsu arranged the marriage of Shigetsu and Tomeko. They were to act as her chaperones.

When Eichoku returned to Japan in 1908, it was because she was pregnant. Sokatsu traveled with her back to Japan and stayed for six months, and then he returned to San Francisco for another year and a half, to lead the center on Geary Street, before deciding that America was not yet ready for Buddhism, before abandoning to his disciple the dream of Buddhism taking root in a new land.

Eichoku's daughters—a second was born after Sokatsu returned to Japan—were raised apart from Eichoku and Sokatsu by a local family and, at least while Sokatsu was alive, acknowledged only as Eichoku's nieces. But they knew who their parents were and felt no shame or need to conceal their circumstances.

It is not necessary to follow the strict monastic life in order to arrive at satori. Sometimes the alternative, a lay practice, may be preferable; at least it is often more available—certainly for women, who were not admitted to the sodo. Without the guidance and acknowledgment of a true teacher, however, lay practice rarely amounts to anything.

Huineng, the Sixth Zen Ancestor, was a lay practitioner who became a Zen master. In the history of Zen, there are many stories of lay students—women as well as men—who cut through the barriers of delusion to demonstrate their enlightenment.

In times of cultural upheaval, as in Meiji Japan—which had seen the abolishment of feudalism and the samurai class and had perpetrated the haibutsu kishaku, a wave of violent persecution against Buddhism in which tens of thousands of Buddhist temples were destroyed—it becomes necessary to refresh the old institutions. Kosen Roshi embraced the modernizing program of the Meiji emperor and sought university students and professionals to establish his lay practice society.

Sokatsu never stopped teaching. He devoted himself emphatically to training lay students—hundreds by the time of his death—among them three who carried his full Dharma transmission:

Goto Zuigan, who had been part of the original group in California and eventually did take monastic ordination, becoming abbot of Myoshin-ji and Daitoku-ji; Kuon-an Eizan, a university man, a professor of natural science at Yokohama, who around age nineteen had a major Zen breakthrough after spending three months doing zazen alone in a cave, maintained lay status his entire life, and eventually became successor to Ryomo-an when Sokatsu retired; and Sokei-an.

It was well known that among the students of Sokatsu there were several over the years who were secretly temple monks, who would come to study under him because he was considered such a brilliant teacher. If Sokatsu found out, the student was banished. Some of Sokatsu's students did enter temple life at some point—they too would be disowned, though occasionally readmitted, as with Goto Roshi.

Later, in private, Sokei-an would often repeat a saying of Japanese Zen students: "May I get what the roshi has, but also may I keep from being like him." His allegiance to Sokatsu as a teacher was unfailing. But not to Sokatsu as a man. He loved Eichoku and was very fond of Eizan—who had also come from a wealthy family and let Sokatsu run through his fortune—and he felt Sokatsu as a man had treated both of them poorly.

Westerners tend to come to Zen practice with expectations, too many illusions of what Zen masters are supposed to be. It can get in the way of their training. There's a gap between the brilliant teacher and the fallible human that can be hard to reconcile. But it should not negate the teaching. The training is to see beyond apparent contradictions.

When you see people who are doing good or evil, of course you will like or dislike them.

The teacher holds a treasure. It already belongs to you. You must untangle for yourself the knot that will release it into your being. The treasure is more precious than anything. When you grasp this, you will recognize that the universe accommodates everything. *Dukkha*: There is suffering. Is this a betrayal? *Nirodha*: There is cessation of suffering.

By the end of his time in Japan, Shigetsu had, as he put it, completed his Zen. What did this mean? He had successfully navigated, through his years of persistence, and not a few missteps, the entire sequence of koans instituted by Hakuin Zenji. He had gotten to the end, demonstrating his awakenings in the Dharma combat of sanzen.

Enlightenment is a process. Within Buddhism, the supreme awakening of the Buddha is considered to be complete, irrevocable. The rest of us, if we are fortunate, arrive at many enlightenments—some profound, some less so; many momentary, fleeting, some more lasting.

The system of koan study in Rinzai training provides a framework for unfolding multiple awakenings; the first kensho, a profound initial awakening into the awareness of original being—dharmakaya—is followed by dozens more koans designed to facilitate deepening, strengthening, more readily available access to the awake state. Within this framework, there are many occasions of satori, small and large, until it becomes a robe that is constantly worn.

Is the sequence of koans necessary? *The gates of Dharma are manifold—I vow to enter them all!* Hakuin, who systematized the use of koans as he revitalized Rinzai practice in the eighteenth century, considered his fivefold sequence to be the most direct path to reality. This is important. There are teachers who make adjustments according to their particular lineage and the needs and progress of their students. This is also important.

There is also in Rinzai Zen acknowledgment of the necessity of post-satori practice. It turns out that finishing is not the end.

At this point was Shigetsu a Zen master? He did not yet have his inka, the final certification to teach, the full Dharma transmission, the title of Roshi, or a new name. That would come. But not yet. First he had to return to America. The koan of everyday life.

Intimations of the Sublime
Hinsdale, Illinois, 1932–1933

No, there was not some big problem. A big problem isn't necessary to begin seeking a more profound reality. Even in America. Or, put another way, dukkha, the First Noble Truth—usually translated as "suffering"—can simply mean unsatisfactoriness. Or disappointment. People get distracted by ambition, gossip, habit. Everyday life feels flat, predictable. Every so often a bright moment penetrates the haze. An inkling of possibility.

For Ruth it began early. She was born into privilege and social aspiration, exposed to the opportunities of America and the entire world. The first child of wealthy Chicago businesspeople, she entered a universe buzzing with pride and possibility. The 1893 World's Columbian Exposition brought representatives of all the advanced nations to her city and demonstrated to all attendees the triumphal excellence of her land, the United States of America, which was quickly becoming a major industrial power. The World's Parliament of Religions, part of the Exposition, brought Soyen Shaku to Chicago, with a discourse about the Buddha's teaching on the law of cause and effect, which his young student D. T. Suzuki had translated into English. Ruth was a year old. Forty years later, this same Dr. Suzuki would introduce her to her Zen teacher in Japan.

Her parents hosted dinners to coincide with the proceedings, as their position required of them. Ruth's father, George E. Fuller, had turned a modest family endowment into estimable wealth as a commodities broker on the Chicago grain and stock markets. George and his wife, Clare Elizabeth Houlgrave Fuller, had come to the United States from French Canada, in the decade before Ruth was born. Ruth's mother had family money; her parents immigrated to Canada from England, where the Houlgrave name hearkens back to Cheshire and Lancashire manors established in the thirteenth century.

In 1890s Chicago, the Gilded Age was in full swing. Fashions were changing; electric streetcars were replacing horse-drawn carriages and cable cars. Chicago grew from less than a million to nearly two million people as the city became an industrial and transportation hub for America. The newly built railroads allowed grain to flow from previously unsettled prairie land into the city, giving rise not just to better food distribution but to a new cohort of speculators who could now buy and sell commodity futures without ever taking physical possession of the grain. Those who were clever and well connected, such as George Fuller, could multiply their investments many times over.

In 1894, the Burlington Northern train line connected Chicago to Hinsdale, Illinois, a town incorporated twenty years earlier in anticipation of this rail line. Enterprising developers had bought up the gently rolling landscape, laid out streets and built houses, enticing young families to invest in a quiet and safe setting with a rural flavor just twenty minutes by train from the big city.

Ruth and her parents moved to Hinsdale in 1895 when Ruth was three; her brother, David, was born later that same year. In 1898 the family purchased a house at 409 South Grant Street— her father could walk the four blocks to the rail station to commute to Chicago for his job. In keeping with their rising status, the family had a live-in servant, from Sweden.

Hinsdale became one of the wealthiest towns in Illinois, with a quaint downtown, old farmhouses, and grand mansions. In 1899 the Hinsdale Club opened in the center of town to host dances, lectures, plays, and meetings. Though the public schools were quite good, Ruth and her brother attended private schools. Immigrants, largely from eastern Europe, flooded in to provide services to the people of the new town.

In many respects George and Clare played out the roles expected of their class, attending and hosting lavish social functions and training their two children to behave appropriately. But not all was peaceful in the household: George, as his business successes multiplied, took mistresses; at some point he contracted syphilis. His indiscretions shook Clare's sense of stalwart propriety, and she banished him from the house when the children were still fairly young. Although George moved out, to a grand, floor-through apartment in downtown Chicago, he remained part of the children's lives.

As a child, Ruth presented herself properly, but she did not refrain from speaking her mind. If something did not make sense, she pointed out the hypocrisy. She read everything she could get her eyes on. She was an intellectual. The reasons for things mattered. From early on, as she cultivated awareness of the great cultural traditions of the world, she developed a deep respect first for the European rationalists and then for what she could find about the lands and religions of the East.

But she had little appreciation for her own family's religion. Her parents were strict Presbyterians: this was the rigid Calvinist sect that believed in predestination, and thus in "infant damnation," which claimed that babies who die in infancy without the grace of baptism are eternally damned. This made no sense to Ruth. Eternally damned? For no crime? Simply for being born, through no intention of their own? This was not justice.

And Ruth's mother, Clare, would also not countenance such an unmerciful view. This became the subject of bitter arguments between George and Clare. Whether it was ultimately the true source of their disagreement, it would never fail to fill the air with a heavy, acrid vapor. Afterward Ruth could walk into the parlor, now empty, and still feel her skin prickle at the lingering vitriol that clung to the wallpaper and dripped from the chandelier.

What was the purpose of this church? Ruth recognized it as an important social institution. It gave her family structure; it provided definition. It set the standards. But the theology? It was utterly irrational. It had no basis in reality. There is no inherent damnation. With no recourse? No possibility of salvation? The very notion practically gave her a seizure.

As soon as Ruth heard of Buddhism she found refuge in its profoundly sensible truths. It was little wonder that expressing and upholding those truths would eventually define her life's purpose. Lurking in the background were the shackles of her Presbyterian upbringing, which, mostly, she managed to shake off by the end of her life.

A human birth is a precious opportunity. There is no guarantee of anything.

Certainly the household one is born into makes a large difference. From a certain perspective—from the Buddha's perspective—one of the seven factors of suffering is contact with conditions that are unsatisfactory. For example, the household you are born into. Which may also, Ruth acknowledged, be a source of conditions that do not directly cause suffering. She appreciated her own privilege. She saw it as useful, providing immense opportunities, and she held to her resolve to live her life making the best possible use of these. As she saw it, some of the more profligate youth of her class squandered what they were given. They took the vehicle of their wealth straight to the scrapheap—bringing suffering upon themselves and their families, and doing precious little to relieve the suffering of others. They should find a destination more worthy of their endowments.

As with other young women in her rarified circles, Ruth's late teens and early twenties were consumed with lessons (languages, music, dance) and parties, charity and debutante balls, theater, opera, trips abroad—all preparing her for a position as the wife of some similarly situated gentleman. Women of her class were taught to restrain their intellectual and argumentative sides. She attended the Kenwood Institute, a prestigious high school affiliated with the University of Chicago, but was not expected to seek a university degree.

Ruth Fuller, senior photo from the Lampadion Yearbook, 1911, Kenwood Institute. Courtesy of Joan Watts.

She had a gift for languages, and she studied French and Italian with a fervent interest in getting beneath the surface, in truly understanding. Where others were content to learn piano as a pleasant entertainment, she pursued it vigorously, developing skill and precision. On her way to becoming an accomplished musician, she traveled to Switzerland for several months in 1913, to study with the renowned pianist and conductor Rudolph Ganz, who had been at the Chicago Musical College and who would later come back to the United States to lead orchestras in Chicago, St. Louis, and Omaha.

When it came to organizing social events for any cause, Ruth spared no detail, making certain that everyone who attended was provided for lavishly. She saw to it that every guest was treated as the guest of honor. She considered social formalities not as a barrier between people but as the framework of civility that allowed

Ruth Fuller, circa 1915. Courtesy of Joan Watts.

people who might not agree on all matters to engage in polite
exchanges and recognize their common purpose.

In June of 1916, when Ruth was twenty-three, Chicago hosted
the Republican National Convention. Ruth and her compatriots
turned their skills toward organizing garden parties, balls, and a
grand parade in support of women's suffrage.

Ruth's parents worried that, as her twenties progressed, she had
not found a marriage. Her determination and sharp intellect might
be admirable, but these qualities did not make her especially mar-
riageable. Girls of her set were usually engaged after their debuts
at eighteen or nineteen. At twenty-five, she might not marry at all.
Ruth was well-liked and respected by her peers, but clearly that
was not enough. Her parents took it upon themselves to find her
a husband. Through mutual contacts, they found Edward Warren
Everett. Warren, as he was known, was wealthy and from a suitable

Edward Warren Everett in his Chicago law office, circa 1917.
Courtesy of Anne Watts.

family. A distinguished trial lawyer, he was a senior partner with a prominent law firm. His grandfather had been a governor and senator of Massachusetts, and had shared the speakers' platform with Abraham Lincoln at Gettysburg. Warren was twenty years older than Ruth and had never been married.

She was not happy about the arrangement, but she quelled her protests and acquiesced.

Everett family dinner. Ruth is on the right of the table; her mother and father are behind her. Courtesy of Joan Watts.

Warren and Ruth married in 1917 in a modest ceremony at the Plymouth Congregational Church in Chicago, followed by a small reception with family and close friends at the large apartment of Ruth's father on Scott Street. They traveled to Honolulu for a brief honeymoon. As a wedding present, Warren gave Ruth a yellow Stutz Bearcat sports car.

On their return from Hawaii, Ruth and Warren first lived on Lincoln Park West in Chicago. Their daughter, Eleanor, was born the following year, 1918. It was a breech birth, which caused Ruth lingering medical problems.

Beyond her busy role as mother and wife, running a household with multiple servants, planning social dinners and parties for her husband's clients, and taking an active role in Chicago's society, she continued her private reading and study. Though these independent forays toward deeper possibilities for a life opened a window she could peer out through, in the early years of her marriage they also made the restraints of her position chafe all the more, until the undefined yearning was able to grow into a more deliberate pursuit.

On her return from Nanzen-ji, back into this contentious household, she considered where she had been. Was she the same person? Before Switzerland, before marriage, before motherhood, before Japan—before the zendo?

If anything she was more herself.

Anyway, this whole business of the self was problematic at best. So many people remain stuck imagining they are destined to live a certain life. In many cases, she supposed, people did find more or less what they expected—if they kept their expectations modest. If they lacked curiosity. If they lacked vision. Now with the Crash, bankers hurling themselves out of windows—someone among them might have expected a disaster, but once they'd been doing well for a certain number of years they stopped being able to imagine that anything could go off so terribly. How could it happen? They had not prepared for it. What was tragic, apart from the waste of human life, was how their imagination ultimately failed them.

She had always been able to imagine how things might be different. In that way she had not so much changed as gained more experience. She had somehow retained the capacity to be surprised—which, it occurred to her, was a prerequisite for true progress. Do you know your next thought? If you imagine you can predict what lies on the other side of the koan, you have already locked yourself out. It requires persistence, but of a receptive attitude. It's not what you expect. Then when it arrives, there's a deep familiarity about it that is itself surprising, a sense of being suddenly not cut off from the universe. And to think that this whole time it was right here with you. But fleeting.

The trick is not to think you can trap it into staying, but to welcome it, to invite it in as a visitor, a welcome guest who comes and goes according to the mysterious demands of one condition pulling at the next, coming and going. With the proper attitude and after many attempts at enticing and tricking it into staying, you and the guest find some way to become more familiar with each other. And next time it may linger a moment longer, and perhaps come back sooner—though to be sure, it is easy to slip, and months may go by between visits. Faith, for Buddhists, is a matter of allowing that it will arrive, it will return—perhaps with this very breath. Even in America. But not with people yelling at her. Much more likely, she felt, in Japan, in the zendo. So she must return.

Her experience at Nanzen-ji had already resolved the question that had been her starting point: would it be possible for a Westerner, rigorously following the system of meditation practiced in Zen Buddhism, to achieve observable results? Her breakthrough had confirmed that, yes, it was possible. But she also grasped that it was only a beginning.

This lack of progress was wholly unsatisfactory.

A Stone May Hear

New York, 1921–1926; Tokyo, 1926–1928; New York, 1928–1933

Sokei-an had to go back to New York. The visa he had obtained gave him semipermanent residency in the United States, but if he left the country for more than two years at a time, it would be void. So in 1921, he had to return. In any case, he was ready. He had accomplished what he had set out to do in Japan. He had completed his koan study. Nevertheless, his training continued. There is no way of knowing when the breakthroughs will occur.

On arrival in New York in late 1921 or early 1922, he again went to live in Greenwich Village. By now he was fully a master carver, and he had earned a reputation as someone who could be trusted to repair the most delicate pieces—jades, woodcarvings, precious antique furniture, statuary. He went to work for a man named Edward Farmer, one of the top importers of jade lamps and porcelain bowls, Chinese ceramics, carved furniture, with a luxury boutique on East Fifty-Sixth Street off of Fifth Avenue. This provided a steady stream of income, which was sufficient to live on.

In Greenwich Village he had found a social climate where he was accepted as a unique individual. Now he seemed somehow more solid than when he had lived here before—less the wispy, youthful poet who had entertained the boisterous patrons of Petrillo's with his flowing waves of verse, though he continued to frequent the ongoing, spontaneous salon of the restaurant's back room. There was somehow a largeness, a deep, quiet presence that filled the space around him, even in the midst of a crowd—a still point that he could project at will, a secret flash of light if you caught his glance a certain way. If you were open to it. Of course if your mind was too busy with your own pretentious assumptions, you would never see a thing. But if you could quiet your mind enough to listen, you might hear something beyond the churning of your own thoughts.

The people in Petrillo's sometimes reminded him of his birth mother's family. His birth mother was an actress and his aunts were geishas.

This birth mother, Chiyoko, had come to stay with his father by arrangement, when it became clear that Kitako, the mother who would raise him, was unable to have a child.

Kitako Kubota was from a large and eminent family. She and Tsunamichi had been married for several years without producing any children. Tsunamichi especially yearned to have a son. At the time, their solution was not so unusual: both sides of the family, Kitako included, agreed that Tsunamichi would take a concubine to help conceive a child. In those days, when a man of the upper classes took a concubine, whether to produce children or for pleasure, it was considered a symbol of wealth or status for the man and a respectable occupation for the woman. It was understood that a chief wife might have to share her husband and household with another wife or a concubine—and be agreeable about the situation.

In any case, they made no effort to hide their arrangement. Kitako returned to her parents' home, temporarily retiring from her position as Tsunamichi's wife, while young Chiyoko moved in. She was seventeen or eighteen years old, the daughter of a tea master and *ikebana* teacher in Osaka, quite pretty and sweet. Their agreement was that she would live with Tsunamichi until she produced a son, and she would stay with the child for a year after that. When she had fulfilled this contract, she would receive a dowry for her own marriage and would return to her family, leaving any children she had with Tsunamichi to be raised in his household.

Yeita was born March 15, 1882—though later his birthdate was celebrated on February 15 to coincide with the Buddha's enlightenment day—toward the end of the first year Chiyoko lived with Tsunamichi. For whatever reason, she stayed on for two more years after the birth instead of one; Yeita was a toddler when Chiyoko disappeared and Kitako returned home to become the boy's mother.

Kitako, a conscientious and loving person, always feared that she could not offer her son the same love she would have given him had she been his birth mother; to make up for that, she lavished him with attention and affection. She need not have worried. He grew up absolutely devoted to her.

It was during his university days in Tokyo that Yeita discovered the whereabouts of his biological mother. They arranged to meet in Ueno Park. A police officer noticed them and came over to make sure nothing illicit was occurring; the officer mistook Chiyoko for a prostitute who had accosted the youth.

She was quite beautiful. Now in her midthirties, she had become a successful actress, with a family and other children of her own. After the initial meeting, she and her reunited oldest son began seeing each other regularly. She introduced him to her sister, the geisha mistress. During his vacations he would go to stay there, at his aunt's geisha house in Osaka. The geishas took him into their world, playfully introducing him to the delights of feminine companionship; he happily returned whenever he had the chance.

Chiyoko had another sister who was a singer of *joruri*, a narrative song form accompanied by shamisen, performed on its own or incorporated into *bunraku*, the traditional puppet theater of Japan. And she performed bunraku along with her husband, who was renowned as a singer and actor. The uncle was also a master of *rakugo*, comedic monologues performed on a vaudeville-like stage.

Yeita relished his newly found uncle and aunts, and he immersed himself in their theatrical world, for a time harboring fantasies of entering that world as a performer himself. He learned their repertoire and showed talent—he was a natural mimic. At least once, he got his uncle to let him come onstage and perform in the uncle's place.

It was a life he could imagine living. Even as a Zen student, even in his early years in America, he saw no need to abandon such aspirations.

When he returned to Japan, however, he did none of those things. He devoted himself entirely to his training. He sat zazen and tangled with koans he thought he had already solved. That was all.

There was a blank spot on the map. It was his mind. He had finished his Zen and entered a state of immediacy that was a form of absence. This is fairly common. There are monks who go into rapture, where they are gone, unreachable. In extreme cases their bodies may appear lifeless. There is a story of a group of Zen students at the end of a Rohatsu sesshin who come upon the body of a senior monk, showing the early stages of decay. The abbot tells them not to disturb the monk: he will return to his body at the end of the evening. And sure enough, the monk returns. The students bow to him. The abbot is furious and chastises them—this is not the goal. Do not follow his example! Where had he gone? Nowhere. He was simply absent.

It is better not to talk to such people—their view is wrong. Like some priests who absentmindedly meditate like a doll looking at the sky—in a thousand years, they will gain nothing. Be very careful of someone like this who calls himself a Zen student—he is not your friend.

Mindlessness practice does not mean being absent—it means that the mind you experience as belonging to you has no beginning or end. After returning to New York, there were months in which Shigetsu floated in such a state of absence. He did not realize it. Somehow he continued his carving and writing, and interacting with people. But for two or three years, nothing. *This is not the correct understanding of emptiness. True emptiness is active. Like the sky, it embraces everything.*

His first public talks were in Central Park. A few people came to listen. The Orientalia Bookshop, devoted entirely to books, art, and artifacts of Asia, had just opened on East Fifty-Eighth Street in Manhattan. The scholar Ananda Coomaraswamy gave talks on the art of Asia and helped arrange for a series of talks and discussions by other teachers and scholars. Thus it was that Shigetsu Sasaki began giving regular talks about Zen.

When I was a boy, I was looking for drinking water in the temple near where I was fishing. I left my rod outside and went inside. There was only one monk in this little old temple and one old woman. He was giving a lecture to one old woman and stones! I understood he was giving a lecture, and I stayed till it was over. I did not understand a word!

At twenty I entered the monastery. Then, when I was twenty-three and studying Zen, I was passing through some place, and I saw many dressed-up ladies and gentlemen going into a temple. It was the same temple, the same monk, and an audience of two hundred! Later my teacher said, "Say anything you want. Don't mind the audience. Stones hear—a stone may hear!"

But to be fully a teacher, he needed his inka. And for America, for Americans, he saw that, however interested they were in his subject, they would only really begin to pay attention and apply it to their lives if they recognized him as a religious official. A temple man. He knew America. He needed to be ordained as a priest. His teacher Sokatsu would not be pleased. Shigetsu would wait before mentioning this detail.

Sokatsu agreed that he should come back to Japan for additional training—to clear up some elements of his practice that still needed improvement. And then Sokatsu would give him the full Dharma transmission, to authorize him to teach and make him the lineage bearer.

In 1926, having spent five more years in the United States, he traveled back to Japan for the last time. He would remain for two years.

His mother was ill. His wife had become mentally unstable. In his absence she had had a severe breakdown.

She had become infatuated with a married man in Tokyo, a Christian preacher and proselytizer. One day her mind snapped in the street: she was down on her hands and knees worshipping a horse, ranting incoherently. They had to carry her away. She was in a sanitarium for two or three years. When she came out she became a Christian—a rather vehement Christian. When Shigetsu went back to Japan, he found living with her impossible.

As a child, upon hearing a Christian missionary assert that humans are inherently sinful, Yeita put the notion to his father for confirmation. His father laughed and told his son, "It is false. Everyone on earth is pure!"

As a child, at times he did things that he knew would anger his father—not from any great desire to antagonize him, but simply out of playful irreverence. He would use his father's samurai sword to cut weeds—highly disrespectful. He stepped on his father's sacred priestly robes—if anything, even more disrespectful, an insult to his father's position.

Once, when he was thirteen, his father was sick and asked him to close up the shrine and put out the candles. Yeita went and tried to blow them out, but they were too high for him. So he took them down and doused them in water. The next morning when his father went to light them, the wicks were still wet and would not light. His father was furious. Yeita was sent away for two weeks, to his uncle's house.

As a young child, during the day he was allowed to roam through the woods and along the water more or less as he pleased. They lived near a river that ran to the sea, and Yeita would spend his mornings catching shrimp. Every day he was down by the water catching shrimp and bringing them home for his mother to cook for him.

One day when he came home his mother was out on an errand. Determined to have his favorite dish, he looked at the cooking fire and his mother's cookware and realized he knew what to do. He had been watching her closely and, without even thinking, understood how to prepare the shrimp. He put water in one of his mother's pots and boiled the shrimp and was very satisfied with his delicious meal.

When she came home she was furious. What? You used my best pot for shrimp? Now it smells like shrimp and nothing else can be cooked in it! She showed him the pot that was set aside specifically for shrimp: "Use only this pot!" But when again he wanted to cook his own shrimp, he found whichever pot was convenient. He did this several times. Finally, exasperated, she came home one day with a special pot for him to use. "This is for you," she said. "Cook your shrimp in it, and when you're finished, wash it and put it away." And he did, delighted to have his own pot.

Japan had changed. There was a *tengu* at work, a demonic spirit. He did not believe in demonic spirits. And yet.

One day he went to the *Chuokoron* office and he was told that they didn't need anything more: there were other writers coming up who were taking his place. He was no longer in vogue. They didn't need an article for the next month. Nothing further.

For some time his teacher Sokatsu had been needling him about this writing, this vulgar way of making a living—how he relied on being an entertainer. A Zen teacher does not rely on being entertaining. Shigetsu acknowledged this but defended his work—it's actually Buddhism in disguise, this Nonsense.

"A disguise—who is there that sees past it? Only one person. The disguise is too clever! Who is there who wants to be enlightened and not merely entertained? And that one—why would he turn to this Nonsense to be enlightened? In any case, it cannot last."

It did not last. When the gate closed, he was devastated. In the *Chuokoron* office, where he had been sending his Nonsense every month for the past—what, ten years, twelve years? where every month Tomeko had gone to collect the check, the two hundred dollars that she relied on for her support, for the children, for his aging, ill mother—they said, "No more. Thank you for your offerings. We will not be requiring anything further."

So that is all? No more?

"The tastes have changed. People want fresh voices, something new. You had your time, now it is over."

At home he dropped down to his knees. He pounded the floor and wailed.

In 1928 his mother died. The same mother who had chastised him for ruining her cookpot. Who had introduced him to his carving master. Who had supported his study of poetry and art and then his entry into Zen training. He had asked her for permission to travel to the United States with his teacher, and she had given it. He had asked for her permission to marry Tomeko, and she had given it. He had sent Tomeko back to Japan to look after her. Kitako had been ill these last few years. Now she was gone. This same mother.

On July 15, 1928, Sokatsu granted him inka, the final seal of approval in the Rinzai school, giving him the title of Roshi and the name Sokei-an. As a sign of the transmission, Sokatsu gave him a fan and a robe, which had belonged to his teacher Soyen Shaku, to take to America.

The name Sokei-an refers to the Sixth Zen Patriarch, Huineng, whose hermitage was in a place called Caoxi—pronounced Sokei in Japanese. The life and teachings of Huineng are important to Sokei-an, but Sokei-an is not Huineng.

Sokei-an, granted inka, 1928.
Courtesy of the First Zen Institute of America.

This transmission of Dharma is a very important and grave matter. A Zen master is not like a teacher of the West, who passes information and intellectual knowledge to students. A Zen master embodies the teachings and transmits nothing more or less than his or her own quality of being. The student becomes the teacher's embodiment of the Buddha's awakening—the direct contact and expression of realization in an unbroken line from Shakyamuni Buddha.

> It can only be done face to face, eye to eye. This eye I am talking about is a very important part of Buddhism. This eye is the physical eye, the eye of wisdom, the eye of Dharma, and the eye of Buddha. In Buddhism, all theories take this hairpin turn. The physical eye and the Buddhism eye are the same.
>
> You must break into Zen in your everyday life, express this profound Samadhi, and in the ever-changing circumstances before your eyes, manifest the lightning-fast intuition of wisdom in action.

Sokei-an went back to New York again in 1928. Now he was a roshi and could teach properly. But he didn't find anybody to teach when he first went back, and he was still quite distressed about many things. He was completely alone with nothing but his Zen.

He got a commission from another magazine, to write a series of articles on the various peoples who lived in New York City. And so, when he got back to New York, instead of going to Greenwich Village, he lived for two or three months apiece with an Italian family, a Portuguese family, several other families, and eventually with a black family.

He needed to do something to eat. He went to Yamanaka & Company, where he had repaired antique carvings, and met with Mr. Miya, head of the New York office. They discussed Sokei-an's situation. Mr. Miya was very interested in Zen; he had studied some Zen previously.

Sokei-an always spoke very appreciatively of the families he had been staying with—especially the Italian family and the black family. He liked them very much, and he never felt anything but gratitude and kindness toward them. But when he spoke to Mr. Miya, Miya found it unfortunate that he must board with these families.

So Mr. Miya himself arranged the lease on two rooms with a little kitchen at 63 West Seventieth Street and gave Sokei-an five hundred dollars.

At that time, before the war, there was a Japan Club in New York, quite a prosperous institution, run largely for the heads of Japanese businesses who were established in New York. They used to go there for dinner and have Japanese food. There were reception rooms where they could play cards or *go*. A group of them had a class. And Sokei-an began to talk to them about Zen a few nights a month. Little by little people began to come to listen.

By 1930, Sokei-an had some regular students, and in April 1931, in that house on Seventieth Street, they incorporated the Buddhist Society of America. He was not happy with the name—he would have preferred it to be the First Zen Institute of America—but was voted down.

Who were these people? What was it in their lives that drew them to seek something other than what the America around them had to offer? Something slight, perhaps; a mere inkling that not all was as it seemed, as it had been presented; that a simpler, innocent past was maybe not quite so; that the lost time of childhood held inaccessible secrets that no amount of talking would reveal; that the winds of foreign places carried wisdom, which might be difficult to translate but which, for someone with the right attitude, was possible to grasp.

Or something larger, perhaps—a not-so-subtle discontent. A dispute with things as they have been promoted, in the glorious America of the modern century. This greatness that is not quite good enough.

Not everyone wants what other people want.

What was it that drew them in?

A friend says, "I heard this man speak—a Japanese Zen Buddhist priest. I went to hear him talk—something happened!"

"What do you mean? What did he say?"

"It was curious. He was just talking—slowly. At first it was difficult to catch his words—his accent, his pauses, as if he were waiting for the words to come from the air, and he pulled them down and spoke them through his mouth. He seemed to be telling a story about—what, I'm not even sure. His childhood. His teacher. Confusion and then not confusion. Meeting someone. A Buddhist concept. And then the room disappeared!"

"What—he's a magician?"

"It's hard to explain. You should come hear him yourself."

Perhaps they were expecting something magical. But it was not magic: it was contact with reality. If they experienced this, if they kept coming, after a few weeks he would give them the first koan and offer them sanzen. But it was important to come first to his talks—not just to show dedication, true interest beyond mere curiosity. The familiarity of hearing him, experiencing dharmakaya, even just in teisho—it was like tuning the instrument. Then they could begin to learn the first notes. The possibility of hearing for oneself.

Some of the Japanese supporters—Mr. Miya and others—had a genuine interest. But they were prisoners of tradition. For most of them, in the beginning, supporting him was merely to fulfill a sense of obligation. To show that they were upstanding fellow countrymen. Buddhism as they knew it, as they expected it to be, was mostly ceremonial, and they were grateful to find someone in their midst who could fulfill these functions, even just the bare outline of them. For them there was no doubt that his priestly services were satisfactory. But what he was doing did not require their presence. They would come to talks occasionally, they would make offerings, the donations that helped keep him afloat. But they would not take sanzen, they would not become his students. As a teacher, he was here for the Americans.

Of course Sokatsu was furious when he found out about Sokei-an's plan to become a priest. But Sokei-an said, "Americans will not pay attention to a layperson."

Sokei-an insisted on going ahead and shaving his head and putting on robes, and from that point on he always functioned as a priest. His master could not forgive him this decision—he disowned him as a disciple and in fact never spoke to him again.

Buddhism at its root is a pragmatic religion: its starting point, the Four Noble Truths, is the statement of a problem (dukkha, suffering), the cause of the problem (ignorance, craving), the potential for cessation of the problem (nirodha), and the method of resolving the problem (the Noble Eightfold Path). All based on empirical observation and refined through practice.

Sokei-an's decision to become a priest was simply practical: based on the available evidence, he had determined that in America he would only be effective as a teacher if he were ordained. Otherwise the trappings of priesthood did not concern him. As a Zen master he fully agreed with Sokatsu that the most capable students were usually laypeople.

Sokei-an had a friend in the Daitoku-ji lineage, a priest named Aono Futetsu, who had at one time been a student of Sokatsu and so was a Dharma brother of Sokei-an. Of course Sokatsu had severed all ties with Aono when Aono entered the temple establishment. When Sokei-an contacted him, Aono Roshi was abbot of Manman-ji, a big subtemple of Daitoku-ji, located in Chiba Prefecture. Aono understood Sokei-an's predicament and was happy to make arrangements for him, formally accepting him as a disciple.

On March 15, 1933, Sokei-an received the priestly precepts and the rank of *jisha* (attendant) at Daitoku-ji. On the occasion of the six hundredth anniversary of temple founder Daito's death, he received a robe and bowl from Aono Roshi, along with the religious name Soshin. All of this, through a complex but accepted procedure, was carried out while he remained in New York. But his real training and authority to teach came from Sokatsu, and he was always known as Sokei-an, the name Sokatsu gave him with his inka.

On Sokatsu's seventieth birthday in 1939, the venerable anti-priest gave a talk about his life. At the ceremony he said that he had taught five thousand students. Of these, nine hundred were initiated into Zen. Of the nine hundred, he had given inka to nine, and of those nine, only four were his heirs. Sokei-an was one of the four. With that statement, Sokei-en was reinstated.

The apartment on Seventieth Street was just one large room with a shrine that could be closed off with folding screens. An old friend from Japan gave him a couch bed, a very large Chinese rug, some thirty folding chairs, a small desk, lamps, bookcases, and a radio. He embellished his tokonoma with brocades, and his small altar had lighted candles and mysterious doors that were thrown open after sanzen. They held celebrations there for Buddhist holidays— Buddha's Enlightenment Day, Nirvana Day—as well as Sokei-an's birthday, and they had parties throughout the year with offerings of food brought to this modest temple.

After each talk Sokei-an permitted six questions. He went straight to the point. If you were an intellectual, you received philosophy, but if you had the Dharma eye, you saw—you were taken beyond Maya, you entered the realm of the immeasurable. Once he was asked if he could see into the future. He answered, "It is too terrible."

This was the first Zen institute in America and Sokei-an was the first Zen master to live in America and write, lecture, and give sanzen in English. He saw the country as ripe for spiritual revolution, since the young were not prisoners of tradition.

> When I came to this country and was tramping through the Cascade Mountains, following the Columbia River, I felt the soil of America had the Zen essence. The people's nature is like those great cedar trees—rather coarse grained, but straight and simple. The wonderful element in the American people is their generosity and bigheart-edness. Tao is already there, but these days human beings have forgotten what religion is. They have forgotten a peculiar love which united their human nature

to great nature. Americans live by their personal desire, isolating themselves until their hearts grow cold. That is the shortcoming of individualism.

My own mission is to be the first Zen master to bury his bones in this land and to mark this land with the seal of the Buddha's teaching.

I am in New York and I open my Zen school, Sokei-an is not doing this. New York is not doing this. After 2,500 years, from Japan, across seven thousand miles, this is the first time the seed of Buddhism has been transplanted into the soil of the eastern part of America. A growing seed is a precious thing.

He lived and taught there with his Maltese cat, Chaka.

I had a house and one chair. And I had an altar and a pebble stone. I just came in here and took off my hat and sat down in the chair and began to speak Buddhism. That is all.

Sokei-an and his cat Chaka.
Courtesy of the First Zen Institute of America.

Two Cats Spitting
New York, 1933

There was always a cat in the picture. It had nothing to do with tradition. For Sokei-an, the cat was an affectionate companion. And also a reflection of a certain sort of consciousness—alertness, ready attention. One should be like a cat at a mouse hole—not sleeping, but relaxed and alert, ready to pounce at any moment.

The universe expresses itself in everything. If you see buddha nature in a cat, who does it belong to?

The temple cat was Chaka, which is Japanese for "tea cake." A confection. There is also a Japanese idiom, *chaka-chaka*, that indicates restlessness.

Sometimes the plain meaning is correct, in Zen as elsewhere: a sweet companion. The unspoken hint about restlessness, however, was not lost on some of Sokei-an's students.

When Ruth and Sokei-an first met, they hissed and snarled like two cats spitting. Ruth thought: This is someone to contend with. Who has the real thing but is somehow not yet expressing it fully.

Sokei-an thought: This is someone with too many ideas. Who thinks she knows something.

In March of 1933, in the throes of conspiring to return to Japan, Ruth received a letter from her friend Dwight Goddard, author of *A Buddhist Bible*:

> My Dear Mrs. Everett: About your coming trip to New York, I wish very much you would meet Rev. Sokei-an Sasaki, 63 West 70th St., N.Y. You ought to know him. In some ways he is autocratic and blunt as the old school Zen masters, but underneath he is true. He has an artist's temperament, is an excellent woodcarver of Buddhist images, and earns his money by repairing all kinds of art treasures for Tiffany's. When you meet him try and turn the conversation to his artwork and ask to see some of his carvings. I think you will like him, in spite of his bluff assertive exterior.

She was in New York looking for a boarding school for Eleanor. She knew the Yamanaka family, and Mr. Miya, who ran their New York branch. Mr. Miya asked her if she would like to meet Sokei-an. He said, "I'll have a dinner at the Japan Club and have you meet him."

She had heard Mr. Suzuki speak of Sokei-an, but Mrs. Suzuki disapproved of Sokatsu and felt therefore that nobody connected with them should meet Sokatsu or know anything about him. And because Sokei-an was Sokatsu's disciple, he was beyond the pale of their interest.

But Ruth had also heard of him through old Mr. Goddard and other fellow Buddhists. So before going to New York she wrote directly to Sokei-an and said she would like to meet him. He made an appointment for her to come for a visit.

On a cold but bright afternoon at the beginning of April, an American woman, alone, wearing elegant but practical clothing—a modest outfit appropriate to her station, with a dark blazer bearing a carved jade brooch on the lapel, simple pearl earrings, and a single string of pearls adorning her neck—stepped out of a taxi onto the sidewalk in front of a solid four-story apartment building a block west of Central Park. The light glinted off the upper-floor windows. She paused to straighten her skirt as she rang the buzzer.

She had hoped to leave enough time to walk through Central Park on this crisp spring day—it was not quite like the grounds of a Japanese temple, but there were certainly spots within that would be suitable for meditation—but the business with looking at schools for Eleanor had gone too late. Another day.

He greeted her at the door—himself, alone. She had not expected attendants, not here, not like at a venerable temple in Japan. But she had also not expected—there was no polite distance—this immediacy. He was right here. A man, a being, fully present. Something about him. She had not meant to be taken aback, but—what? What was this? A tingling at the base of her skull. There was something—everything—unexpected about him. Something in his eyes. She felt her breath deepen. She had expected him to be large for a Japanese man, but this was different. The space around him seemed brighter—somehow even brighter than the bright day outside. And yet—

"Please—come inside. I am happy to see you. You can put your shoes there."

She felt somehow more awake. She had not expected to be reminded of the zendo at Nanzen-ji—after all, this was only an apartment in Manhattan, with just one man . . . In any case, it was not at all like the zendo. It was something—she could not put her finger on it. It was him. But who was he? How did he end up here, of all places?

He led her past three rows of folding chairs to a smaller room. To one side there was a cat lying comfortably on a cushion.

"Please—sit."

"Thank you."

She immediately sensed a fullness in his presence—a power somehow both raw and refined. An animal power, but more than that. A human power. A gateway to forces of nature. But there was also the curious feeling that no one was here. And what about herself—was she really here?

There was something like impatience in his attitude. A theatrical scowl. He was not smiling. He was not taking pains to put her at ease. And yet she did not feel any discomfort. In fact, she did feel strangely at ease. As if she could speak her mind completely and openly. Is this what sanzen with him would be like? She was not looking for a teacher. She already had a teacher. But what was she looking for?

"So—you have been in Japan."

"Yes, I am fortunate to have the acquaintance of Dr. Suzuki, who was able to secure an introduction for me to Nanshinken Roshi. After several weeks of zazen outside the sodo of Nanzen-ji, I was invited to join the monks in the zendo during osesshin."

"That is quite unusual. When I hear of American women going to Japan, I think, what can they possibly hope to find? They bring too many ideas with them."

"Yes."

"Not the right attitude. Missionary women, especially."

"I have met some of them as well. Their interest may be genuine. But being Christians—how can they possibly experience Buddhism as it truly is? As for Christianity, I don't really see what good it does—the way it is typically expressed. My only purpose is to study true Buddhism. I believe it cannot be experienced fully by someone who clings to another set of beliefs."

"But Christianity is important—the message of love. Americans have real need for that."

"The message of love, of course that is important. But Americans, I think, have difficulty hearing it."

"Then how can they hear Buddhism?"

"As I said, if one holds too tightly to another belief— "

"In any case, there are teachers of Zen here now. In America."

"Yes. I have been very interested to meet one."

"Have you read *Alice in Wonderland*?"

"It is a delightful children's book."

"I do not consider it simply a book for children. The author possesses insight like a real man of Zen. If you consider it from the perspective of studying koans, you may recognize this."

"Yes."

"I use it with my students. Some of them are beginning to make real progress."

"I suppose it merits further examination. Under the guidance of Nanshinken Roshi I have been working primarily with koans from the *Mumonkan*."

"But you will return to Japan? Tell me, Nanshinken Roshi—he has a reputation as being very stern. They say he does not spare the nyoi."

"He has shown me nothing but kindness. As for using the baton—are there not always one or two monks who are lazy and deserving of that treatment? Who must be dragged in by their ear for sanzen? Because they never have an answer."

"And your own sanzen?"

"That is between my teacher and me."

"But you are working with koans."

"Yes. And your students—you do not offer zazen?"

"They would not stay."

"How can they have the true Zen experience without zazen? Sitting meditation—"

"Of course meditation is important. But they are beginners. They will not see the purpose—they will be discouraged."

"You should expect more of your students."

"They must become hungry for it themselves. This is not Japan, where it is normal to push students hard and not offer any explanation. With Americans, if I do not offer them something they can grasp, they will question the purpose immediately. And then they will disappear."

"They can sit zazen."

"They come back for my talks, and if they show persistence in their interest, I offer them sanzen."

"They can learn the correct posture and quiet their minds."

"At least I have a roof over my head."

"I think you underestimate your students."

"Since you have so many ideas about what is proper between a teacher and his students, perhaps you will help me consider a puzzle I have been contemplating. Look at it as a koan of life if you will. I have been thinking about my teacher Sokatsu Shaku. He has a very sharp and direct manner. For the student, it can be uncomfortable. He is very effective. In my estimation, there is no greater teacher in his generation."

"I have not yet had the pleasure of meeting Sokatsu Roshi."

"I also have had another important teacher. My deceased father. He was very patient and kind with his students. So my question— which is the correct attitude for me to take with my own students?"

"Why not just be yourself?"

It was Sokei-an's turn to be caught by surprise. This woman clearly had achieved a degree of penetration that he had not anticipated.

"You will be in New York a few more days? Perhaps we can continue our conversation."

"Mr. Miya, with whom we are both acquainted, is arranging a dinner at the Japan Club this evening. He is hoping for your presence. And I also would be delighted to see you there." They snarled and hissed and at the end of their meeting Ruth felt she had made a dent in him.

This was the beginning of their relationship.

The dinner at the Japan Club that evening was well attended—it developed into a full-blown party. There was not much opportunity for Ruth and Sokei-an to talk, but they recognized in each other the spark of mutual interest that had been ignited—interest that would at first smolder and then burn strongly in the years to come. Yes, this is . . . perhaps unforeseen. But here it is.

Sokei-an wrote to Ruth: "Do we have any more opportunity to see each other before you sail? Perhaps not. There will be no more staring contest in our next meeting."

Thereafter, each time Ruth came to New York, they would meet for dinner.

Sokei-an was coming to Chicago. During the summer and fall of 1933 the city presented its second world's fair. Like the Columbian Exposition forty years earlier, with its Parliament of World's Religions that Soyen Shaku attended, the current proceedings included a World Fellowship of Faiths. Throughout the summer, forty-four thousand people came to events in which representatives of the world's faiths discussed practical matters—how their respective beliefs and practices, in dialogue with each other, might help alleviate the crises of the modern world.

Sokei-an, though skeptical about the potential for such an endeavor, attended. He stayed with Ruth as a guest in her home in Hinsdale.

He wrote to her afterward, "I am very glad I find Buddhist friends. These days it throws some music in my loneliness. Here in New York I am simply living among the deaf and mute."

RETURN TO NANZEN-JI
Kyoto, 1933–1934

Ruth is back in the zendo. The great dim zendo in the pine forest of Higashiyama. Back among the dark, motionless figures. Around her is the same deep stillness. Through the stillness again she hears the singing of the wind in the trees, the rushing of the mountain stream. As if from far, far away, the deep, sweet tone of the bell of Eikan-do comes floating toward her.

What is it about this place? The quiet—such deep quiet. The shadows and dimness. All the surfaces glow with the polish of dry cloths and generations of monks walking in procession. The simple devotion, *gassho*, hands together, bowing low from the waist; quiet offering. The incense, slightly sweet, a hint of spice. The opposite of distraction.

A certain athleticism also. Some things must be done quickly, with vigor. Give an answer! Full attention! The nyoi useful for counteracting sleepiness. Gassho and then a sharp blow between the shoulder blades. Wake up! As if your life depends on it. Not as if: Your life depends on it. The world depends on it.

In this place all of her concerns dissolve. All of her frustrations as insubstantial as vapor, drifting away even before the slightest hint of breeze whispers through the silent hall. In this moment everything is completely satisfactory.

Who she is does not matter. The wind through pine trees. Who she has been does not matter. Water rushing over rocks. Who she will be does not matter. Wisp of acrid incense smoke. Who? Does not matter. Dry leaf on path. Buddha nature: Mu!

Warren was livid. "You're abandoning me! You're taking my daughter, my only solace!"

Eleanor, of course, would not be left behind. Her prospects for school in New York were secure. It was not necessary that she begin immediately. A year in Japan would open the world to her in ways that boarding school never could. It would certainly set her apart from any of her peers. It had been her idea, actually, presented with her developing arts of persuasion. Of course Ruth did not need much convincing. Of course Eleanor did not want to be stuck nursing her ailing and ever more irascible father.

They arrived in October 1933. As before, Ruth rented a house on the Kamo River, this one called Shounso (Pine Cloud Villa). Eleanor, now nearly sixteen, was delighted to be there. She spent her days studying Japanese with a private language teacher, interspersed with studies of flower arranging and tea ceremony, explorations of the city with her teacher, visiting temples with her mother. She found a rich affinity for Japanese culture and, through this immersion—even without practicing meditation formally—as a teenager arrived at a deeper understanding of Japanese Buddhism than most Americans would have access to for at least another generation. She no longer felt abandoned.

Eleanor, who from a young age had shown sharp intellect and a curiosity and insight about life and the world that verged on mysticism, was developing an elegance that Ruth had so far not encountered and an entertaining wit that would, before long, make her an enjoyable companion. Her debut would be impressive. All in good time. For now, Ruth was relieved that her daughter's tendency toward illness and the ill-humor that accompanied it seemed to be less in evidence.

Warren, now retired and barely able to walk, was left in Hinsdale in the care of his widowed sister. That was about as close to satisfactory as possible, given the situation and the persons involved. Perhaps he could be brought here. But not now. Not yet. Ruth, otherwise a diligent and often passionate letter writer, maintained a perfunctory, though familiar, correspondence with her husband and sister-in-law.

In her first osesshin, at the beginning of her previous summer here, Ruth had come to within a breath of cracking the Mu koan. She pushed at it and teased it, gave it breathing room, came back at it stronger than before, pulled and twisted and turned it around, saw it from both sides, from no side—but, alas, still from the outside. She had pulled layers of husk off its kernel, freeing it to better penetrate the seed inside. Getting past that "no." Of course it was she, herself, whose layers were being peeled away. She was so close. But in the end, she was too exhausted to fully crack it open.

Returning here, at first she had to recover from some slippage that resulted during her time away, in the outside world—the lesser, less-true world, as she was coming to recognize. This was, perhaps, inevitable. Senior monks are often too busy with work and other activities, apart from during sesshin periods, to avail themselves of regular sitting meditation. But for them, regular zazen is no longer necessary. Every movement, every gesture, is fully enacted in a state of meditation. They live in it. For someone like her, not even a novice—in spite of more than a decade of study, useful preparation for beginning an active, direct practice, but not the thing itself—zazen is the necessary vehicle. It would, before long, carry her through the gate of the first koan, and then the next several in succession.

On the first of December, the Rohatsu osesshin began. This weeklong intensive training period would culminate on December 8, celebrated in Japan as the Buddha's birthday. As before, the monks would get little sleep, and none at all on the final night. It was the most auspicious time of year for penetrating through to the core of reality.

When the meditators got sleepy at about 1:00 a.m., Nanshinken would come through the zendo and rouse everyone for walking and chanting in the hondo. This sutra chanting penetrated through the silence with stirring unison, forming a buoyant raft of rhythmic sound that lifted them out of the haze that had gathered over hours of sitting silent and motionlessness. The sound and vibration coursing through each body carried them beyond any thought, beyond the desire for sleep, lifting everyone's spirits into a realm of sparkling, radiant emptiness. The boundary between body and breath vaporized.

They would get their breathing adjusted and begin to chant with exactly the same rhythm. The sounds of the Sanskrit words and the repetitions cleared away everything. There was nothing left but the sound. Deep, full, emptiness. Chanting and bowing, the respect of bowing, the mudra of exposing yourself, making yourself vulnerable. Very important. Here you are. Here I am.

Ruth believed chanting and bowing practices should be kept in anything that would someday become American Zen.

As before, in the lulls between intensive practice sessions, Nanshinken Roshi would come to her kitchen to relax, read, and eat her American cooking. She would feed him the tomato sandwiches that he loved.

In December, at the end of the Rohatsu osesshin, Ruth took vows to formally dedicate herself to Buddhism. During the induction ceremony, Nanshinken gave her the Buddhist name Kuge, which means "noble."

After the formal closing ceremony of Rohatsu, Ruth addressed the monks:

> I am an ordinary, everyday American woman. My life at home is that of the usual American woman of some means, a life which I judge does not differ much from that of Japanese women in the same situation in society. But it has for many years seemed to me that most of us live this brief span of years allotted to us between birth and death only half-conscious, half-awake to what life really is. There are times in the life of almost every human being when one becomes conscious of another hunger than that for food—there comes a great yearning to understand the "why" of existence and a longing to find one's own place in and relationship to the great Universe. It was not until I came to the study of Zen that I found that simple and eloquent truth again reestablished.
>
> I consider the months which I have given to the meditation as productive of the most valuable experiences of my entire life. And from what might be called "religious experience" which have resulted from these many, many hours and weeks of silent sitting, there have been

opened up to me a world of which I had previously
been only partially conscious. When one has experienced even slightly, through meditation, the unity of
all life, never again can one look upon one's neighbor
as quite so much a stranger as before. That is to me,
the great social value of meditation, the establishing
of the consciousness of the identity of oneself with all
people. Meditation is of value only in terms of everyday activity.

In early spring, before the cherry blossoms bloomed, Ruth had a
friend bring Warren to Japan, and she hired Ikeda, their stalwart
guide, translator, and secretary on the earlier trip, to care for him
in Kyoto.

In late summer the family traveled to Manchuria and Peking.
They visited the provincial city of Changchun, which the Japanese
had been remaking into the new capital of Manchukuo.

Since the Everetts first traveled in Asia in 1930, the Japanese
had consolidated their authority over Manchuria. Puyi, the last
emperor of the Manchu Qing dynasty, had in 1912 been deposed
from his nominal rule over China—he was only six years old—but
was allowed to remain in the Forbidden City until 1924, when he
fled to Tianjin under Japanese protection. In 1932 the Japanese
made him chief executive of Manchukuo—the Japanese puppet
state—and then in early 1934 elevated him to the title of emperor
of Manchukuo.

Warren and Ruth were granted an audience with Emperor Puyi
and Empress Wanrong. Wearing their finest—Warren in crisp tail-
coat and striped pants, Ruth in a shimmering gown and her best
pearl jewelry—they were led into the audience hall in a modest

office building, certainly nothing on the lavish and ornate scale of the Forbidden City.

Emperor Puyi was friendly and approachable, not at all pretentious. When he spoke with Warren about political matters, he spoke carefully; with Ruth, talking about Buddhism, he became more relaxed, and revealed a sincere longing. It was clear that his interest in Buddhism was genuine, and his access to its potential for relieving suffering was constrained by circumstances. Here was a man who was somehow incomplete. He had been born into a certain family and taken as a two-year-old into a strange ritualized world of adults he did not know or trust, who bowed to him as they attempted to control him, with no companions his own age, without his mother, only his ill-at-ease father and a wet nurse, who was his only solace during childhood.

Empress Wanrong remained politely in the background. She was delicately beautiful. In fact, she appeared fragile—she looked like she could be easily broken. Unknown to them, the emperor, who had long favored her, blamed her for driving away his second consort, Wenxiu—her co-wife—and had ceased communicating with her. Wanrong was also becoming increasingly addicted to opium, which would eventually be a factor in her death in a Chinese prison.

Puyi was himself a prisoner. He had grown up—if that were a wholly accurate assessment—in an exquisite prison, first in the Forbidden City and now in this polite exile. He longed for freedom. This is what he told Ruth: "You have found in Buddhism a peaceful refuge. I would welcome such an opportunity to also have a long period of retreat from the world."

This is what he did not tell her: As long as he remained in any sort of public position—which was hardly up to him—his yearning would remain unfulfilled. And even, later, when the last vestiges of worldly power were stripped from him, he would find it difficult to access the freedom available to one who could renounce the world completely.

Ruth had met a man who was completely free. He was named Sokei-an.

Hermitage in Manhattan
New York, 1932–1939

And yet freedom, the freedom within the rigor of dedicated practice, at first arrived in fits and starts, mere glimpses. This was Ruth's experience in the zendo. Gradually, eventually, it would return more readily, would linger, until for someone like Sokei-an who had truly unlocked it, it could be entered easily, at will—freely. When this freedom arrived, when Sokei-an embodied it—which was the foundation of his teaching—it illuminated the space entirely, dissolved all boundaries and assumptions of where space began and extended.

Not everyone was able to witness this transformation immediately—there were those whose Zen eye was not yet open. But in the room, when he was talking, the light would become so strong that even these people were transported.

One morning in 1932 the scholar Dwight Goddard came to the apartment on Seventieth Street to meet Sokei-an in person for the first time. In China as a Christian missionary in the 1920s, Dr. Goddard's profound encounter with Buddhism had led him to take vows of practice and declare himself a Buddhist. He had spent a year at a Zen monastery in Japan, and he had just published *A Buddhist Bible*, a selection of translations compiled in consultation with his friend and collaborator D. T. Suzuki. He had written to Sokei-an and wanted to meet him.

Sokei-an did the *osoji*—the cleaning—himself. At that time he was doing carving and repair work for Yamanaka, and he had work clothes he always wore in the morning when he was working and for cleaning up—an old *mompei*, a sort of padded jumpsuit, often worn by children and working women in winter.

Dr. Goddard knocked on the door. Almost immediately it opened. The man who answered had a broom in hand and rumpled work clothes on, and scowled at the visitor. The dignified, seventy-year-old Dr. Goddard, in his humble black suit and bowtie, was taken aback. "Does the Reverend Sasaki live here?"

Sokei-an said, "No," and slammed the door.

Afterward Sokei-an got to know Goddard well, and they became friends.

Years later when Ruth asked Sokei-an why he would slam the door like that, he said, "If that man had eyes, he would have seen I was the Reverend Sasaki; he wouldn't have looked at my mompei." These were immediate responses to the situation, not in any way an attempt to be eccentric.

The public portion of an evening at the Buddhist Society of America would begin with one of the senior students greeting people as they came in for the talk. Sometimes, in the beginning, there was a mere handful. Sometimes eight or ten. Sometimes, after a while, twenty-five or thirty. The guests would sit in the folding chairs and wait. Those who were new, who had never visited and did not know what to expect apart from a talk by a Japanese religious master, were invited to sit quietly, maintaining an upright posture, and allow their breathing to relax. Those who had come once or twice already, if they arrived a few minutes early, might have asked a senior student for tips on how to sit without feeling agitated and might have received some simple suggestions. This was the basic meditation instruction at Sokei-an's hermitage.

At eight thirty, a woman with large eyes that seemed on the verge of overflowing stood near the reading desk at the front of the room and announced that Shramana Sokei-an Sasaki, abbot of Jofuku-in, would be reading from a translation he had made from the sutra of the Sixth Patriarch of Zen in China and would comment upon it.

Through a pair of sutra-papered doors at the north end of the room, a large Japanese man in priestly robes and shaved head entered. He paused at an altar and performed a brief ceremony, bowing, burning incense, and chanting syllables that sounded more like rhythmic tones than recognizable Japanese words. He intoned them fully, though somewhat quietly, as if to himself, or simply to the altar, rather than to the room—with gentle reverence and a relaxed, seemingly casual grace, not in any way ponderous. Then, without directly regarding the audience, he seated himself at the reading desk, where his manuscript, inscribed in red Chinese characters, awaited.

As he settled into his seat, all of the rustling motions of the audience quickly ceased. Sokei-an sat before the group like a boulder on a mountaintop—still, immovable. He became the mountain. His immovable silence stilled all possibility of chatter in the room, absorbing even the scattered thoughts, anxieties, and preoccupations of the roomful of people sitting there, until everyday concerns dissolved and the possibility of fully listening emerged.

After about twenty minutes of sitting in this silence, the serious students were called up for sanzen. One by one they rose from their seats, bowed or nodded or briefly paused before the altar on their way to the sanzen chamber. What did they encounter? Behind the folding screen—this was the sanzen chamber, set up in a corner of the room—Sokei-an did not withhold anything. He fully transformed into the absolute state. This was his direct teaching.

The bell would ring, the sanzen student would return to the main room, the next student would rise, pause at the altar, and enter the master's chamber. What was spoken behind the screen was usually too quiet for those outside to hear—though occasionally a shout or roar would punctuate the murmurs. Then the bell would ring, and the student would emerge with a look of determination or exasperation or studied indifference, and the next would enter. When the last student came out—there were never more than six or eight taking sanzen at any time—the gong or wooden-fish clapper would signal that sanzen was complete, and Sokei-an would come out and take his seat at the table in front where his notes rested on a wooden stand. Next to the stand was always a crystal glass and a metal water pitcher for refilling the glass with cool water, much needed on hot summer nights when the ceiling fan labored rhythmically in an attempt to keep the drowsing, sweating students cool.

Sokei-an raised his *hossu*—the ceremonial fly whisk. Then he began talking, starting in a low, deep growl that would swell into words. He spoke extremely slowly. His delivery was full of pauses—a pause between phrases, a pause between sentences. A pause between thoughts. Those who were taking notes would be able to transcribe his words. But when he entered the dharmakaya state, those who were taking notes forgot themselves, and their pencils stopped moving.

The notes for this teisho were from the *Platform Sutra* of the Sixth Zen Patriarch, which provided material for 190 talks Sokei-an presented between 1935 and 1939. He read a passage, then began discussing it, giving it context, chewing over its meaning and relevance. If there was a technical term, he translated then discussed it for a few minutes. He expressed that the Buddha's teaching could only be correctly interpreted through Zen teaching.

> I translate the Sanskrit word *samadhi* into English as "tranquil meditation," or you could call it "absorption into Reality." Habitually, you think of this and that with names and forms. This mind activity is quite natural, but it is a nuisance. When your brain has nothing to do, it takes a vacation and makes this mind-stuff, which has little to do with the real life you are confronting, and it is very, very annoying. When I was in Manchuria, in a truck that might be blown up at any time, there was not much time to think, but there was still this mind-stuff. In tranquil meditation, we annihilate this mind-stuff, not by force but by practice.
>
> In the last lecture, I explained to you the meaning of samadhi and wisdom, but I shall explain it once more because many were missing at the last meeting. These lectures are very important. I am sorry that those who are absent are not hearing what I say only once in a lifetime.
>
> *Samadhi*, intense meditation, means to be absorbed in the depths of Reality. It is different from the abandonment of your mind in sleep, when you are absorbed in the chaos of darkness. In *samadhi*, you are absorbed in Reality.

In the course of talking, Sokei-an would insert stories to illustrate his purpose and draw the listeners yet further in. He would speak in the voice of any character, any person, male or female, old or young. It did not matter that his accent in English was poor; he became the characters. If there was an animal in the story, he would become the animal. If there was a pebble, a pond, a golden mountain, he would become it as he spoke. It was a special gift, beyond what an ordinary, or even extraordinary, actor could do. Sokei-an, the man they affectionately called Osho (revered teacher), disappeared entirely, replaced by the fox or ox or pebble or pond or mountain, right there for all to see.

At any second, while you are working at your desk, in a factory, or depositing a coin in the subway turnstile, you get a glimpse—Ah!—and it is all over.

In China, a monk was sweeping in the garden. A pebble struck a bamboo root and—Ah! Do not think this is a marvel. It is Reality. It is not like a flash in the eye, making the world look different. It is not so foolish. It is the diamond of the mind, the source from which spring all the laws of the universe.

This is the Sixth Patriarch's school of Zen. But, as a foundation, we must practice meditation, the foundation of Zen. If you haven't much meditation, you may pass koans, and you may attain wisdom, but it will shine dimly. But when you find IT, the whole universe shines, and you are its master. Only such meditation practice will enable you to discover intrinsic wisdom.

When you study painting, you are not given paints, canvas, and brush for a long time. For many years you have only charcoal and a piece of paper in your hand. You make light and shadow, light and shadow, until light and shadow are swallowed in your mind. Later, when your eye is developed, you will see light and shadow in color. When you look at a nude, you will not see this light and shadow, but only the outline of the body. So in Zen, one must be in *dharmakaya*, the first stage.

Later, when Ruth had become part of the group, she would say to him, "Sokei-an, you started out tonight explaining a technical term, and you were going along beautifully. And then before you knew it you were back in the dharmakaya again. Tonight's lecture theoretically had nothing to do with dharmakaya—how is it you're always getting back to the dharmakaya?"

He said, "There is one thing the West knows nothing about as yet, and that is the dharmakaya—that there is an absolute state people can experience, which must be experienced. I don't expect in my teaching life to do any more than to inculcate some people in America with either the feeling or the understanding or the realization of this dharmakaya state. That is the basis for our Zen study. Until they come to realize that—first of all to know about it and then to understand it and then to realize it—they cannot go on to real Zen study. And because nobody knows about the dharmakaya state in the West, I must come back. I must come back and teach it to them, talk to them about it."

He lived in it all the time. They had never seen anybody do something like that.

Nobody who ever listened to him could have any doubt: this was a thoroughly enlightened being. Once you had heard him and seen him you couldn't forget it. He would become so radiant it was almost hard to look at him. He glowed with what he was experiencing.

The room was completely filled. With what? Light, energy, an
unnamable quality. His face would change to a soft focus. As
he breathed in, everything was drawn into him and held there,
poised, shimmering with this electric charge. Heightened awareness: it was this active, ready state that was to be cultivated—"I
shout to wake you up!"—not peace of mind, which he disparaged
as "tranquil vacuity." *Become the cat at a mouse hole—not sleeping, but relaxed and alert.*

Sokei-an's woodcarving The Dancer.
Courtesy of the First Zen Institute of America.

In the moment when intrinsic wisdom penetrates throughout the universe, your enlightenment is there. Like a cat watching a rat—intrinsic concentration. Both cat and rat are in *samadhi*. When the rat moves, the cat moves too. When the cat's concentration becomes weak, the rat runs away, the samadhi is lost. You can observe samadhi in the swordsman. It must be like an artist at work. When you watch a Japanese artist drawing a plum branch, he does it in just one stroke from top to bottom, and he shows the exact motion of the branch. The plum tree is living.

There were two signs in the room. The first said, "This Society Is Supported by Voluntary Contributions. Rules: Regular Members Monthly Contributions: $5. Lecture Members Monthly Contributions: $3." The other sign said, "Those who come are received; those who go are not pursued." Each regular member's donation for the year would pay a month's rent. Sokei-an, who had seen his own teacher make too liberal use of his fellow disciples' fortunes, was determined to tread the opposite path. He relied only on himself to cover his own living expenses, with his writing and carving work. The donations from students were for the rent, for the electric, phone, and water bills.

He applied no pressure, no persuasion; if at some point the donations were too paltry to see the rent paid, that would be his signal to pick up his hat and do something else. If the people stopped coming, he would accept that it was not yet time for Buddhism in America. There were in fact months when it was uncertain whether the rent would be paid—this was, after all, the Depression, and none of the members, until Ruth arrived, had money—but somehow they always scraped by.

At the end of the evening, Sokei-an would stand at the door with his monk's bowl and accept donations. When Ruth first came for a lecture in 1934, she arrived early with an offering of an orchid that must have cost at least five dollars—more than the expected monthly donation. At the end of the night, she matter-of-factly placed a folded dollar bill in the bowl—as much as the typical donations would amount to for the entire evening, with seventeen people in attendance.

The others were grateful but also somewhat wary of this woman whose means were beyond most of their imaginings. And she seemed to have caught their teacher's attention, though perhaps not because of her wealth. She had been in Japan. She had spent a year in a Zen temple there. She seemed to have ideas about how things should be done here. She was not immediately popular with the others. In fact, there were some who thought it would be better if she did not make herself a frequent visitor.

ELEANOR AND ALAN
London–New York, 1932–1938

*Observe carefully: all conditioned things are
unsatisfactory; all conditioned things are impermanent;
all conditioned things are void of self.*

To me Zen is daily life—there is not much to talk about.
[UNSIGNED by Sokei-an (1932)]

In 1932, a young Englishman named Alan Watts had written to
Sokei-an:

Dear Mr. Sokei-ann Sakai 18 Feb. '32
Many thanks for your most interesting letter of the 1st.

From what you say there and from what I have read
elsewhere the essence of Zen is to regard Existence uni-
versally or impersonally, or so I understand. Instead of
thinking "I walk," you think "There is a walking," until
you begin to see yourself as a part of the Universe not
separate from other parts while the "I" is as the whole.
I have tried this and the result is that there comes a feeling of calm, of indifference to circumstances.

In the Sutra of Wei-Lang [Huineng] 6th Patriarch, I
read that one should get rid of the pairs of opposites—
good and evil, joy and pain, life and death. Surely it is by
the personal attitude to Existence that these opposites

arise; by thinking "I do," instead of "There is a doing."
By regarding oneself objectively in this manner one
becomes detached and an idea of "one-ness" prevails.
Is this what you mean when you say: "The master reg-
ulates his cognizance of the body of relativity (i.e., the
pairs of opposites?). Ceasing to follow its movement
(ceasing to think "I like" or "I do" or "I hate"?), he
realizes serenity."? Surely this is seeing Existence from
the standpoint of Tathata, which is the very basis of
Existence and yet is undisturbable by it? It is really
rather hard to explain! But I somehow feel that as soon
as I start looking at things impersonally, the "I" which
thinks about opposites vanishes, while a sort of calm,
"universal" feeling takes its place. Am I on the right
track?

Yours sincerely,

[SIGNED] A. W. Watts

[April 1, 1932]

My dear Mr. Watts,
It seems to me that you are on the track that all Zen students have passed along, but it is very difficult to judge
through correspondence whether you are surely on the
main track of Zen or not. Conceiving the general idea of
Zen and realizing the Samadhi of Universal Life is not
sufficient. It is very hard to judge the ultimate attainment of Zen without observing the daily life. Unless a
close contact is established between teacher and disciple

in order to make certain whether attainment is one of
mere conception or that of really standing in its center.
From my standpoint life must be Zen itself and we do
not care much about the mere conception of it. I am
quite sure you are on the way of Zen and I hope some
day in the future we will meet each other.

[UNSIGNED by Sokei-an]

A mere nineteen years old when he wrote *The Spirit of Zen: A
Way of Life, Work, and Art in the Far East* (and twenty when
it was first published in England in 1935), Alan Watts had composed that book—written in evenings and weekends in little over
a month, as he was employed raising funds for London hospi-
tals—in order to better understand the subject of D. T. Suzuki's
Essays in Zen Buddhism. He set himself the task of digesting this
baffling feast of profound, yet reluctant wisdom—yes, with the
thought of translating it from the somewhat mystifying formu-
lations he encountered in Dr. Suzuki's rendering, which, though
presented in English, were still difficult to penetrate, in spite of
Watts's several-years acquaintance with the subject. He imagined
that, if he could do this successfully for himself, it might prove
useful for other English speakers who perhaps had even less direct
experience.

He was the youngest member of the Buddhist Lodge in London,
founded in 1924 by Christmas Humphreys, a prominent lawyer
and avowed Buddhist; Alan's father, a founding member, was
vice president and treasurer. Alan had been its secretary from the
age of sixteen, and he also served as editor of the society's journal, *Buddhism in England.* When Dr. Suzuki first came to lecture
at the Lodge, Watts had been entranced, as much with the Zen

elder's presence—playing with a kitten with complete absorption while some underqualified speaker droned on and on—as with what he said.

In 1936 Dr. Suzuki returned to London for the World Congress of Faiths, and Watts made it his business to be present every time Suzuki spoke. In the young man's estimation, Dr. Suzuki was the brightest light of the gathering: with ease, directness, and humor, he deflected tiresome questions—without ever quite explaining anything. Watts began meeting with him as well, certain he had found his teacher. There was never anything formal about it. They would meet and talk, or not.

At the time, Alan was working on his second book—also largely based on the writings of D. T. Suzuki—*The Legacy of Asia and Western Man: A Study of the Middle Way*. In spite of his developing knowledge and expertise, and in spite of the clarity and opening toward insight he conveyed in these books, he felt he was not really much closer to the thing itself, the direct experience that would take a person—himself—out of isolation.

It was with such thoughts and intentions that he had first written to Sokei-an. The responses he received were moderately encouraging but still somewhat equivocal. He gathered that Sokei-an, though seated in America and teaching in English, might not be so different from the legendary masters of China and Japan, who would never so much as acknowledge anything but a direct, face-to-face encounter. To them, there was no way around it. In fact, there was nothing else. Dr. Suzuki had indicated as much. He had spoken respectfully of this living master in America and encouraged Alan to contact him—though in Suzuki's guarded response Alan suspected more was left unsaid—that perhaps the two teachers, in spite of Dr. Suzuki's recommendation, did not see eye to eye.

If it meant traveling to America, Alan resolved that he would find a way, in spite of having no money or career as such. Dr. Suzuki had suggested Japan, but that seemed even less plausible. In any case, it was not the tradition as such that he wanted, in its calcified forms and encrustations of local custom—it was the thing itself, which ultimately must be liberated from the forms. He appreciated the forms—his Chinese was improving, and he was enraptured with the calligraphy and other arts of East Asia—but he could already see that, for him at least, a modern man of the West, they were not from whence the kernel of wisdom would emerge. He had an inkling, of uncertain origin, that in Sokei-an he might find a kindred spirit, who valued the freedom that was the core of Zen experience as much as he did—and held the key to unlocking it.

There was also the matter of finding a willing companion to join him in exploring the secrets of ecstatic physical union. In his voluminous readings, Alan had encountered the sexual manuals of the East, and he held strongly to the positive attitudes expressed therein—that there was nothing shameful about the physical body, that in fact it was to be celebrated, that physical pleasure could be a vehicle for spiritual ecstasy as well—quite to the contrary of what the stern Anglicans had admonished him and his fellows at King's School in Canterbury.

The English girls he had consorted with thus far were not so easily persuaded. Even those few he had found compatible were constrained by propriety. They would have to be married before they would let down the last barrier. There was Hilda, who was not English but Danish, an au pair working for a family in London, who acted somewhat more willing, but still not to the point of satisfying his full desires. It did not help matters that just as they were entwining themselves in each other's grasp, he always had to catch the 11:55 train back home or be rather awkwardly stranded. He did not risk it.

When the Everetts returned to the United States in 1934, Ruth took Eleanor to New York, where Eleanor was to begin at the Masters School in Dobbs Ferry, Long Island. But before driving the final stretch to Dobbs Ferry, they took a room for a few nights in the Plaza Hotel in Midtown Manhattan, overlooking Central Park. Together they visited Sokei-an, having him out for dinner, attending his Wednesday evening lecture. For both of them, this brief visit somewhat cushioned their reentry to living in America.

At the end of their trip to Asia this time, Warren had been with them, and his condition seemed to worsen only gradually as long as they were there. Now he was back in Chicago, barely able to move. It was as if the effort of joining them in Asia had sustained him, but briefly; upon returning, he deteriorated even more rapidly than before. His arteriosclerosis was affecting his extremities, including his head. He remained in Hinsdale, at Swan House, in the care of his widowed sister.

Eleanor, for her part, had found her year and a half in Japan and travels to China more satisfactory than she had ever found life at Swan House. In Chicago, she somehow always felt as if she were in exile. From what? From the fully lived life she found in nature. From mountains—which were sufficiently abundant in Kyoto. There were friends she thought of, and corresponded with, but to be honest, she had missed so much school because of her ailments and family travels that she practically felt like an outsider when she did pick up her classes again.

In Japan, her mother had been occupied with her own pursuit of wisdom, which suited both of them, relieving Eleanor of much of the burden of otherwise near-constant pressure and demands to be better than she possibly could be. In Japan, Eleanor had teachers and companions who became fast friends. Even old Nanshinken, the stern roshi of grand Nanzen-ji temple, seemed to genuinely enjoy her company, chatting amiably and casually with her when he visited their house on the Kamo—even in preference to her more proper mother—when the opportunity presented itself.

Eleanor was possessed of what to her peers at Dobbs Ferry seemed practically mystical knowledge. She was fluent in Japanese. She was precociously talented at ikebana and tea ceremony—the latter she was invited to perform before members of the Japanese imperial family when they visited the United States, and she acquitted herself skillfully. Like her mother, she could write eloquently, which allowed her to mask the gaps in her formal education. And, like her mother, she was an exceptional pianist.

It was winter, then spring, and Eleanor arrived at the end of the school year marveling simply that she had made it all the way through—in fact, it had been the most complete school year of her life.

She spent a rather dismal summer back home in Hinsdale, beset by migraines, looking after her invalid father, while her mother was batting around the country. With high hopes, in September she returned to Dobbs Ferry.

At first all was well, and her spirits held up. But mostly, by winter, she was ill. Her asthma was worse again, and these debilitating migraines would put her out for days at a time. A series of fevers slid into chronic bronchitis. It seemed like it would never end. She spiraled into depression. She spent weeks in and out of the infirmary, unable to attend classes or complete her work. The headmistress called Ruth: it was agreed, Eleanor would be sent home.

But what was home? Hinsdale had never been much of a refuge. She had her own car, which was kept there—not the Italian sports car of her fantasies, but a sensible black Chevy sedan she had been given when she was fourteen, once she had proved she was master of the beastly Packard convertible that handled like a two-ton truck. That vehicle, wondrous in its own way, had been replaced briefly with a horribly ostentatious chauffeur-driven limousine that embarrassed her to no end—her mother's car—driven always too slowly through grim Chicago neighborhoods where crowds of unemployed men glared at them until she shrunk herself down below the window in the back seat, wishing she were anywhere else. Her Chevy was a vast improvement over that, at least, and many were the times she slipped out of the house unnoticed—her parents in the midst of one of their screaming tirades at each other—to drive country roads and release herself from the unbearable confines of that house.

But having the car was not without its own burden: she had to be her father's chauffeur. Before his retirement, every morning she would deliver him to the commuter train station for his trip into Chicago—at least he had relented that, yes, it would not be necessary to drive him all the way into the city—and every evening she would retrieve him. While in the car, he was congenitally incapable of relaxing into a comfortable silence. None of those three qualities—relaxation, comfort, silence—was within his grasp. He spared no opportunity to berate her for every miniscule or imagined infraction—until one evening, in the snow, with the windshield frosted over, she had to hold open the door as she drove, slowly, in order to see anything at all, and he sat in petrified silence until she guided them safely into the driveway.

Then she had gone with her mother to Japan, and her father had retired. He had fought his way through fifty years of intense competition and trials, made his million, never let up. He was completely worn out. Here he was, at Swan House in Hinsdale, unable to feed or bathe himself. Again it fell on her, Eleanor, to take care of him, even if she herself was ailing. Her mother was away, mostly, traveling around the country giving talks and trying to make something of a publishing career. It promised to be a grim winter.

In spite of all that, Eleanor did recover sufficiently to go out with friends when the opportunity presented itself. Among the many things she excelled at, she loved dancing, and she found herself on the dance floor at parties and debutante balls. And through her mother's acquaintances, she began doing clerical work for the Library of International Relations.

Her own debut party, the afternoon and evening of her eighteenth birthday, December 30, 1936, was an elegant tea at Swan House, produced by her mother.

The *Chicago Daily Tribune* society page had this to say:

> Monster motors were blinking in fabulous circles round Swan House, and from the open door came music of Hungarian gypsies, the hum of many voices. Eleanor's hair is golden red, her eyes topaz. Her frock was emerald satin. She is one of the few debutantes, I fancy, who speak Japanese and are conversant with the magnificent art and long history of Japan.

In the spring of 1937, Ruth took Eleanor to London, again leaving Warren in the hands of his sister. For Eleanor, it was an opportunity to study piano with George Woodhouse, a renowned performer and teacher who had arrived at insights about musical practice with parallels to Zen: "It is an impossibility to feel musically well and play with your head full of methods, muscles, and pianoforte mechanism. The first duty of the student is to forget these things." The first chapter in his 1910 book, *The Artist at the Piano*, is titled "Cause and Effect."

Ruth, at the invitation of her friend Christmas Humphreys of the Buddhist Lodge, gave a talk about her experience at Nanzen-ji. Eleanor was present, as was Alan Watts. It seemed inevitable that they would meet. Christmas Humphreys thought they should, and introduced them. They quickly found that they had much in common, much to talk about, and a vivid curiosity toward each other.

Here was this high-class American girl, confident in her bearing, energetic, pleasantly pretty rather than inapproachably beautiful, who seemed to know as much about Buddhism as anyone in the room—apart from her formidable mother, who clearly knew as much about the subject as any native speaker of English. Eleanor had lived there in old Kyoto, breathed it, been in the temple— perhaps not with the severe dedication of her mother, but she had real experience of meditation, had been with masters. She, along with her mother, had an air of easy wealth. It didn't hurt that she had beautiful clothes and knew how to make the best of them, moving with a dancer's elegant grace. She had a light humor, and a light touch in other things as well. He found her intriguing, and at the same time he felt at ease in her presence.

Who was this charming fellow? He seemed awfully self-possessed. His speaking was a curious mixture of utterly calm and at the same time completely excited. He had a precocious natural authority—in fact, nearly everything seemed precocious about him, though perhaps his enthusiasm for dancing, which Eleanor had at least one hand in inspiring, and his attentions toward an attractive and intelligent young woman were in keeping with his youth. Perhaps, eventually, his infectious enthusiasm for nearly everything he turned his attention to would become tempered, as the years accumulated. But that could wait.

A child of the Great War and its grim aftermath, he had little interest in politics, except in the most general way, as something that people had been trying for such a long time and couldn't it really work a bit better? Actually, there were things that might work better: at relieving suffering, at crafting an artful, peaceful, happy life—and what else could be so important? The joy of it—that's what he was getting at. Not just having a good time— though he certainly did not scoff at that—but cultivating deep pleasure, in everyday things, in the company one keeps, in food and song and wine.

He was balm for the weary soul. It felt good just to be around him. Eleanor lit up immediately when she met him. Even Ruth came around rather readily, in spite of understandable suspicions on behalf of her only daughter, which he quickly disarmed with attention directed to her as well—interest in her travels and knowledge and experience of Zen—and his own genuine devotion to unfolding the wisdom of Buddhism in the modern world.

Eleanor was as happy as she had ever been.

They would talk for hours. She went with him to Buddhist meetings. They practiced zazen together at her apartment. Though he had been meditating for years, and had tips from Dr. Suzuki, he constantly struggled with mental agitation. She remarked, "It's as if you're trying to get somewhere more quickly than the train will carry you. But where are you? You're just on the train." She had a steady and relaxed discipline that set an example for him. Once, when walking back with her from a meditation session at the Buddhist Lodge, he expressed how difficult he found it to concentrate on the present. Eleanor said to him, "Why try to concentrate on it? What else is there to be aware of? Your memories are in the present, just as much as the trees over there. Your thoughts about the future are also in the present, and anyhow I love to think about the future. The present is just a constant flow, and there's no way of getting out of it." This comment shook something loose for him. The air sharpened, the evening light reflecting off buildings as they walked became brighter. He was present. He looked at her and saw a deeply familiar being, and felt more whole. He would remember this brief epiphany for the rest of his life.

She always had money at the ready, and she knew how to spend it on life's finer pleasures. When they went to the opera, to the ballet, to piano concerts, they always sat in the best seats. This suited his tastes. She taught him to dance—the hula, which she had picked up on a stopover in Hawaii, demonstrating with her swaying and shimmying hips for his enticed eyes, as well as the more familiar ballroom varieties that she was a master of. He was smitten.

He took her to tea with his parents at Rowan Cottage, his family's modest country house in Chislehurst, Kent, not far from London. Eleanor found them gracious and charming—if Alan's mother was a bit stiff, clearly she had done all she could to make a guest feel welcome and comfortable; his father, more easygoing, did not conceal his delight at meeting her.

Ruth had returned to the United States at the end of summer, leaving the two to their own devices, complicit in their budding romance simply by not impeding it—in fact providing an open opportunity for them by leaving the apartment in Eleanor's hands, knowing full well that Alan would be a frequent guest, and more than likely an overnight one before long. She saw what was happening and, if she was skeptical of Alan's earning potential, she did see that her daughter was happy. Her one comment on departing for the United States was, "He's all right. But he'll never set the Thames on fire." But Eleanor, for once, was not looking for her mother's approval.

He did become an overnight guest. There was no stopping them. Eleanor was willing. More than just willing, she was an eager explorer, a passionate collaborator, with none of the inhibitions of the English girls he had once hoped to know better. Not that she had any experience to speak of—they were both still virgins when they met. Not that she would have gone ahead with anyone else. It was entirely because of him, because she had known immediately and without question they were meant to be together, which gave her the confidence to be adventuresome, to follow him wherever he led—and to take the lead herself at times.

They tried all the exotic techniques he had read in books, and she realized that she found them distracting rather than satisfying—she preferred the more conventional approaches after all. It really was quite simple: sexual ecstasy took her outside herself. And then the self did return, after not very long perhaps—but at least without the heaviness. Loneliness was banished. Love was real.

She doubted her mother had ever experienced real satisfaction—or real love, for that matter. She wondered if her mother was capable of love. If she, Eleanor, had felt love from her, which perhaps she did from time to time, it was at a remove, caged by too much expectation and propriety. If there had ever been love between her mother and father—well, they had produced her after all, though that only indicated they had once had physical relations—she was not its witness.

Alan proposed to Eleanor, and she immediately accepted. They announced their engagement, without establishing a date for the wedding, and made arrangements to sail for America to spend Christmas with Eleanor's family.

On December 17, 1937, they sailed for New York on the *Bremen*, a fast German luxury liner—which sailed under the German flag, the Nazi swastika—well-appointed, with comfortable cabins, delicious food, and opportunities for dancing on deck to a Bavarian band playing Viennese waltzes. From New York, they took a luxury overnight train to Chicago, and they were met at the station by the Everetts' Philippine chauffeur, driving their sleek limousine.

The trip was pleasant and congenial. Alan was happy to see Ruth again, and she seemed pleased to see him. And to everyone's surprise, Alan and Warren hit it off. They would retreat after dinner to smoke cigars and drink whiskey, trading off-color jokes like old school chums.

Alan had been a guest of wealth before—a close friend from King's School had invited him for extended forays to a chateau in France—and was not one to be intimidated by his surroundings. Still, he marveled at the lavish scale of Swan House and the Everetts' lives.

Ruth's brother, David, was there as well—Alan found him picturesquely problematic, a gay, frustrated actor. Other Fuller and Everett relatives he did not find so interesting, but he enjoyed meeting Eleanor's friends. Then it was time to return to London.

They still had not set a date for the wedding. But in February, Eleanor became pregnant, and they decided to get married in April.

Here was someone who was emotionally present. He was right there. He knew how to look at and talk to her as if she were the most important being on earth. Not at all like her stern, distant mother, whose apparently generous bosom had never expressed milk or real generosity—personal, emotional kindness—and who had consigned Eleanor to the governess who made her life hell for her seven earliest years. To be fair, her mother could appear kind, she could act kindly. Eleanor supposed she was capable of a certain form of actual kindness, which truly could be helpful to people. And in many situations—social gatherings, certainly—she could project an attitude of confident ease that actually did put other people at ease, even if it was all part of the form. She was so formal. Everything had to be done exactly right. People who worked for her, if they lasted, quickly became experts at keeping all the details and procedures exacting.

Form is emptiness. Eleanor could see how Zen seemed so perfect to her mother. Emptiness was a positive thing—the opposite of loneliness. Eleanor wasn't so sure. The closest she had come to really experiencing this was in the mountains, the high desert of Indio, where she'd been sent into a blissful refuge of rocks and horses and wranglers and symphonies of light. She supposed music moved that way too—after all, wasn't music just harmonious patterns of sound? Empty forms, but capable of carrying such emotion.

And Alan—what was it that so appealed to him about Zen? The freedom, as he saw it. He had all his reading—and Lord knows, he had read everything, at least what there was in English; if there had been Buddhist writings in Latin he would have read those as well. And now he was learning to read Classical Chinese. He spoke with authority, as if he really knew something about Buddhism—which was true, he knew *about* it—even if what he said did not always coincide with what she had experienced in Japan. Though who was she to judge? They wouldn't even let the likes of her into the zendo, a mere girl of sixteen.

And now another three years, here she was in England, a woman, another life growing inside her, finding many happy moments with this generous and brilliant man, who *saw* her, and liked what he saw. Her Prince Charming. Was marrying him her road to freedom? Though in certain moments she also found herself wary of her fiancé's enthusiasm.

She supposed her mother's Buddhism, like Alan's notion of freedom, was a sort of escape from the miseries of her own childhood. Or not escape perhaps, but a refuge. Could it be both safety and freedom? Couldn't it? Eleanor herself was more Buddhist than Christian. The first time she had set foot in a church was at age six, for her Aunt Irene's funeral. It had felt strange to her—she was a stranger at church. But never mind the church—six-year-old Eleanor's indelible experience from that event was gazing at the very dead body of her aunt in the open coffin. Eleanor was aghast, repelled by this startling deadness before her. It did not look like somebody sleeping. In spite of the mortician's gestures toward making Aunt Irene presentable, the body looked somehow deader than dead—aged, exhausted, ill, drained of the very essence of life—as indeed the blood had been drained.

Their wedding was at St. Philip's Church in Earl's Court—later they chuckled that two Buddhists had been allowed to get married in a Church of England ceremony. Ruth arranged a lavish reception for them at the Royal Stuart Hotel and then set them up in a palatial apartment in an Edwardian mansion in Courtfield Gardens in London. Eleanor was nineteen and Alan was twenty-three.

Waves of fear and anxiety were palpable in the air, beating against the edges of everyone's life with more persistence and ugly strength day by day. In England in 1938 everybody knew the war was coming. First nobody wanted to talk about it. Then it was all anybody could talk about: Are you getting out?

In reality it had already started—Japan had invaded China and was clearly not planning to stop there. Hitler had come to power in 1933 and never made any secret of his intentions. In England there were those who thought he had a point, that Germany had been treated with unnecessary harshness after the Great War. Absolute rubbish, of course—they had started it, hadn't they? But people—some people, for a brief moment—pretended that Hitler would not bother them, if they only gave him what he claimed already rightfully belonged to Germany. Besides, there was money to be made—the upper classes had taken every opportunity to make deals with the Germans.

But that was all beside the point for Alan, whose background was middle class and for whom making money—something that under normal circumstances he did approve of, at least in the abstract, and entirely for the access to life's pleasures that wealth might provide, never as an end in itself—would have been a crass consideration at a time like this. The prospect of war—bloodshed, violence of any sort—repulsed him viscerally. He would have no part in it. And if avoiding conscription meant a choice between the public humiliations and risk of imprisonment that were the lot of a conscientious objector, or relocating to America with his American wife and her family, there was really no question.

The war was coming, everybody knew it. Really it had already started—the so-called civil war in Spain, bombings carried out by German planes. And then the Anschluss, Germany absorbing Austria in a single day and then holding sham elections—a week after Eleanor and Alan's wedding—in which 99 percent of the voters said *ja* to "re-joining" a Greater Germany. Eleanor briefly considered what must have happened to the 1 percent who voted against Hitler, casting their ballots under the glaring eyes of German soldiers. The whole thing sickened her. The child growing inside her twitched. They had to get out.

In Japan she had gone to see movies. Not every week, but regularly. "Easterns"—Japanese samurai movies—and the latest from Hollywood and Europe.

But in Kyoto, before the main features were shown, there were always nationalist documentaries—brief, gruesome newsreels about Japan's military expeditions in China. They were unbelievably brutal. Eleanor found them appalling, sickening. They confused her: showing such atrocities, how could they have any purpose other than to display the horror and futility of war—to convince citizens with belligerent sympathies to embrace peace instead? She had an inkling, however, that the original intention was otherwise, the opposite in fact: to arouse patriotic fervor. How they were meant to accomplish that end mystified her. How could you not turn away?

In 1934 they had traveled to Peking, on a train that bore little resemblance—apart from having wheels to roll along a track—to the luxurious coaches that had conveyed them along the same line four years previously. This time they had been warned they must carry their own food and so boarded the train prepared with baskets of supplies. Their compartment was a cramped room with one small window and two tiers of planks jutting from the walls, each plank supported by heavy chains. There was a communal toilet in the dining car.

Though no food was served, boiling water and tea were available, for those who could stomach the condition of the pots and cups, which may have received a cursory rinse, with questionable water, between uses—washing facilities were minimal. The floor of the dining car was a shambles, littered with food scraps, cigarette butts, gobs of spit teeming with whatever strains of infection the humans who coughed them out were carrying. Eleanor spent most of her waking time there, fascinated by the flow of humanity that ventured through to sit down at the wooden tables and hard-backed benches to eat the food they had brought or managed to purchase from hawkers at stations along the way. She saw Chinese, Manchu, Mongolians—no Japanese—eating, talking, laughing, spitting. A red chicken ran across the car pecking at crumbs, squawking and flapping under the tables and benches, to the delight of everyone but the desperate owner trying to recapture it.

It took more than two days and nights to reach Peking, which previously had been a routine overnight journey. Much of that time their train was shunted onto sidings—sometimes in village stations, often in open country—waiting an hour or more for the higher-priority troop trains to pass. In those endless troop trains, open freight cars were jammed to capacity with standing Japanese soldiers, their rifles with bayonets pointing to the sky.

These boy soldiers—children, none of them more than twenty, many appearing to be barely teenagers—stood rigid in the open cars, their faces clenched into masks of barely contained panic. Children being railroaded to the front lines where they would slog through the muck and slime as Eleanor had seen in those horrifying newsreels, to be shot and bayoneted, to have their guts spilled over Chinese soil for the glory of the Japanese Empire—or doing the same, and worse, to the Chinese, and not just to other soldiers.

Peking was transformed as well. The most beautiful city on earth, as Eleanor continued to picture it—where flocks of trained pigeons had trailed mellifluous whistles from their legs as they wheeled overhead in the bright blue sky, where orderly avenues of stately courtyard houses with gray-slate roofs surrounded lotus ponds. All this had been replaced by a tense clamor of Japanese soldiers barking orders and crowds of desperate, hungry people. The pigeons were nowhere in evidence.

The world had gone mad. But had it not always been so?

The memory of those faces on the trains would never leave her.

In 1938 Ruth moved to New York, to an apartment at the Park Crescent Hotel on the Upper West Side, overlooking the Hudson. She had found a nursing home for Warren, now sixty-five, in Hartford, Connecticut, close enough to visit him.

Alan and Eleanor arrived in New York in July, to live in the apartment next door to Ruth. In November, Eleanor gave birth to a daughter, Joan.

In spite of Eleanor's own less-than-happy experience being watched over as a young child by a governess rather than her mother, she brought in a nanny to help care for the infant, leaving the young parents free to venture out and maintain an active social life.

Alan loved being in New York—the food, the excitement, the constant parade of people in the streets. He loved being married to Eleanor, being with her, being part of her world. He loved going to parties; they were invited to many—weekends in country homes, dinners with scientists, painters, musicians, psychologists, people who were excited to converse about art, mysticism, the life of the mind. Alan, always an engaging and entertaining talker, was immediately popular.

And he met Sokei-an. Within a few days of arriving in New York in midsummer, Ruth brought Eleanor and him to the Saturday evening talk at the Buddhist Society. Alan immediately became a regular and enthusiastic attendee of Sokei-an's talks. He also had regular opportunities to be around Sokei-an otherwise, as Ruth often invited Sokei-an over for meals, and they—soon all four of them—would take small trips together.

Sokei-an and Ruth Fuller Everett, Eleanor and Alan Watts.
Sokei-an is wearing a fake mustache and hat for a masquerade
benefit party. Courtesy of the First Zen Institute of America.

Alan had been baffled and entranced in equal measures by
Dr. Suzuki—and, in spite of quiet admonitions to the contrary,
thought of this as the definition of Zen. Here, by Sokei-an in
person, he was startled, stunned in fact. Here was a man who
was clearly, directly, alarmingly *present*. Where Dr. Suzuki had
a vast grasp of scholarship, could simultaneously draw from
Classical Chinese, Sanskrit, and Japanese religious sources, refer
to German philosophers, and still caution his English-speaking
audience to be wary of a strictly intellectual attempt at understanding—who would continue lecturing, without adjusting his
speaking volume or pausing to accommodate his listeners when
an airplane roaring overhead rendered his voice inaudible; who,
in spite of his neglect of zazen for many years, could enter a state
of samadhi at will, effectively absenting himself, taking a break
from whatever commotion surrounded him—Sokei-an would cut
right through you with his gaze. He was not going anywhere.
In his public talks he was determined to clarify, not befuddle.
He had no need to warn anyone about too much intellectualizing because he was completely at ease in both mind and body,
and there was no danger of that. He was earthy, robust, full of
humor.

Alan had found his teacher. Over the weeks since first encountering Sokei-an, he felt his own awareness opening up. Now he
was prepared to begin the inner practice. He had not given up his
reluctance about submitting himself to any teacher or system, but
he yearned for the full experience that koan practice with a master
would provide.

In October 1938 Sokei-an accepted Alan as a sanzen student.
"Before mother and father: what is your original face?"

I know how this works. I will crack this koan. I have practically already solved it. And so Alan Watts applied himself with gushing enthusiasm.

He quickly had an answer.

He bowed to Sokei-an and presented it.

"No." Sokei-an rang the bell. *Out.*

Alan returned to zazen. Well, if that wasn't it, then what?

He arrived at another answer. With nearly as much confidence, he presented it.

Sokei-an rang the bell. *Out.*

Alan returned to zazen. *If that wasn't it, okay then. It will come.*

A CITY REFUGE
New York, 1938–1942

H ave you noticed them together?"
     "How could I not?"
"They're like children. Like they've never been in love before."
"Well, she hasn't been."
"No, I suppose not."

They watched it happening before their eyes—Eleanor and Alan
saw it before Ruth did, before Ruth could admit that anything
unusual was happening. But they saw it, and then she realized
what she felt for this man was not something she had known
before. Sokei-an had cracked her shell.

He cut through her rigidity with fart jokes. "For a whole week
the *tenzo* prepares only *natto*—fermented soy beans. Very gooey,
stinky. Many Japanese love natto—you have tasted it? Like some
English cheese, I think? For a whole week, the monks eat nothing
else. There is one monk—not very bright—who struggles painfully
for every koan. This time he thinks he has the correct answer. But
when he bows for sanzen, he opens his lips, and there is nothing.
Nothing! There he sits, shaking, crying in fear—he knows he will

be struck yet again, for this is a roshi who uses his nyoi vigorously. Suddenly an enormous fart drops out of his ass! The monk smells his answer—much more fragrant than natto!—and waits for the blow to come. Nothing. He opens his eyes, not even realizing he had them closed. And Roshi says, 'So—your capping phrase?'"

Ruth, driving, blushed and giggled in spite of herself. Eleanor, in the back seat, whispered to Alan, "In Kyoto, our housekeeper Kato-san always said natto would cure flatulence."

"How does it taste really?"

"Something like Epoisses. But stringy and lumpy. It's quite good, once you get a taste for it."

"Maybe that monk had something else besides just the natto."

Ruth was continuing her Zen studies with Sokei-an, taking koans from him, more or less picking up from where she had been with Nanshinken, though their methods were different. In sanzen Sokei-an was very strict. He was the powerful teacher—this was not a man sitting in the roshi's chair; this was an absolute principle you were up against. Nobody went in without their knees shaking, paralyzed with fright. His intuition of what was going on in your mind and how to force you to crystallize for yourself what you were moving toward penetrated any vestige of delusion.

In the years Ruth knew and worked with him this never changed: as intimately as she came to know him, in sanzen she never had any different feeling—she was face-to-face with an absolute state.

The other students were upset with Ruth. She made every mistake possible to make in a group.

"She comes here and immediately starts wanting to change things. What business does she have trying to change things?"

"Please be patient. From her experiences she brings very valuable perspectives. And her enthusiasm is an enormous asset.

Please, for once in my lifetime, I ask you to let me handle the situation without interference."

It took time, but the other members were obliged to give grudging assent.

Ruth at forty-five became one of the principal supporters of the Buddhist Society of America. Sokei-an was fifty-five. There were about thirty students, most of them women. In 1938 the group included a number of distinguished members, including Edna Kenton, one of the longest standing, a writer known as an authority on Henry James, with a number of books to her credit; Helen Scott Townsend, another long-standing member and the Buddhist Society's secretary, who was a professor of phonetics and a Sanskrit scholar; a Mrs. Reber, editor of the *Evening Journal*; a Mrs. Stern, psychoanalyst; George Fowler, professor of history; a Baroness Dorpowska, who had come of age in the imperial court of the Hapsburgs; Madam Bluestone, a yoga teacher; Audrey Kepner, another of the Society's oldest members, an editor and retired history teacher, who had begun the project of transcribing Sokei-an's talks in 1932; and Mary Farkas, a writer and documentary filmmaker, who had recently arrived and would soon join the project of transcribing and editing Sokei-an's talks, and who eventually would take on the publishing of *Zen Notes* and later become director of the First Zen Institute.

In private Ruth had been arguing with Sokei-an, from their first meeting, that a true Zen experience required formal zazen. "How could anyone even know what it's like to enter training without sitting meditation?"

"The serious students sit at home."

"They won't abandon you if you offer zazen. Make it available. They need it. The serious students will be here."

Finally she prevailed, volunteering to help anyone with questions about the correct posture and other demands of proper sitting.

She was there every morning at 8:00 a.m. to ring the bell. It was true: the serious students began attending zazen regularly.

As Mary Farkas later commented:

> Her unflagging industry and perseverance dismayed as well as impressed those of lesser energy, as presently appeared when Sokei-an's faithful were obliged to work with her, or watch from the sidelines while she accomplished what they had scarcely dared to dream. As can be imagined, her innovations did not come into being as a smooth, continuous growth. Tempests of words swirled around Sokei-an. Arguments about each domestic improvement, about grammar, about the translations, about all kinds of things, constantly arose and were quelled.

The apartment on Seventieth Street that served both as Sokei-an's lodgings and the meeting hall of the Buddhist Society of America lacked amenities. To some it was charming, but Ruth was determined to make improvements. It needed a refrigerator. New drapes. Redecorating. Her experience in industrious homemaking extended well beyond entertaining and decorating: she had designed Swan House, essentially serving as its architect, overseeing the entire construction. There was only so much that could be done within the limitations of this inadequate space, but it had to be done.

Formidable though Ruth was, Sokei-an was enjoying her company a lot.

In the first week of December, the group celebrated Rohatsu—
the festival of the Buddha's enlightenment. There was no formal
sesshin, as at a traditional temple, but they met every night for the
week and extended the zazen and sanzen sessions. The culminat-
ing day of Rohatsu, usually on December 8, was the traditional
moment for inducting new members fully into the sangha.

On December 10, 1938, Sokei-an formally initiated Ruth into
the sangha of Buddha, saying that he was substituting himself
for the master of Nanzen-ji. He gave her the name Eryu, which
means "dragon's wisdom," explaining that the sutras held a tale
of a dragon's daughter who came to see the Buddha and attained
the highest realization in that first interview.

Eleanor and Alan were among those present. They greeted her
as Eryu.

Alan's frustration in sanzen was beginning to wear on him.

He bowed to Sokei-an and presented his answer.

Sokei-an rang the bell. *No. Not right.*

"But I'm right!" Alan shouted.

Sokei-an replied, "No you're not right," and that was the end
of Alan's formal Zen training.

The curious thing about Zen training is that it must be undertaken
for oneself, through oneself, yet nothing can be accomplished if
self-improvement is the object—the self is both impetus and obstacle. Alan understood that well, intellectually at least, and wrote
about it. Still, the intellectual understanding was not sufficient. He
thought he had gotten over it—over himself, over intellectualizing.
Apparently Sokei-an disagreed.

The whole master-disciple tangle was not what he was looking
for after all. He realized he had never been able to submit to it

wholeheartedly, which was perhaps much of the issue at hand. Part of the matter, of course, was that he—Alan—ran through his patience for koan practice before he unlocked the first one. He thought he had solved it. In fact, he was so convinced, he tried to argue with Sokei-an. That was not the correct solution either.

But personally he loved Sokei-an and admired him deeply, looking to him as a model of a life well lived. He found ways to observe his teacher frequently—Sokei-an was often with Ruth, and often Eleanor and Alan were included. Beneath the earthy humor and sense of ease in the teacher's company, Alan felt or imagined that Sokei-an shared his ambivalence about the strictures of tradition—here was a man, a fully awakened master, who was completely free, who would say things to the effect that Buddhism does not matter, it was only how human you were. This was where Alan found confirmation of his personal insights.

Alan's observation of Sokei-an increased and deepened his admiration. Sokei-an's calm and relaxed attention to what was going on around him, his laugh, his humor, his scholarship in the Buddhist classics, his skill as a sculptor, greatly impressed Alan. And though Sokei-an had arrived at his awakening through strict Rinzai practice, there was something in his being that acknowledged the possibility of another way. Dr. Suzuki had dropped hints about Jodo Shinshu—Pure Land Buddhism, more popular in Japan than Zen—containing a simpler, more direct expression of nondual experience: it is not necessary, or really even possible, to arrive at reality by striving, because in fact *you are that*, already, immediately and absolutely. There is no going, getting, arriving, any of that. *You are already there.* Could it really be so simple?

Alan pointed out that even Sokei-an had publicly expressed ambivalence about Zen Buddhism—it was not the tradition that mattered, but the essential core. Perhaps the method was effective, if one was willing to abide by its severity, but once that had done its work, it could be discarded. As Sokei-an said:

> When I started to study Buddhism and was studying koans, Zen and Buddhism seemed from my height to be the size of the whole universe. Today, I must confess Buddhism and Zen are just some old furniture in the corner of my mind. I, today, a man at the age of fifty-five, really enjoy my own mind more than Zen and Buddhism. But this was a gift from Buddhism, so I appreciate the kindness of Buddhism. This, our heart, is important. We must have something that is original, that is not Buddhism or Zen, that is science, religion, or philosophy. I did not find it for a long, long time—and Buddhism and Zen were a hard burden. Now I speak about Buddhism and Zen in lectures; but when I am alone I do not speak or think about Buddhism. I enjoy something that has no name but that is quite natural. Perhaps you call it the Pure Land. It is wonderful, the Pure Land. Someone asked me to go for a vacation to Nyack for one month, but I refused. I just stay here and live in my own pure mind.

It was possible for Sokei-an to be at home in New York City as nowhere else. He never wanted to go outside of the city. Here he was completely free. *Sentient beings are numberless. I vow to save them all.* Many of them, at any given time, are in New York. Everything is here.

Sokei-an could be prickly. He had quick reactions and a quick temper.

Ruth invited him for lunch. "I'll send a car over for you."

"I can walk."

But the next time: "I'll meet you at half past noon."

When he arrived, he was annoyed. "You could have sent a car. What a way to treat a roshi."

Often for lunch Ruth would meet him at Childs, the branch in their neighborhood at Eighty-Second and Broadway, and then they would go up to her apartment in the Park Crescent to work on translating *The Sutra of Perfect Awakening* together. He of course had already been translating it from the Chinese and teaching from it. It had been her idea as well as his to prepare an edition for publication in English.

He had translated and taught from the *Record of Rinzai* as well, but when he had presented to his teacher the idea of publishing an English edition of that work, Sokatsu discouraged him, suggesting that he, Sokatsu, would have to approve it, assuming that Sokei-an was working from the Japanese version the master had given his disciple many years earlier. It was too complicated to have to please Sokatsu—one of the wonderful things about New York, about America, was freedom from such obligations—so Sokei-an set aside the project. He never abandoned it, though, intending to return to it later. In fact he and Ruth spent many hours with that book as well, and she was determined to have it published.

Ruth's idea was that publishing these texts would provide valuable material for the English-speaking Buddhist world—however small it currently was, it would grow—and also raise income for the Buddhist Society of America. Since returning from Japan, she had ventured into publishing, producing an elegant volume of Chinese and Japanese calligraphy prints under her own Swan

House imprint. She had also assisted Dr. Suzuki as a proofreader for his 1934 *Essays in Zen Buddhism, Third Series.*

They would have lunch and then work for a couple of hours. If it was a teisho day, they would return together to his apartment—the Buddhist Society temple—to prepare for the evening. Other evenings, he would often stay for dinner.

"Sokei-an, did you know that for a time Childs provided a vegetarian-only menu?"

It was his turn to raise his eyebrows in stunned silence. How could that be possible? It seemed incredible that his favorite all-American eatery—the sparkling-clean, white-tiled establishment where a waitress in white skirt and blouse would graciously take their order—would have abandoned the skillful preparation of succulent beefsteaks.

"Apparently the founder of the restaurants was a devout vegetarian, and once they were well established, he imposed his will."

"So—a spiritual man. Probably he was poisoned by bad meat as a child."

Sokei-an loved to eat steak. It's not that he lacked compassion for animals or respect for the Buddhist training precepts. He saw cause and effect more complexly than simply equating the avoidance of meat with refraining from killing, and he shunned any pretense of personal virtue that might accrue from such a view. He did not want to separate himself from people. He was a man of the world, immersed in the world, and here for the benefit of the world of people. What he had to offer was for people—Americans. His teacher had instructed him to get to know America and Americans. So he became American—not least by what he preferred to eat. And, as it happened, the land and its people and ways were more compatible for him than Japan could ever be.

Sokei-an decided to take a walk from the bottom of Broadway in Lower Manhattan to the Broadway Bridge at the northern tip of the island, something he had done in his earlier years in the city on numerous occasions, among his many crisscrossings of Manhattan.

He started at Battery Park, where he had often gone to meditate in his younger days, when he lived in Greenwich Village. These days there was not so much meditation, actually. He could enter samadhi at will, whatever he was doing. He could modulate his state of mind, activating whatever degree of intensity he desired. Usually in public he carried himself with a calm, available aspect, engaging those he was inclined to interact with, simply by being awake and present. If he wished to avoid a conversation, he would make himself uninteresting and would be ignored.

There was also less walking now than in his younger days. In his late fifties he had less energy than in his youth, when he walked across the mountains of Japan and the Pacific Northwest, walking all day for sometimes weeks on end. Even when he first lived in New York, it was as nothing to walk up and down Manhattan. Now he would have to stop and rest. The distance seemed more significant. His heart—well, his heart was fine. But his blood pressure was high, he knew; he was getting headaches, sometimes he felt faint. Ruth kept trying to bring him to her doctor. But what could a doctor do?

By the time he crossed Houston and walked up to Fourth Street, a thought crossed his mind to turn left and spend a little while in Washington Square Park. But he kept going north. It was a warm mid-October, 1939—a week ago the thermometer had reached 90 degrees, and everyone at his teisho had been dripping with sweat, even in the evening, in spite of the ceiling fan. Now, late morning, it was not so hot—pleasantly warm for a walk.

He did pause at Union Square, another favorite place for observing the populace. There were a few people out, but it was not crowded, and he did not stay long.

He continued up to Times Square. In front of the Childs at Forty-Second Street a butcher was making a delivery, hoisting a full side of beef on his shoulders. Sokei-an stood near the side door, watching, curious that the delivery had not been made earlier. After a few minutes, the butcher stepped back out onto the sidewalk and regarded Sokei-an. "You the inspector? Top quality product we got here—" and froze. Sokei-an's unfathomable gaze erased everything. The man silently mouthed a stunned "Oh." Sokei-an nodded, the merest indication of a bow, turned away, and walked in the front door.

After lunch he spent the remainder of the afternoon walking the rest of the way up Broadway. Most of the people he saw in Midtown seemed preoccupied, which was typical. Once he got to Columbus Circle and the Upper West Side, there was still a certain amount of bustle in the air, but the canyon of skyscrapers gave way to a more open view of the sky. There was a shift in attitude as well, not precisely more relaxed, but perhaps less hurried. Sokei-an entered a deeply familiar walking reverie, passing through the neighborhoods with all of his senses open and alert.

He had enjoyed his brief sojourn living in Harlem a decade earlier, with the black family that had welcomed him into their house for a few months. He had enjoyed how they spoke to each other, their forthright attitude. As he crossed Harlem now he sensed the same underlying desperation that accompanied humans elsewhere, but also a liveliness that lifted his spirits. He had recently given a talk at a church here and had been received kindly. He had talked about Buddhism, of course, as well as expressing the idea that keeping the true message of Christianity alive in their hearts was quite important. They had expected him to arrive as a missionary; he was not. He was simply interested in discussing human truths.

The shadows of the late afternoon stretched long as he reached the Broadway Bridge. Suddenly he was weary from his walk. His headache had returned with a strong throbbing. He had expected to take the subway back to his neighborhood, but a cab was waiting at the curb, and as he approached, the driver was already opening the door for him. He got in.

In January 1940 Edward Warren Everett died. His last years had diminished him physically. His authority eroded to a meek shadow. In the nursing home, he chafed at his reduced state of chronic ailments and dependence on his family and hired caregivers—and did not take pains to conceal his misery. His passing, though publicly mourned, was for Ruth and Eleanor accompanied by relief as much as by grief.

Ruth was concerned about Sokei-an's health. Against his objections, she had made an appointment for him with her doctor, to check his blood pressure and heart, after lunch. But now he was eating so slowly. Not like a dawdling child: like a monk, savoring, studying each morsel, investigating its flavor and texture, the transformation from one form of matter into another, from energy to matter to energy—the sunlight energy to the grass to the animal, matter, to his body, energy again, to sustain another life—and onward to become waste, excrement. Birth, growth, death, decay. Another birth? Perhaps not.

My Lord, he's taking forever. He is not going to finish in time. He is determined to miss this doctor's appointment.

"What does he see in her?"

"Are you serious? She's a brilliant, powerful woman. Who else could match him? She has it, and he sees it. I'm sure they both knew right away, from the first, about each other. Just as we did. When you know it, you know it."

"I think he was lonely."

"He's surrounded by interesting, intelligent women. He enjoys drinking tea with them. And flirting. But your mother is exceptional."

"When he was a student, he used to play with the geishas. His aunt was a geisha mistress."

"Maybe he'll reveal some secrets."

This gate that gate empty gate open gate gateless gate grateful gate. So many gates. Her moon gate. She had no idea. It was a revelation. It was a revelation to have no idea. His pointing to the moon gate. He could touch her and reveal gates that had not existed, as far as she imagined, until he opened them all. He opened them all. She was immensely grateful. They were matched in power and passion. She wanted to advertise her bliss but knew it would be too disruptive to reveal in public.

Sokei-an still wrote for Japanese publications, though only as a source of income. He still sent money to his Japanese wife, along with more and more frequent appeals for divorce—considering that in reality they had not been husband and wife for many years already, at least since the first time he returned to Japan in 1919, and certainly since 1921 when he came back to New York. She would not grant it. Whether or not she accepted the reality of their separateness, she refused to acknowledge it in legal terms. She sent a sarcastic reply.

This did not hinder his romantic pursuits—in earlier years with his girlfriend Elizabeth Sharp and others. Now with Ruth. It did restrict the possibility of marrying Ruth until it was practically too late. He asked her many times. They were together, taking trips, sharing their meals, working together on translations, and before long living together. She was more than a girlfriend. Actually she was the love of his life. Why should they not cement their bond in the eyes of the law and their community?

Their previous marriages had been arrangements of circumstance—in his case not without affection, at first—and, for both, with intentions of finding at least a satisfactory compatibility. But anything approaching love, for both, had been an early casualty. In the beginning Tomeko had shared a teacher and sangha with him, but that did not last.

What did Ruth and Warren have in common with each other? Wealth and membership in the elite social class that wealth provided. Interest in aspects of the world beyond Chicago and America, but for drastically different reasons. There had been no real conjunction of like-minded individuals or enduring affection to offset the contentiousness and volatility in the household. Ruth was a master of endurance and, as of her first sojourn at Nanzen-ji in 1930, had established herself as an independent agent.

For Sokei-an's part, the more important bond had always been with his teacher. Which was another complication. His first marriage occurred because of his teacher, and to seek a divorce would be an unforgivable insult to Sokatsu. Still, he did seek it.

As discreet as she and her lover had to be, Ruth did not hide her happiness from Eleanor. She told Eleanor that Sokei-an was the love of her life—she would say so again many times over the years. She was finding a passionate love for the first time.

Eleanor was walking. Her mother was in love but she, Eleanor, felt heavy. In Chicago, when she had felt this heaviness, she would go for a drive, out past the edge of the city, into the open prairie. It helped, somewhat. Here, in this closed-in city—their apartments were over the Hudson, but that almost made the feeling of being boxed in more immediate—it was simpler to step out of the door and set off on foot. She might hail a cab at some point. She might go shopping. Often she would just be walking, surrounded by the urban commotion, sunken into herself.

This heaviness. It was physical too—she was putting on weight, becoming physically heavy. They were all eating too much. It was all connected; she felt gravity pulling her down, the heaviness of the world. The whole world was tearing itself apart—Europe and Asia in flames, and nothing seemed to stop Hitler. The Americans were not going to do anything; everything was going to pieces. *The whole world is in flames. What samadhi will save you?*

She knew she was supposed to feel joy and delight with her baby, now already two years old—how did that happen? Joan was walking and inventing her own adorable words and, yes, really delightful. But even with her, this uncertainty crept in. Eleanor's own mother was always too certain. It was false—it made Eleanor desperate for a more solid reality, one that accepted real uncertainty, not just in koans but in life, and somehow got beneath it to solid ground. She was not finding it in Buddhism. At the moment, her dedication was weak. In a way, Buddhism was just what she had grown up with. On the veranda of Pine Cloud Villa, their house on the river in Kyoto, with their very important visitor Nanshinken Roshi—really a sweet, simple old man who had never married or probably even been with a woman—together flipping through sumo magazines, Nanshinken teasing her about which wrestler she should marry.

As heavy as she felt, the ground kept shifting. She yearned to feel the firmness of nature underfoot. Not concrete, but earth, rock, mountains. To look through crystalline air, to see clearly for miles, as she had in the desert of her childhood. She felt out of place on this cramped island, in this city with its crowds and skyscrapers and busyness and clamor.

Her father was in his grave now. He died in January and they had taken him back to Chicago and buried him in the family plot at Oak Woods Cemetery, with his parents and his brothers and their spouses, those who had gone before him. He was so much older than Mother. Ruth was forty-eight now, as of October 31— born on Halloween, of course—and might well have a whole life ahead of her. In any case, she seemed relieved Father was gone. At least that would put her in the clear to fall in love. For the first time, she kept saying.

True, Father had been an awful burden for Eleanor as well, and she did find some relief at his passing. But she also realized it went much deeper than that. He was part of her, as disagreeable as he often was. And if there was relief in his passing, it was not accompanied by any sense of lightness. Not with the world as it was. As disagreeable as he was, he had provided some stability. It was not quite that she missed him. And yet . . .

Eleanor, on Fifth Avenue, walked past the ornate west front of St. Patrick's Cathedral. That at least was a solid edifice. Should she stop? Should she step inside? There was no reason for it really. She kept walking.

Alan, bless his heart, did as much as he could for her when she was down like this. But it was not always the right thing. How could he know? He wanted to help, but sometimes she just needed to step out. Into the desert. Instead here she was in this gray, noisy city. He blamed himself for her worries. There was some truth to that—she worried about money, and how his unconventional career did not seem to be actively producing it. True, they never lacked for anything, but it all came from Mother, and that only added to the sense of constriction—in fact, it was one of the great sources of it.

Eleanor's brilliant, unconventional husband had just published another book, *The Meaning of Happiness*—which, in her current state, touched her as an ironic title. Though actually it was full of wisdom, and she agreed with it fully. But how much could any book help her or anyone with this desperate gloom? And in practical terms—as a source of income, that is—the books were okay, but not really something to rely on with any sort of consistency. Not with the Germans plowing across France like a lumbering ox over molehills and eager to do the same to England, and America dithering across the ocean. At least they were safe here, for now. But what was the world coming to?

The book was getting favorable reviews and selling well in spite of the prevailing dismal mood. As a result, *Harper's* had offered him some regular editing work, and he had some new articles in the works. And yet . . .

She walked past St. Patrick's Cathedral again. This time she went in. She had been out all afternoon and, weary, sat in a pew near the back. For a few moments she bowed her head forward, not in prayer, but in something like a loosening, as in the first moments of zazen, in which her mind relaxed and began to settle. She lifted her head and looked up the aisle toward the altar: there before her, in a pool of brilliant light, was radiant Christ. There, here, right here, himself—there he was, standing, garbed in white robes, his beard, the distinct hairs of his head—his arms outspread wide to embrace her, looking directly into her eyes with a gaze of fathomless depth, unbearable kindness. She was paralyzed. She closed her eyes and opened them again. He was still there, smiling his impossible smile. She felt herself trembling and burst into tears. How could this be happening?

In the weeks that followed, Eleanor tried to make sense of her vision. First of all, what was she, a Buddhist—however imperfectly—doing in a Catholic church, confronted with a searing vision of Christ? It was utterly real. She could still see every fold in his robe, the flow of his hair, his sharp features. She needed to consult an expert. Were there any? Alan thought it unlikely and cautiously suggested she consider that many students of Zen, in deep meditation, had experienced visions, which were acknowledged as mental images, however startling and apparently real they appeared.

"No—you weren't there. If you had seen it as I saw it—him— you would have been as dumbstruck as I. I need to figure this out."

"Then something like one of Jung's archetypes?"

"So far beyond that. Anyhow, it was personal. There was a full presence. He looked straight at me. Into my soul."

She consulted the priest at St. Patrick's, who was not able to offer much beyond, "Well, you had a vision." And there were no other presumed experts she could find.

Alan had been reading. He was shocked that so few Christians knew about their own mystical traditions, traditions that could give Christianity vitality and meaning. To revive these lost mystical practices and integrate Christianity with the other great religions sparked his imagination: he contemplated becoming a Christian minister. He was a natural theologian, speaker, and singer—good skills to have as a parish priest. And there were practical reasons for looking into Christianity as well—he needed a more identifiable career. Being a Christian minister would provide a stamp of legitimacy for something that was already present. If a brand of Christianity could be found that was open to one such as he.

They went exploring. They ruled out most denominations, set-
tling on the Episcopal Church. It was the most liberal form of
Christianity, essentially the Americanized version of the Anglican
Church in which he had grown up.

Those who knew him as a freethinker, and a fathomless source
of bawdy limericks with a propensity for outlandish dancing, were
dubious. Did he not find every sort of organized religion oppres-
sive? He had often said as much. And those who knew him as a
Buddhist were suspicious—Ruth, in particular—that he imagined
Buddhism was somehow deficient or, perhaps more damning, that
his commitment was shallow, which would indicate a more per-
vasive weakness of character.

He explained that it was not an abandonment of Buddhism or
of any of his principles whatsoever, but indeed a deeper welcoming of the essential qualities embodied in the lives of the great
Buddhist masters—and that he had discovered similar qualities
concealed, buried as it were, in the lives and teachings of masters
within the domain of Christianity itself. He intended to reveal
these more forthrightly, so that they not remain hidden from a
world that desperately needed such insights. Though inherently
mystical in nature and expression, such Christian wisdom might
yet be more accessible to Westerners, Americans, than thus far the
teachings of Buddhism were, in spite of their efforts.

"Yes, it will take time for Buddhism to sink in. All the more
reason to persist diligently."

"And so there may be those who find their way to the truths
of Buddhism through a more genuine expression of Christianity.
Does not Sokei-an suggest as much?"

"The message of love of course. But Sokei-an has never presented anything more or less than the direct truth of Buddhism,
through his very being."

"Of course. And that is Sokei-an."

Ruth was not convinced. To her, it represented an abdication, a watering down of something so rich and complex, something that could only be truly grasped within the fullness of the expressed tradition, through the direct presence of a realized master. And here was Alan, who had lost patience with the first koan before he had unlocked half of it. At least now he would be setting aside pretensions of teaching Buddhism.

Watts saw in ancient writings—Pseudo-Dionysius the Areopagite, and an anonymous medieval work called *The Cloud of Unknowing*—clear parallels with Buddhism: A God that existed beyond any capacity of humans to apply a description or definition. Unknowable through the intellect. Nondual. *Form is emptiness, emptiness is form.* And that the human aim should be direct experience of reality, beyond the realm of concepts, beyond the impossible attempt to reconcile opposites through thinking—for in fact the opposites were already fully reconciled, beyond the comprehension of the grasping mind. This reality of reconciled opposites might be called a message of love.

Ruth was unconvinced. "How nice that you dear children have found a belief that really means something for you."

Alan and Eleanor visited all the Episcopal churches in New York. The service in one was too dour. In another, there was no Choral Communion. Eventually, they stumbled into a long, lofty French Gothic structure on West Forty-Sixth Street, neatly hidden between the two taller buildings on each side. It was Palm Sunday, 1941. The ritual was full and stirring, with polyphonic Gregorian chants resonating in the theatrical sanctuary and the attendees arriving with a calm, unhurried, natural grace. This was what Alan was looking for.

In 1941, Ruth purchased a building at 124 East Sixty-Fifth Street, with apartments for herself and family on the top two floors. The top floor was for Ruth's ailing mother—they had an elevator put in, unusual for a private residence—but Clara Fuller died before they moved in.

The third floor was for Sokei-an, and the second and ground floors became the new home of the Buddhist Society, with the public meeting hall at street level and the second floor holding

The building at 124 East Sixty-Fifth Street in 2006.
Courtesy of Janica Anderson.

the roshi's sanzen chambers and study as well as the society's library—much of it from Ruth's large collection of books on Buddhism and related subjects. Ruth designed the interior in the style of a traditional Zen Buddhist temple and furnished it with many of her beautiful works of Asian art and furniture. She had also taken over editing the Buddhist Society's journal, at the time called *Cat's Yawn*, later *Zen Notes*—which began as simply a way to catalog Sokei-an's talks for his students and soon became a monthly publication, printed in a pamphlet edition of a few hundred copies and distributed to a slightly wider circle of students, institutions, and interested members of the public. (In 1947, a compilation of these talks would be published as a book—again called *Cat's Yawn*—as the inaugural offering of the First Zen Institute's publishing project.)

On the eighth of November, 1941, the Buddhist Society of America reopened to members in its new quarters on East Sixty-Fifth Street. Sokei-an addressed the group:

> I am very glad to see you all assembled here tonight, after a long, long vacation. Mrs. Everett designed this hall after a Japanese temple, and she worked by herself to command workmen. Her service to Buddhism is very great. This hall is unique in the United States. I am very grateful to her. I don't doubt that many people are grateful to her. Hereafter, no people dance at night, no one plays the piano, no children shout in the street. In quietude we can enjoy our meeting. But there is one I will not name who created the circumstances that Mrs. Everett came and picked up and put in a nice place, and there are others whose energy and money

have upheld the temple for ten years. Without them this temple would not be here today.

The first public meeting at the new temple quarters was held a month later, on December 6.

Sokei-an would take six questions at the end of a lecture.

"Is war necessary?"

"This question is concerned with the possibility of avoiding war, avoiding conflict. Is war inevitable? Not necessarily. Is war probable? Probably, if we do not resolve conflict another way. Is conflict avoidable?

"The manifestation of dharmakaya in the human mind is like a wave, a storm, like lightning. Sometimes it is harmonized and sometimes it falls into great conflict. When it is harmony, the human being lives in peace; when it is not harmony, the human being lives in agony and struggle. It appears as law, and, subjectively, we call it morality. That is all. That is Buddhism.

"It is because of the innate nature of Perfect Awakening that I believe people will at some time give up their traditional faith and come back to natural faith; really find the common ground on which to build their temples! Before this time, we must encounter many tragedies—struggles, wars.

"War has always been one way that Buddhism has spread. Buddhism came to Japan from China with war. It is possible that war between the United States and Japan will help bring Buddhism to America."

The Japanese bombed Pearl Harbor the following morning. Infamous day.

"There's that car again."

"Which car?"

"That black one. Those two guys pretending not to be watching us."

"Don't be silly, dear. New York is full of people. Why imagine it's anything to do with us?"

"What else would be interesting to them? They've been here every time we come and go."

"Nonsense. You've seen too many movies."

"Don't you think they'd be interested in Sokei-an? Or have you forgotten that the nation of his birth just attacked us?"

"He's hardly even Japanese. He's lived here his whole adult life."

"Except when he was in the Japanese army."

"He was hardly an adult."

"Wasn't he about the age I am now?"

"And that makes one an adult?"

"Mother, I have a child of my own."

"Do you suppose maturity is inevitable merely as a consequence of age and childbearing?"

"Of course not. I understand it's a lifelong undertaking. What would Sokei-an say?"

"Ask him yourself!"

"About the war."

"He has nothing to do about it, obviously!"

"I guess it might not be obvious enough to those government agents in the car."

"Government agents! What a lot of rubbish you've concocted in your imagination."

"When we were in Japan, I never got the idea that ordinary people wanted so much war. It was all over the papers of course, and those awful newsreels. But it was all from the government. People just went along with it."

"In most places people will go along with their leaders. That's always been the way of it."

"Sokei-an talks about his time in the army. He says it was good training for a Buddhist, never knowing if today you'll get blown to bits. He must have been paralyzed with fear. And he came out of that and went right back to his teacher—and then came to America."

"I've always thought of him as fairly fearless. Oh, to be sure, he was a hopeless neurotic as a youth, before he met Soyen Shaku and Sokatsu and started his training. His first kensho, it was very powerful—that was before he went into the army. His teacher held him back to build it up and make it more powerful."

"Do you suppose that's what he was doing—trying to do—with Alan?"

"Really now, that's between the two of them. It's not anyone else's business—not yours or mine. It's a deeper bond even than the bond of marriage."

"Alan felt like he was getting somewhere and Osho sent him out."

"If he thought he had the answer when he didn't, and tried to argue—well, then, he must really not have been ready."

"It might have taken another year or two."

"In any case it won't work to bully your way through. One must have absolute faith in the possibility."

"Maybe his faith isn't so strong."

"It's a lost opportunity—he'll never know it fully. I'm sure he'll find a convenient way to reconcile himself with it, if he hasn't already. And absolve himself of any embarrassment over giving up."

Immediately after the attack, everything Japanese became suspect. At first, in the early days after Pearl Harbor, leaders of the

Japanese community on the West Coast, Shinto and Buddhist priests, and anyone associated with Japanese cultural groups or martial arts groups was arrested—because they were considered to owe allegiance to the emperor of Japan.

On February 19, 1942, President Franklin Delano Roosevelt signed Executive Order 9066: "Instructions to all persons of Japanese ancestry living in the following areas . . ." All persons of Japanese descent in these areas, regardless of citizenship—in fact more than two-thirds of them were American citizens, and many of the rest, like Sokei-an, had lived in the country for decades and had permanent residency status—were now considered enemies.

There were two FBI agents conducting round-the-clock surveillance from the veranda of the Cosmopolitan Club across the street. Ruth and Sokei-an were followed and questioned repeatedly. For the time being the meetings at the Buddhist Society were allowed to continue—sanzen for the senior students and the Wednesday night lectures—under the watchful eye of the government.

It hurt to sit. It hurt so much that Sokei-an could not concentrate on anything without being interrupted by the pain. He finally went to Ruth's doctor. His hemorrhoids were so inflamed, it would be necessary to operate. And his systolic blood pressure was up around 180—but there was little they could do about that. The doctor explained that it was simply hereditary.

He went in for the surgery for his hemorrhoids during the first week of June 1942. If there were no complications, his recovery should proceed smoothly and quickly.

On the fourteenth of June, a week out of the hospital, Sokei-an felt sufficiently recovered to give sanzen and teisho. A dozen of his closest students were present. The atmosphere in the room was somber. It was not just his health. There was a sense of foreboding. He dispensed with discussions of technical terms and spent only a few minutes with the text he had translated for the occasion. The bulk of the talk concerned what Zen had meant to him. He said, "There is only one thing. I got nothing, but there is only one thing I want, and only one thing that matters, and that is to be a human being." That was the last public talk he ever gave.

The next day, June 15, 1942, Sokei-an was arrested by the FBI as an enemy alien and taken to an internment camp at Ellis Island.

A Forsaken Sojourn
and a Strange Marriage

Ellis Island–Fort Meade, Maryland–New York–
Little Rock, Arkansas–New York, 1942–1945

Ellis Island. He had never been here. It was not the gate through which he had entered America.

It was his first prison. He might be released immediately after his hearing. Or he might be forced to live out his days here, a prisoner in the shadow of Liberty's torch, within view of his city, which he might never walk through again.

Not that he was up for walking at the moment. Getting to the latrine forced him to trudge through mud to the far end of the next building—much too far for anything resembling comfort. He had not really recovered from his operation. It hurt just to move.

He wrote to Ruth: "I have dreamed of Chaka, golden eyes looking at me from among the weeds in the garden. I sleep well these nights, but I don't look over the sea from my window, for the shadow of the city aches my heart."

Ruth was beside herself. Could they have anticipated this? Could they have prepared? They had talked to those government agents willingly, openly. How many times had they been taken aside and questioned—a dozen? They had not hidden anything. There was nothing in Sokei-an's life or work that merited this indignity. It was absurd that anyone would need convincing at all, but she would convince them.

The day of the hearing arrived. She was prepared. She had consulted her lawyer, who thought there should be no problem. There was no evidence against him. He had not been in contact with Japanese forces, military or political or really anyone at all, apart from the papers and journals to which he sent material purely for the entertainment of the readers.

There were questions from the panel. They did not sound like questions.

"He writes about America."

"True, America and Americans have often been his subjects. For entertainment."

"He writes in Japanese."

"Yes, that is his first language and the language in which his audience is able to read."

"In his writings he has criticized the United States. He is a Japanese propagandist."

"He has no political affiliations."

"We suspect there may be coded messages."

"There are no coded messages. He has no political affiliations whatsoever."

They pulled up a piece, a Nonsense column he had written in 1936. It made reference to war between Japan and the United States. The prosecuting officer had determined that it was advocating war, a call-to-arms from the writer to his countrymen: that Japan should attack the United States. The column was written by Shigetsu Sasaki.

"Do you recognize this name?"

"Of course."

"He is an ordained minister in a Japanese religious institution. May I remind you, we are at war with Japan; they are our sworn enemies."

"He loves America. He is absolutely not an enemy of America."

"His religion is the religion of Japan."

"Buddhism in Japan—if I may explain—Buddhism is not the state religion. It is no longer commonly regarded as even particularly important there."

"Madam, you have lived in Japan?"

"I have."

"And you subscribe to Buddhist beliefs?"

"There is nothing political or anti-American about it whatsoever."

"Thank you, Madam. That will be all."

This was such utter nonsense that Ruth could barely contain her frustration. She was fuming, furious. But they would not hear any logic; they were not interested in a simple explanation. They could only gather the most superficial idea of his writings—a complete misreading, a complete misunderstanding. They really had no idea what to make of it, so they called him a propagandist. They would not release him.

The ineptitude of the hearing was inexcusable. They had no evidence. They were disorganized. It was as if his internment was a forgone conclusion, the hearing little more than an announcement of his fate. A farce, a tragic farce. What use was a hearing if there was no listening? We have to get him out, Ruth thought.

Eleanor and Alan had moved to Chicago for his seminary. There were only the others in Sokei-an's group for Ruth to turn to. They witnessed a change in Ruth. It shook her confidence. Here was a woman who had always been certain she could handle anything.

Now she began to realize for the first time that Sokei-an's strength was not in her alone. She was not sufficient. He needed, and now she understood that she needed, the whole group.

Sokei-an was shocked. Was it possible he had so misunderstood America and Americans? After nearly four decades, he expected to be treated fairly. His adopted country. His home. In New York City it was possible to be free. In his training, in his religion, it was his responsibility to be an agent for freedom. How can this now be possible?

He wrote again to Ruth, heartbroken. "The Island is shrouded in drizzling rain. Avalokiteshvara weeps over me today. I am waiting for Alice in the Wonderland to come."

He wrote to Ruth. He wrote to his students, as a group, and to a few as individuals. He wrote to his son, Shintaro, and daughter Seiko. His American children, born in America, land of liberty. Now adults, just past thirty and nearly thirty years old. They were in America. They were being held in camps.

Shintaro, born in San Francisco in 1909, was brought to Japan for the first time at age seven. He never fit in. He never felt at home there, never felt at ease. As a child, he mostly kept to himself. When this was not possible, he would get in fights. Other children mocked him, or he imagined they did—in any case, he reacted as if they did and mostly preferred to avoid other people. He always felt misplaced. In Japan, he immersed himself in studying, especially Chinese, and Buddhist literature. He also studied English, looking forward to the day he could escape to America, the land of his birth, where people would not scorn him.

In 1930, when he was twenty, he sailed to Seattle. He had a

hard time sticking at anything very long. He would find work as
a houseboy for a while, or as a gardener, and then would move
on. He went down to San Francisco, worked on farms around
San Jose and Fresno, went back up to the Northwest again. America was better than Japan, but he had trouble here too. He was
always suspicious that people had ill intentions toward him. He
met with his father's old friend who owned the *Great Northern
News*, who took him on as a printer's devil in the press room.

Shintaro's sister Seiko, born in Seattle in 1912, came to America
to look after her older brother. Their mother sent her—he needed
looking after, he was never completely okay on his own. Seiko
came and met him in Seattle. But Shintaro soon left again, heading
down the coast to California.

He was always in touch with his father. Sokei-an, when Shintaro was in San Francisco, asked Nyogen Senzaki to keep an eye
on the boy, which he did, perhaps with some ambivalence—why
was Sokei-an himself not looking after his son? Why did he not
bring him to New York? In fact, Shintaro had an open invitation,
and plans to visit the great eastern city, but for whatever reasons
was unable to follow through with those plans.

In Seattle, Seiko met a man—a *nisei* named Ted Inouye, whose
family supplied fishing boats and ran a salmon cannery in Alaska.
He was a kind man, but he drank heavily. One summer in Alaska
he got in a fight with his family, and they disowned him. After
that, he and Seiko settled in California as well. Before the end of
the decade, they had three children.

Ruth first wrote to Shintaro on July 10, 1942, to inform him
that his father had been taken to Ellis Island. Shintaro had been
back in Seattle for a few years. He had managed to settle into
newspaper work, first in the pressroom for the *Great Northern
News* and after a while as a reporter and editor. Sokei-an had

been encouraging him to come to New York—he would very much like to see him. They were working on a dictionary of Chinese Buddhist terms and would like his assistance. They could arrange funding and would pay for his travel expenses. Please, find a way to come!

The newspaper had been allowed to continue publishing after the war began because the owner and all of its editors were American citizens. With the evacuation order, there was no one to run it. The paper closed. Shintaro was taken to Camp Harmony in Puyallup, Washington, and after a few months to Camp Minidoka outside of Hunt, Idaho. There were dust storms. He wrote to Ruth, "Minidoka is no place fit for people to live. The climate is unhealthy and the air somewhat rarefies. The weather runs from an extreme to an extreme."

Ruth tried to get him released to her with a translating job in New York. At first it seemed possible.

After four months at Ellis Island, on October 2, 1942, Sokei-an was transferred to Fort Meade in Maryland.

He could walk again. Not well—his energy was gone, he was tired all the time. Sometimes he would feel it in his chest, sometimes his eyes. When the headache came, it felt like a claw clenching the base of his skull, and then sticks tapping his temples, smacking him in that tender spot next to his eyes, striking harder and harder with each blow. Sometimes he would see a white flash and then nothing. The guards showed him kindness. They gave him aspirin, which provided some relief, though when the headache subsided, he was useless for doing anything; he had to lie down, he could not lift himself off the cot.

It came in waves. He would have a few good days—he could read, write letters, work on carvings. Then it would hit him again.

His blood pressure would spike—the headache, nausea. He had
to lie down.

The moon rose between rows of hutments, the plywood-reinforced
five-man tents that lined the dusty dirt lanes of the camp, each
with a Sibley stove in the center as the only heat in winter and
a bare forty-watt bulb the only light. In winter it was muddy; in
summer it was dusty.

Rows of hutments. This same moon. Here there was no flowing stream to reflect it, no wild Oregon river, no lotus pond. This
dusty place. Only the partially obstructed view to the sky, and the
stream of his recollection. What is memory to an awakened mind?
Not a trap, not a prison. A place to visit or not as desired. Dust.

Unavoidable betrayal of misunderstanding. Mistranslation.
Mistaken identity. How could they possibly know him? His essential purpose was of no interest to them. They only saw an alien
cult. But he was more American than Japanese—if not a citizen,
at least a permanent resident. He would marry Mrs. Everett. He
would find some way. She would find a way. To get him out of
this forsaken place.

They accused him of making inflammatory statements. Something he had written in 1936: Buddhism has always spread through
war—when it came from China to Japan, it was through conflict.
War brings countries together. Perhaps Japan should attack the
United States—then Buddhism would spread here more quickly.
But of course they could only read the surface, seeing only incite-
ment, never irony, never an open question.

The Zen master never explains. Of course there are explanations—the background, perhaps, the Buddha's teachings on
impermanence and the *skandhas*, on cause and effect. But this is
just to help guide the student along the way. There is no reaching

dharmakaya by explanation, only through experience. The student must make the discoveries. Then there can be confirmation. Not explanation.

Not good enough for the government. The government needs an explanation.

He did not wish to be in this position. When he first arrived in this country, he felt the prejudice acutely. In San Francisco it was like an invisible screen blocking off neighborhoods, theaters, trolleys: you are not wanted here. It permeated the Art Institute. But then he found none of it in Oregon, and not so much in Seattle or the rest of the Northwest. In New York, there was not so much either. He had stayed with Italians, Portuguese, blacks. There was no problem for him; they were very welcoming. No one tried to hide the differences. They could be American. He could be American.

In the camp, he avoided the other Japanese. He had been apart from them so long, they looked at him suspiciously; he had little interest in associating. He made friends with the American guards—which made the other Japanese yet more suspicious, though to his eye the guards did not subject them to abuse, at least, beyond the essential fact of enforcing their residence in this unfortunate place. Conditions were sparse, uncomfortable. Miserable.

The colonel in charge of the camp tried to make things easier, and for that Sokei-an was grateful. They were willing to let him have his books. And his carving tools. By way of thanks, Sokei-an carved a cane for the colonel, in the form of a dragon.

On May 27, Shintaro wrote to Ruth:

Dear Mrs Everett,
You wrote me in your letter that my father was fairly

well when you saw him in the Camp. Sound is very lonesome to me. When you see my father next, please tell him that I love my father as well as I love my sister, Seiko.

It is very hot here in these days. The sun comes out glittering in the morning and passing upon the head it sinks glittering in the evening.

The headaches were getting worse, much worse. In the morning not always bad, but by evening the dull pain was constant, throbbing, squeezing from the base of his skull to the sockets of his eyes. And his heart—sometimes it jumped; the rhythm was off. It would last for a few seconds, his chest felt tight, he would have to lie down. He who had walked across mountains. He who had walked for days, for weeks. He could barely stumble from his cot in the tent to the canteen without pausing to rest. It was breaking his heart.

The summer has come to Fort Meade. In the evening I sit down upon the weeds. I read books at random till I find myself in twilight's deep; then I take a shower and go to bed. Again, I have something to carve these days. In the daytime, therefore, I take refuge into the work of woodcarving; and it deprives me of the mind tantalized, awaiting for the news of my pending rehearing. I was so glad to hear, through Ruth, that my son will soon be freed from the relocation center, and that something for him to do was already arranged.

I am carving again. I have my tools back. It is unprecedented—against the law. But there is an exception in my case! The colonel is pleased with his cane, the captain is pleased with his box, and another captain is pleased with his gun. Really the army has been very kind to me.

Sokei-an's carving The Koan.
Courtesy of the First Zen Institute of America.

Ruth marshaled all her resources to getting him out. It became her single-minded mission. She hired Hugo Pollock, a lawyer who had worked with her husband, who knew many people in government and how to get the attention of those he did not yet know. She gathered Sokei-an's students and friends together at the Buddhist Society to strategize and write letters. George Fowler, one of Sokei-an's senior students, was now a commander in the navy. He set to work on his teacher's release through whatever channels he was privy to.

One day in the middle of August 1943, the Japanese inmates at Fort Meade were lined up to be transferred by bus to Missoula, Montana. An officer pulled Sokei-an aside, saying simply, "Come with me." They arrived at a room where two immigration officers were waiting for him. "This must remain a complete secret," they said. They gave him all of his dictionaries. Then they put him into a limousine, got in with him, and drove off. He was being released.

Sokei-an had been interned from June 15, 1942, until August 17, 1943.

> September 7, 1943
> My dear Shintaro,
>
> We have been waiting to have some word from you as to your situation, but as yet none has come. Your sister sends me continuously the little camp paper, "Denson Tribune" and I have been reading it with great interest.
>
> I gather from it that all those in relocation centers have been divided into four groups. Those in the first and second groups are to be sent to Tule Lake on or about September 15th. At least that is the program for the Denson center.
>
> I also gather from your letter and from reading the articles on this classification that you must be in Group 3, a group whose loyalty to America is doubted, but who will be allowed to have a thorough hearing to determine their attitude toward America and the American way of life. If it is proven without question that they are loyal and devoted to this country, they will be transferred to Group 4, and then be eligible for indefinite leave from the relocation center. I certainly hope you will be successful in proving your allegiance to America.

Your father and I have discussed your situation in detail and there are certain things which he wished me to write to you. Please read this letter over carefully, many, many times if necessary, so that you clearly understand everything I am saying to you. It is most important for your future that you understand your father's position and his attitude very clearly. So, even if this letter is very long, take time to read it and digest it completely.

Your father's re-hearing took up the better part of two evenings and lasted in all more than six hours. Your father was most carefully examined personally by the members of the Hearing Board, as were also the ten witnesses, Japanese and American, who appeared in his behalf.

At the conclusion of his re-hearing Attorney-General Biddle released your father on parole. What the basis of this decision of the Attorney-General was of course we do not know exactly, but we understand that his conclusions were these:

1. Your father had no intention of carrying on any propaganda work for the Japanese government;

2. Your father's writing could not be considered to be in any sense propaganda;

3. The money which he received from Mr. Muraoka, while it was recompensation for his contributing a column to the "Japanese-American" for a period of over ten years, was in reality contributions to your father's Buddhist work and *not* direct payment for his writing;

4. Your father did NOT receive any money directly or indirectly from any Japanese agency.

Your father thinks for himself. His intention in

writing his Nonsense was only to amuse himself and to amuse his readers. He employed the slang and colloquial expressions in use by Japanese on the Pacific Coast, but the backbone of his writing was his Zen expression, not his intention to disparage the way of life or the political policies of the United States of America. In a figurative sense he pill-coated sugar, while other writers sugar-coated pills. The reason why he speaks of his writing as pill-coated sugar is because in it there was no pill. The core of it was simply sugar. By taking this pill-coated sugar people amused themselves.

Now it appears that you, Shintaro, will have to go through some kind of hearing if you belong to this Group 3. Your father sends you this particular message and you must follow his advice when the time comes.

You must state clearly that you are loyal to the United States of America and that you will do anything to help America win this war because you love America as your native land and because you believe that a man's life must be for a man, not for any hypothetical idea or for any vain aim. You believe that the American democratic attitude stands for man's life as an individual, not for vain glory or for imperialistic aggression.

These words are not a temporary concept of your father, adopted for today's situation. Your father has lived continuously almost forty years in this country, except for four years spent in Japan, and as a result of long consideration he has awakened to this understanding. Of course you remember that your father has many times in the past stated to you that when you grew up you would have to work for the United States because it was the country of your birth and the country which you have chosen to be your home. At the hearing which you are likely to have to undergo you must protect yourself, protect your father, and protect the land which is your home.

Your father has been thinking very deeply about your sisters and your mother. He is ready to do something for them when the time arrives. These words have been stated by your father from his own heart and his instruction to you is: "Listen to your father. You are no longer a child. In any plight consult your father."

Before your father was interned and before you were sent to the relocation center, the Buddhist Society of America, Inc., by whom your father is employed, tried to arrange for you to come to New York and to find employment for you here. We sent you $225.00 for your railroad fare and necessary expenses, but you failed to receive permission to come here because the time of removal was near.

If you are asked in your hearing about the source of this $225.00, you must state clearly from whom you received this money, and not prevaricate in any way about it. The money belonged to the Buddhist Society of America, though it was sent by me in my name because that was the simplest way to handle the matter. No danger can come to you from explaining the true circumstances which occurred. Perhaps some straight statement about this money will help to clear up your situation. I am sure you will be asked about the source of this money, since the government keeps strict watch on all money transactions.

When you have finished reading this letter, keep it or destroy it according to your own judgment. DO NOT carry it around and show it to other Japanese in the center. That will do you no good and might do you harm.

All my best wishes to you. Your father sends his regards.

Seiko and her family had been in California when the war broke out. Along with many others from the Los Angeles and San Joaquin Valley areas, they were sent to southern Arkansas and interned at the Jerome War Relocation Center, in the humid, mosquito-infested marshlands of the Mississippi River.

My dearest daughter, I was released on parole. My usual mode of life was restored and I am living in the residence of Mrs. Everett. I have high blood pressure, but it does not annoy me much except that I have a little headache sometimes. I think my death will not come so soon, and there will be some period of cool October hereafter toward the end of my life. Write me by-in-by and tell me about the conditions of your life in the relocation center. I have been saved from the jaws of death. You don't know what that camp was like.

Sokei-an had suffered at least one mild stroke in the camp. On a good day, he felt his strength return somewhat, and he would do some walking if he could. His students would visit frequently, but he did not have the energy to give sanzen or teisho.

"Marry me!"

"How can I marry you? You're still legally bound to another woman."

"She is a lifetime away. You know there is no longer anything to it."

"Of course I'm completely . . . it's not so simple. For me—well, my husband is deceased. Your wife is alive. So there is that. In any case, what business does a roshi have being married?"

"Only tradition! Of no consequence!"

"But how do you get past that one practicality?"

"A Japanese divorce. It can be done."

"Without her consent?"

"That is not the only problem."

"No, I suppose not."

"My teacher."

"Sokatsu, yes, you have said."

"It was because of him that we married. It would be a grave insult."

"At a certain point—has he not insulted you? By disowning you?"

"He has taken me back. It is a very difficult matter. It would be difficult to live with."

"For how long?"

"Yes. While there is still time. You must marry me! You will carry on the work in my name."

"An American divorce. It may be possible. We shall have Mr. Pollock look into it."

Sokei-an's younger daughter, Shihoko, who was born in Japan and had always lived in Japan, remained more or less in communication with Sokei-an, and he would send her some money when he had it. The girl was bright and her mother wanted to send her to university. So Sokei-an sent money over for her education. And then, when she graduated, he found out that the college was—her mother had lied about it—a Christian theological seminary. When Shihoko graduated, she was a minister, a Christian minister. And she promptly married another Japanese Christian minister.

Sokei-an knew not to expect reasonableness from Shihoko's mother, this woman who had rejected Buddhism long ago, who had deceived him about her youngest daughter—their daughter. Yes, he wanted to support her, but he had never known her, had lived near her only for four years, long ago. Tome had pulled her into Christianity and poisoned her against her father. What would any of them care about his Buddhist life, his teaching, his legacy? It was a hard root to stub one's toe upon.

Sokei-an had been out of the camp a few weeks when he was called in by the government again. There was a lingering question of whether he could be allowed to remain on the East Coast or would have to go to the central part of the United States. The West Coast was still a restricted zone, while on the East Coast there was more room for a tribunal to make decisions, according to their discretion, considering the details of each particular case. They were evaluating whether his remaining on the East Coast would be a danger to America. Several of his students, including Ruth, were subpoenaed as well. There were six or seven ranking officers—colonels and majors—sitting behind the table. This examining panel kept him in the room a long time. The four or five students who had been questioned first had been in the room, all together, for fifteen minutes or so. They began to worry when he was still in the room after twenty minutes, a half hour, forty-five minutes. Finally he emerged into the lobby where they were waiting, expecting the worst.

When he came out, they rushed to ascertain whether everything was okay. He said, "Oh no, they've been very nice. They wanted to know about Manchuria." They questioned him about everything he knew of the region—the terrain, the climate, the people—everything he'd learned or seen or knew as the result of his time in the army.

Afterward Sokei-an and Ruth and the other students got into a cab and headed downtown to Longchamps for dinner, to celebrate getting clear of this hurdle—presumably the final one. It was mid-September, a hot afternoon and evening. Sokei-an was sweating. At the dinner table, as they were sitting down to eat, he got very quiet. He turned to Ruth and said, "I don't feel very well. I think I'd better go home." They got him into a cab.

Before they had gone very far he began vomiting violently. They all knew about his high blood pressure, and they knew the camp had made everything worse—it had broken his health. They did not want him dying right now—not yet, not right here in this taxi. The driver raced him to a hospital. It was a long, torturous night of waiting. Finally some relief as his condition stabilized—acute coronary thrombosis. At least he was still alive.

The thrombosis impaired his speech, his movement, his ability to concentrate. For the next seven or eight months he was a complete invalid. He couldn't give lectures or do anything in public. People came to see him, but it was not until the spring of 1944 that he felt he had recovered enough to consider teaching again.

And then he was not getting well. The doctor, the best New York doctor Ruth knew, was very worried about him. Finally the doctor took her aside and said, "Now look here—if you want Mr. Sasaki to get well, you have got to marry him. You have got to." He knew the lawyer, Hugo Pollock, who had worked to get Sokei-an out of the camp. They had discussed the matter. Pollock thought a divorce could be arranged in this country.

The doctor explained, "It's the only thing that will keep him alive. He is determined he's going to die, and the only thing that will bring him any kind of peace of mind, and possibly facilitate his recovery, is for you to marry him."

Pollock, who by this point had become a steadfast friend, set it up for them.

"Here's how it works. You go down to Arkansas. In Arkansas, you can get a divorce after a period of six weeks residency and public advertisement in the newspapers—assuming there is no one who contests the divorce. You need not be concerned about that."

"My daughter is there. In Arkansas."

"You'll be able to see her. She's at the Jerome camp? We'll make sure she gets clearance to leave for a visit, one way or the other. Her presence will be neither an advantage nor a hindrance."

"I have been in frequent contact with Sokei-an's daughter. She understands the situation and will be fully supportive—she will be simply thrilled to see her father after such a long time."

"You go down to Arkansas—you both have to go, of course. It doesn't matter if you go together or separately, you just have to establish residency, both of you; have it documented and notarized. I've been in touch with associates down there—we'll take care of any paperwork. You just have to go down there."

"Mr. Pollock, you're quite aware that Mr. Sasaki's health will not permit him to travel alone."

"Of course. There is nothing legally to prevent you from accompanying him. I would advise it, in fact—as will his doctor. Mr. Sasaki, you will need a local sponsor, of course, because of the war and your situation. There is a minister of the Congregational church in Little Rock with whom I am acquainted. He has expressed his willingness to serve in this capacity—and in fact is quite interested to meet you."

"Will there be any difficulty with the traveling—crossing state lines?"

"I will accompany you on the journey as well. There will be no questions."

They set out by train in late May 1944. At first they had thought of going to Hot Springs, so that Sokei-an could use the baths, but the doctor decided that would not be the right thing for him in his condition. When they arrived in Little Rock, they found a hotel that suited them, near the river, with a kitchenette apartment for Ruth and a room in another part of the hotel for Sokei-an.

After a couple of weeks it seemed that Sokei-an's condition was finally improving. They were spending all of their time together. Some days they would go walking through Little Rock's Riverfront Park along the Arkansas River. After so much trauma surrounding the internment and Sokei-an's health, their conversation danced away from grave matters and began to turn again more toward Zen.

The news was all about D-Day. It appeared that the Allied invasion of Normandy was a great victory, but it was unclear if the reoccupation of France would finally be successful enough to turn the tide in the Allies' favor. And German bombs were still falling on London—thank goodness Eleanor and Alan had come to the United States. At this point the war in the Pacific was not so clear, either. Sokei-an felt that he could see its end. But it was too terrible to talk about. So they turned their attention elsewhere.

"Eryu, you know I will not live long. When my father was in this condition, he survived only a few months. Less than a year. When I am gone, it will be up to you to continue this work."

"Of course."

"The worst thing is not having found a successor. It will be up to you to find someone. You must find someone. I have written many times to Sokatsu and Goto Roshi. There is no one. With the war, it is even worse for Buddhism in Japan."

"It must be someone who speaks English. There is Goto Roshi."

"He says he is too old. Perhaps his English is not so good now. But when the war ends—of course it must end soon—he may wish to see the United States again. He may be convinced. In any case, he is my devoted brother and will certainly help in any way he can."

"I will write to him. And Sokatsu."

"Sokatsu of course cannot do anything himself, but perhaps he will help. He has retired now and is not in good health. We can hope he still favors our project, as he once did. He is not so easy to predict."

"And do you suppose anyone will pay attention to me?"

"You will be Mrs. Sasaki. In any case, when you go to Japan you must visit Sokatsu."

Ruth had heard about Sokatsu before the war, first from Dwight Goddard, who had managed to go see him. But the Suzukis would not allow her to go.

Mrs. Suzuki in particular was opposed. She belonged to the Episcopal church. She had married Mr. Suzuki, a student of Sokatsu's master Soyen, and they had a little house inside of the Engaku-ji compound. But she never liked Soyen, because he drank too much and played with geishas.

Soyen made no bones about his inclinations. One warm summer night in Kamakura he had been at a geisha house, on the second floor. All the shoji screens were open, all the lights in the room were on. He took off all his clothes and danced around stark naked, the populace watching.

So Mrs. Suzuki was violently antagonistic to Soyen. She took sanzen from him for a short time and then couldn't endure it. This she herself told Ruth.

Soyen was followed as the roshi at Engaku-ji not by Sokatsu but by an extremely ascetic, tall, thin man, about whose morality nothing unfavorable could be said. Mrs. Suzuki showed Ruth his picture and said, "You see, he's so spiritual. He's the kind of teacher I wanted; somebody who was spiritual, not like Soyen."

Ruth described the conversation to Sokei-an. "Did you know how it pleased Mrs. Suzuki that Sokatsu did not get the position after Soyen Shaku retired? She began sanzen with Soyen but considered him appalling. And she had heard about Sokatsu and his mistress and wanted nothing to do with him. But the priest who did follow Soyen as abbot, who got the job instead of Sokatsu—she found him very spiritual."

Sokei-an replied, "Oh, spiritual. How could he be anything else? When he was a kid he got kicked in the balls by a horse.

"In any case, your friend's husband—he never completed his training. Suzuki-san, he puts out his own ideas and calls it Zen—pure self-manufactured nonsense. But the teacher you find to follow me—he must be a real roshi!"

From the day he became a priest, Sokei-an had been writing to various priests he knew, telling them they must try to send somebody to him in America, someone he could break in and prepare to follow him. He felt bitterly disappointed that he couldn't get one bit of reaction from anybody. Nobody was interested, nobody offered him any help of any kind. He would say, "They're so blind, they're so stupid, they're so steeped in their old ways they can't see beyond the edges of the island. They can't see what's happening in the world; they don't know how to."

They returned to working on the *Rinzai Roku*. Sokei-an was getting restless. He missed New York. He looked forward to beginning sanzen again with his students, who had been without him already for the fourteen months he was at Ellis Island and Fort Meade, and then for the months he was incapacitated. Some of them had been making real progress. Bringing Zen to America was planting a lotus on a stone—it would be three hundred years before coming to full fruition. But it had begun.

There were so many loose ends to wrap up. He had confidence that his Eryu would be equal to the task, but she could not be the teacher herself. They needed to find someone who could take up that piece—which of course was the basis of all the rest of it. The translations would be useful, but ultimately only to those who had the direct experience, the eye-to-eye, soul-to-soul encounter. Without that—only so many words.

Seiko came to visit. She received the clearance and brought her three children. Sokei-an lit up when he met them. Her youngest, a boy called Timmy, was just a little baby. The older boy, Mineru, was four or five, and the oldest, a girl named Mary, was eight.

Seiko had artistic talents—in painting and writing—and in looks she resembled Sokei-an the most of his three children. His fondness for her was undiluted by time or distance. It was visible in his face, in his voice, in the way he stroked his baby grandson's forehead.

They talked about life in the Jerome camp in a general way. She did have opportunities to paint. She contributed to the camp newspaper, the *Denson Tribune*. Her husband was busy as a camp mechanic. Quarters were tight, the mosquitoes were annoying, but overall the worst of it was simply the constant reminder of being so completely subject to the government.

There was a great deal that remained unspoken. He was concerned for his daughter's well-being—he sensed an unexpressed,
if not unexpected, anxiety beneath her cheerful demeanor. She
was concerned about his health. They both knew this could be
the last time they saw each other. Though they had been in close
correspondence, she had never tried to visit him in New York—
her life was on the opposite coast, and then the war complicated
everything—but now she was simply happy to have a few days
in his company. It would, indeed, be the last time they ever saw
each other.

The divorce was finalized. Everything was ready for the simple
wedding Mr. Pollock had arranged—a civil ceremony with just a
minister and the lawyer present. They had a ring. But it turned out
that in Pulaski County, of which Little Rock was the county seat,
they were not allowed to get married. They were not both white.
It had not occurred to them, or their otherwise astute lawyer, that
Southern antimiscegenation laws would apply to them.

It was a Saturday, July 8, 1944. They had tickets for the train to
Chicago departing later that afternoon. They would not miss that
train. But the plan to have the wedding in the morning and allow
plenty of time to board the train was not holding up. The lawyer
made some phone calls. Somehow he found a judge in another
county who would overlook that law. They got in a cab—because
of gasoline rationing they could not use the lawyer's car—and
speeded to the tiny crossroads town of Benton, about twenty-five
miles outside of Little Rock. Apart from a grand brick courthouse
building with a four-story clock tower reminding them how little
time they had, there was nothing to the town beyond a couple of
rundown country stores with a couple of old men sitting around
on a hot Saturday afternoon. Even so, it was the county seat of

Saline County, and the judge would conduct their wedding—not at the courthouse, which was closed, but in his own home.

The judge welcomed them sweetly. He had a bouquet of flowers for Ruth, and his wife brought out tea for everyone. The judge performed the ceremony. They were legally married. They thanked him and rushed back to try to catch the train. Because of the gasoline rationing, the cab was not supposed to go outside of Little Rock. But somehow they managed it. They got to the train just in time, falling exhausted into their Pullman car.

They were bound for Chicago to spend a few days with Eleanor. With the heat and all of the stress and excitement, Sokei-an had a restless night.

The train was due to arrive in Chicago about 11:00 a.m. They got up in the morning to go to breakfast. They had to stand in line—the train was quite full, so they had to wait in a corridor to go into the dining car. Sokei-an was standing in front of Ruth, as the train was passing through the middle of Illinois. She was looking out the window at the open land rolling by.

She looked back to the line and there was nobody in front of her. She looked down—he was on the floor. He had collapsed. Some other people helped drag him to a seat, and they called the conductor. Ruth sent a telegram ahead to a doctor she knew in Chicago, told him to have an ambulance ready at the station. After a while, Sokei-an came to, groggy and weak. When they got to Chicago, they lifted him off the train, into a wheelchair and to the ambulance.

Getting back to New York was the same: an ambulance to the train, and an ambulance from the train to the house. And from that time, Sokei-an's blood pressure would go up to around 240. He could hardly stand it.

The doctor assessed that by now his high blood pressure had caused permanent damage to his cardio-renal-vascular apparatus. It was imperative for the sake of his health that his life be free of any worry or strain, mental or physical.

Dec. 24, 1944
My dear Eryu-san,

Thank you very much for your Christmas present. I received your letter, too.

I work now at the drygoods section of the warehouse which belongs to canteens in the Camp as a shipping clerk.

My hearing was held a few days ago for the purpose of determining whether I can be included in the list of those persons who will be permitted to leave War Relocation Centers. I shall be notified at the earliest opportunity of the decision made in my case.

How monotonous is the life in the Camp! How flat is my job in the warehouse every day! How shabby is my environment, being hemmed by the sagebrush desert, looking at the barracks standing in rows in the morning and evening! I hope the day I can see you and my father may not be far distant.

I am in good spirits and good health.

A happy new year to you and my father.

Sincerely yours,
Shintaro Sasaki

January 16, 1945
My dear Shintaro,

Your father received your letter some days ago. He

has read it over carefully and we have discussed its contents together several times.

We are glad to know that you do not have to go to Tule Lake. We felt that your opinions could not have been antagonistic to the country of which you were a citizen and we are happy that you were able to make yourself understood.

According to the paper which you enclosed with your letter you are not allowed to go into all parts of the United States unless you have another hearing or an army hearing which results in the rescinding of the present order as it stands. If you do not have any other hearings, or if you do not succeed at another hearing in having your status changed, then you cannot come to New York.

Your father thinks that perhaps it would be best for you to join with friends you have made at the camp and go with them to some city in the central part of the country and make a home for yourself there where you would know people. Certainly the W.R.A. is still continuing to have their employment offices in the larger cities of the country, and through one of them you should be able to get work.

If you have another hearing and if you are able to get your status changed so that you can come to the New York area, do you want to come?

The position which was open to you with the society two years ago, the position of translation work, is no longer available. The person who was to provide the major part of the funds for that work cannot do so now. So you cannot hope to get that work.

Your father is almost sixty-three years old. On February 15th he will have his sixty-third birthday. He is a little better in health, but he is still very much an invalid and can do very little work each day. He must rest and sleep the major part of the time. He is *not* able to support you if you come here. You would have to do that. Furthermore he is not able to make any promises to the government about you in relation to your standing with the government. When you have received permission to come here and decide to come and take a job, he will help you to find the job. But he cannot write letters to the government in your behalf to ask them to let you come here. That you must handle yourself.

Your father and I send you our regards.

Sincerely,

Eryu

"My good friends. Three years ago I predicted that the day of my death would come soon. I have already outlived that day. In such a circumstance it is customary to be given a new name. So I ask you: what shall I be called, who have surpassed my appointed hour?"

Mary Farkas blurted out "Tigerheart." Sokei-an accepted this offering.

May 8. The Germans have surrendered. The Japanese are still fighting.

It will not go well.

On the twelfth, Saturday evening, Sokei-an was stricken with a kidney thrombosis. It appeared that he might not survive the night.

On Tuesday afternoon he raised himself on his bed, folded his legs, and asked for some pillows to be placed behind his back: in this way he was able to sit nearly erect. He asked, weakly, "Am I in shape?"

Then he started talking. His voice was a hoarse whisper. He turned to each of them—Ruth on a chair at the right; Sakiko, one of his students, on a chair to the left; Edna on the foot of his bed at the left edge. Beyond Edna was a large, long window overlooking the little garden. His gaze shifted past Edna, to the world outside. A world he had once inhabited, as he still, briefly, inhabited worlds inside.

He said a few words about working on koans. There was nothing new or notable about these words: he was only testing his voice. He paused, for a long time, as if gathering up strength— from the ground, from his timeless and difficult life, from the many thousands of miles he had walked in his days, from his very nature, from the depths of his being. He spoke again, still very slowly, but this time his voice resonated with the power of the universe: "You must consider, very intensely." He fixed his eyes on Edna, "What you are doing. Every moment." He fixed his eyes on Sakiko. "Not depending. On any. Other. Way." His eyes held Ruth's. "It is. The *only* way."

Two days later, at 6:00 p.m. on May 17, Sokei-an died.

My dear Eryu-san

I received your telegram yesterday (May 20) in which I was informed by you that my father passed away.

I sent a letter several days ago to Leave Section here inquiring if I am still under stop order, because I was prohibited to leave the Camp by the W.R.A. after receiving the exclusion order by which I was prohibited from entering the West Coast and East Coast.

A Japanese man in charge of relocation at Leave Section came down to my place and told me that I can go to New York at any time, I can go anywhere except the West Coast.

I wish you to find a job for me in New York City so that I can visit my father's tomb and see his study or library.

Sincerely yours,

Shintaro Sasaki

June 7, 1945

My dear Mrs Ruth Sasaki

I received Herald Tribune yesterday which came from you.

I received permission to go to New York City and live there from the W.R.A. the day before yesterday.

I shall set out from the gate of the project in June 10 for Chicago, from there to New York at once.

Sincerely yours

Shintaro Sasaki

Sentient beings, those which abide within my mind,
are numberless. I vow to enlighten them.
Worldly desires, those which disquiet my mind,
are endless. I vow to bring them to an end.
The gates of Dharma, the doors of which open
within my own nature,
are manifold. I vow to enter them all.
The goal of Wisdom, through which my mind will
awaken to its own nature,
is ever beyond. I vow to attain it.

REMAINS
New York, 1945–1949

W hat was she left with?
Ashes. There were letters back and forth to Japan. A priest in the Daitoku-ji lineage—where was he to be buried? In America, of course.

What, not Japan?

He gave himself to America. He stated his intentions quite clearly: "My own mission is to be the first Zen master to bury his bones in this land and to mark this land with the seal of the Buddha's teaching." They had purchased a grave at Woodlawn Cemetery in New York, and that is where he was buried, after a service at their house on Sixty-Fifth Street.

The whole tangle of funeral arrangements for a Japanese Zen priest. But he had been very clear—do not be troubled with all the traditional trappings. After all, those are for priests who lived and died in Japan. This is a new situation.

She could not say it: A new death? In what way could dying be new? But she got the point. He would have a stone—it was not ready yet—that would simply say "Sokei-an." Nothing more. Ashes. Dust.

Shintaro had come, finally, to pay respects to his father's grave and to meet Ruth and the other students. There might have been something for him to do if he had been inclined to stay. He was polite and deferential, but dispirited. He did not make friends easily. After so many years on the West Coast, he found the clamor of New York overwhelming. After nearly three years in the camps, he felt anxious in crowds. In fact, other people—even one at a time—made him uncomfortable. And his father was not here, after all—not where he could meet his son's gaze and offer solace for the long absence.

After a couple of weeks in the city, Shintaro determined that New York did not suit him. He thanked Ruth for her hospitality and returned to Seattle.

Dust and expectations.

It was time to do something. But what was to be done? There was plenty to organize. This was something she excelled at. More people to contact. Two hundred cards of thanks for condolences and donations. Did they need to be from Ruth? As Mrs. Sasaki, certainly. As the executor of his estate—this was somewhat more ambiguous. His entire estate consisted of some books, which already belonged to the First Zen Institute; his carving tools, which had been offered to Shintaro but which Sokei-an's son did not take; some artwork, which would be distributed appropriately; his robes, monk's bowl, nyoi, and flywhisk, which would be held by the institute until a successor could be found to receive them; and his words. The words would continue to occupy Ruth and the entire First Zen Institute of America—they had changed its name from the Buddhist Society of America, as a birthday present for Sokei-an in February 1944—for many years to come.

It was not satisfactory. There should be a special stone—not just any stone, but the right one. From Japan. It would be done, someday. But not now.

And one day Ruth would join Sokei-an in the ground as she had joined him above ground. Some remnant of her, at least. She would not be buried with her family in Chicago. Nor with her first husband, interred five years already in Chicago with his brothers and parents.

Now with the dust and commotion settling down after the funeral, she did go to Chicago, where her brother was recuperating from a serious injury, and to Evanston, where her quite alive daughter and son-in-law were conducting a spirited ministry in a curious rendition of Christianity that resembled only in the most superficial details the grim church of her childhood. This variety of worship seemed to be—well, it was practically as if Alan had invented it.

He had read so voraciously that the masters at the seminary had released him from the classroom after barely a year, allowing him to continue his studies directly with tutors. In 1944, he was granted a bachelor of divinity degree and ordained as an Episcopal priest, and then he was immediately made chaplain at Northwestern University. Alan and Eleanor and their two young daughters—Joan was seven, and Anne, born in 1942, was three—had moved into the chaplaincy, a building called Canterbury House, which Alan, whose high school chapel had been Canterbury Cathedral itself, found personally meaningful, as if it confirmed the rightness of his current path. Eleanor hired a maid to help with the girls and threw herself into decorating the home and giving teas, which inevitably evolved into cocktail parties.

Alan loved music, and before long he had young instrumentalists from Northwestern's School of Music to play during services, a choir singing Gregorian chants, and composers helping set soul-stirring arrangements of hymns from the Book of Common Prayer. He conducted a high church mass that was designed for

Alan and Eleanor Watts, and children Joan and Anne.
Courtesy of Joan Watts.

beauty, full of colorful vestments, candles, high drama, and good music. He banned all "corny hymns" and the God of guilt from his chapel, substituting the God of love and joy. He preached for no longer than fifteen minutes, on topics that were close to the students' lives. Usually about love.

So preoccupied with Sokei-an's health and circumstances and the whole aftermath, and trying to maintain the First Zen Institute, Ruth felt she had neglected her children.

They were quite capable of looking after themselves. Or so her daughter protested. When Ruth arrived, she found this was not the full picture.

Alan was expounding, magnanimously—expanding into some sort of inspired latter-day singing mystic priest. The fact that he had become a priest at all still struck Ruth as somewhat dissonant, in spite of his enthusiasm and the ardor of his congregants. They adored him, and he basked in their adoration. A little too much. It was all a bit much for Ruth to behold.

And Eleanor? On the surface she was enjoying herself, enjoying being the preacher's wife. Underneath, she seemed to be shrinking. The role of dutiful pastor's wife perhaps did not suit her so comfortably after all. She seemed hemmed in. All this merriment did not assuage her black moods, which, if anything, were rearing up more than ever. Ruth suspected she had given up meditation—Alan was still studying Chinese and practicing calligraphy, but beyond that . . . When Ruth asked if they were sitting zazen regularly, Eleanor came up with an annoyed pout and "Of course, Mother. Every morning." The evenings were given over to more entertaining sorts of observance.

The young pastoral couple had turned their modest chaplaincy into a sort of temple. This, at least, was tastefully done, even exquisitely. Here, at least, Eleanor had not faltered.

Ritual and pageantry. Ruth recognized the appeal of this. The modern world, the world the war had made, was too stark, and young people understandably were grasping for something that stirred them emotionally. She did not trust it. To her, it obscured a deeper, more penetrating truth. And if there was pleasure in it, it would be fleeting.

It might be as simple as this: Alan loved people, and people loved him. It was effortless. He spoke with a silver tongue, soothing away any doubts, singing praises of simplicity, ease, and worldly pleasure. Eleanor, on the other hand—everything about her required effort. It seemed that people who might once have found her charming were beginning to find her moodiness trying. The more Alan went up, the more she went down. Ruth did not foresee the situation improving. She wondered how long it could last.

"Eleanor, my dear child. I expect I will need to travel to Japan before long. Why don't you come with me?"

"Mother, don't you see what's happening here? How could I leave? We're just getting started."

"I certainly do see what is happening. A trip might do you good."

"At the moment I miss the desert more than Japan. It's usually that way, in fact. And Joan and Anne are so young."

"Don't be silly. Of course you must take your daughters with us. Just as we always took you on our trips."

"Not always."

"In a manner of speaking. In any case, there's plenty of room in the New York apartments, when you need a break from this hootenanny."

Ruth's brother, David, was in Chicago. He was not really recuperating from this latest incident. He was in pain; he could not walk. He had been beaten by thugs—they had broken and dislocated his hip. It was not the only injury, but it was the worst. He was openly gay and had a tendency to attract confrontation. It was not the first time he had been targeted.

When Ruth returned to New York, she brought him along to care for him. In fact, he would never be able to walk again without assistance and remained confined to a wheelchair.

Our beloved Osho is gone.

A pile of notes. Manuscripts in various stages of completion. The *Record of Rinzai*, which Ruth and Sokei-an had been working on most recently. The Sixth Patriarch's *Platform Sutra. The Sutra of Perfect Awakening.* A short time before he died, Sokei-an entrusted Ruth with editing and publishing these texts:

"Bring them out into the world: do everything you can. The important thing is to carry on the work. Goto Roshi will help. And he will help with the search for a successor."

On August 6, 1945, American forces dropped a single bomb over the Japanese city of Hiroshima. It ignited with a flash of brilliant light and such force that immediately the center of the city and eighty thousand human lives were vaporized. Three days later, on August 9, a second atomic bomb exploded over the Japanese city of Nagasaki, immediately killing another sixty thousand people. On August 15, the Japanese surrendered and the war was over.

There was work to be done.

Meetings, zazen, and study sessions continued at the First Zen Institute. George Fowler was president, Ruth was vice president, Mary Farkas was secretary. An editorial committee was formed. Every Wednesday and Saturday the public meetings were held as before, beginning with silent meditation, and then one of the senior students would read a selection from Sokei-an's notes and translations, with some consideration and conversation regarding its meanings and nuances. There was no sanzen.

In the summer of 1946, Ruth got a call from Sokei-an's son-in-law, Ted Inouye. She could tell from his voice there was something wrong.

"Tell me. What happened?"

"My wife ran out. We had been fighting. I did not hurt her but she was very upset. She ran out across the field to the river. The farm where we are now, it's on one of the islands in the Delta. When she did not come back right away I went out to look for her. But could not find her. In the morning her body was found floating among the reeds."

"Seiko."

"Yes. My wife. Your husband's beloved daughter. She drowned."

"Are the children safe?"

"Yes. They are very upset of course. We are—all of us are."

"This is terrible."

"Mrs. Sasaki. I am being held for murder. I did not even touch her."

"I see."

"Please, can you possibly come here to help explain? They will listen to you. They do not believe me, a nisei ranch mechanic. They will listen to you. Please come."

So in late summer she went to California to sort out this terrible situation.

After being released from the relocation camp in Arkansas at the end of the war, Seiko and her husband had returned with their children to the San Joaquin Valley to look for work. Ted was a skilled mechanic and found a position on a vast vegetable ranch on an island in the Sacramento–San Joaquin Delta outside of Stockton. He was in charge of maintaining all the trucks and tractors.

Seiko was unhappy there, and they had been quarreling. He came home one night sizzling drunk, and they got into it again. It was too much for her. She ran out into the dark night.

Ruth came out for a week. She stayed in the ranch house that belonged to the owner, a friendly and supportive big man who liked Ted and valued his work, had hired him in fact, who believed that there was no malice on his part and certainly no injury caused by his hand.

Ruth was able to explain to the sheriff that she had known both Seiko and Ted Inouye, and she knew that Seiko had been distressed. She had recently lost her father. They had all been in the camps, which was an enormous disruption, and she had a hard time adjusting to their new place. It was clearly suicide, without a doubt. Even if Mr. Inouye had a reputation as a drinker, he was not a violent man—in fact, he was absolutely kindhearted, the best imaginable father, a good husband, a steady worker.

The sheriff was sufficiently persuaded that he dropped all charges and released Ted to the ranch and his job.

After that Ted did not want to stay there. Once he saved enough money, he bought a garage in Los Angeles and moved the family there. Ruth remained in contact with him and with Sokei-an's grandchildren the rest of her life, particularly the older boy, Mineru, whom she would visit any time she came to California.

For many years Sokei-an's students had been taking notes on his talks—in some cases there were four or five versions of a single lecture.

The institute now asked for copies, and the editorial committee began compiling and editing them for publication. The edited notes, as they were gathered, became the material read aloud at the institute's biweekly meetings.

In 1947 the First Zen Institute released its first publication, an edited collection of Sokei-an's talks from 1940 to 1941, called *Cat's Yawn*, drawn largely from thirteen volumes of *Zen Notes*.

Ruth solicited reviews from Alan Watts and his friend Aldous Huxley, and from Ananda Coomaraswamy, an old friend and supporter of Sokei-an's from his earliest days giving talks at the Orientalia Bookshop. Watts wrote of *Cat's Yawn*, "It is a collection of material of the greatest value. Sokei-an's editorial articles show the deepest insight, and we should be grateful to the First Zen Institute of America for making available for the first time writing of one who is without a doubt among the greatest exponents of Zen in our time." Huxley said, "It is hoped that the *Cat's Yawn* will startle or delight some of its Western readers into taking the step that leads from mere nature mysticism or mere existentialism, to an actual trial of those expedient means to man's Final End, which experience has proved to be effective."

At first Eleanor had entertained Alan's notions of sexual freedom, but long before they had their first child she recognized her misgivings. Over the years he had convincingly outlined his driving belief that organized religion had been oppressing individuals for thousands of years, confining sexuality within monogamous matrimony in order to diminish its destabilizing potential—otherwise the hierarchical social order that allowed the church to continue wielding worldly power would crumble to dust. But true religion allowed for the passionate embrace of one another, made room for conscious, loving individuals to express themselves sexually—not merely spiritually, as if that could somehow be divorced from sexual passion. In fact to awaken the divine spirit by welcoming sexual ecstasy would lead to a more complete fulfillment of a human life. It was not something that could be restricted by mere oaths and vows.

Eleanor actually agreed with all this, in her head at least. It's not that she thought he was wrong. It's that when she listened to her emotions, she felt his so-called freedom as a form of neglect, a lack of commitment. She did not tell her mother that she secretly agreed with her. She was feeling neglected. She witnessed Alan ensnaring more people with his charms—women and men, though it was with women where she felt cast aside. His sexual liaisons were out in the open—in their house, in fact, which was also the meeting hall for their congregation—and the women who were exploring these sexual possibilities with him, members of the congregation, were right there in the house with them. With him. He brought them in, and sometimes they stayed. And she, Eleanor, his rightful partner and legal wife, could not prevent it. The line that he crossed was one he considered illegitimate. She felt otherwise. But there was no possibility of convincing him. It was a core part of his personal philosophy, which he imagined would benefit the world, the more it spread.

There was a talented young pianist and composer named Carlton Gamer who was part of the congregation. Eleanor began taking weekly piano lessons from him, at first as a way of rekindling her own artistic passions and relieving her loneliness. Carlton met her with a deep well of kindness that she found unexpected, almost startling. He took a personal interest in her, and they found they had many tastes in common. Though ten years her junior, he carried himself with a steadiness and maturity that she welcomed into her life. He became a true friend and confidant, and Eleanor felt their friendship developing into love. Alan was witness to this, and he encouraged the relationship. He still wanted his wife to be happy—and it made his own indiscretions more palatable, taking some of the pressure off their marital stress, at least as far as he imagined. He invited Carlton to move into the house.

In June 1948 Eleanor took a trip to New York to try sorting out her confusion. Ruth recommended she see the psychiatrist who had helped her in the past, which she did. Eleanor returned to Alan with the demand that he seek help.

Alan balked. Help? What sort of help? If there is no problem, what sort of assistance is needed?

In 1949 Eleanor and Alan ended their marriage. It was also the end of Alan's job as a chaplain. Eleanor went to New York by way of Nevada, where she secured an annulment in Reno; within a year she would marry Carlton Gamer. Eight months before leaving she had given birth to their boy, Michael Gamer. Eleanor and Carlton moved with Joan, Anne, and baby Michael into the fourth-floor apartments of the building on Sixty-Fifth Street that housed the Zen Institute, above Ruth. But Ruth was on her way to Japan.

Japan After War
Kyoto, 1949–1950

The land Ruth arrived in was shattered. The country was almost unrecognizable. If Eleanor had been traveling with her, she would have been unable to restrain her horror, would have gasped and exclaimed how it reminded her of Manchuria under the Japanese military occupation—when they had visited the puppet emperor and young Eleanor had shrunk back from the window at the sight of hungry children, the hollowed-out eyes of people begging for rice, and open train cars packed with terrified Japanese troops barely older than Eleanor.

But Eleanor was not with her, and the Japan Ruth saw reminded her of nothing. It was not the place she had known and lived in, full of trust in an expansive national vision. The morale was destroyed. It was a hollowed-out version of itself, a ghost of itself, an inside-out place. The devastation was unfathomable.

And yet . . . The place was still here. The hills of Kyoto, the bamboo forests, the river. Nature was still nature. And the old buildings that were still there still resonated with a thousand years of potent silences. The restraint of a wisdom deeper than words can carry, than bombs can destroy.

Kyoto was the only major city that had not been bombed—its thousand temples remained standing. But even here, the people

Ruth knew, had known, were stunned. Many of them told her they welcomed the Americans, the occupiers—who had been mortal enemies so recently; who had, in fact, destroyed so many lives and places; who had been painted as inhuman, demonic, lesser beings. There was great confusion. The Americans here— servicemen and -women, army administrators—were friendly. They had orders to be friendly. Or it was in their character, in spite of what they must have been taught to believe—*is this not what they were taught? as we were taught?*—during the war.

These strange Americans—or now somehow not so strange— saw human suffering and responded humanely. These tired, shocked old women and men, these disoriented orphaned children—who, when the bombs fell and shattered the glass and collapsed the ceiling on mother and grandfather and grandmother in the next room, and father dead from dysentery or an American bullet in Midway or Mindanao, children who had not known where to go, who had nowhere to go and no one to take care of them—the American troops went out of their way to treat them with kindness at least, if not quite respect. Because the war was over. It was over, and when the Americans arrived in Japan they were stunned by the devastation. They had believed the lies that the enemy was still strong in their homeland, when in fact they were already collapsing and the land and the country and the people were a tragic, shattered husk. It was too much to grasp. Suddenly there were no more enemies. Only humans confronting other humans as suffering humans. After all, what else was there?

Before mother and father, what is your original face?

Above all else, Sokei-an's father taught him what it means to be human. Ruth could see it, all around her. But such extreme suffering—is this somehow necessary? For what? The koan, which she had solved years ago, closed in on her.

It had taken months to receive the necessary military permission to enter the country. She arrived in October 1949. The occupation forces under General MacArthur had established a certain degree of order amid the destruction, but it would be more years before anything could be considered a true recovery. The occupiers would remain until 1952.

At Nanzen-ji, which had been overflowing during osesshin in 1932, there were just a handful of monks, and they seemed listless. At Daitoku-ji, the premier Rinzai temple in Japan, there had been more than forty monks. Now there were four. Goto Zuigan Roshi was abbot and kancho. He was very gracious. He served Ruth tea—there was no sugar for cakes—and he reminisced about his time in America with his Dharma brother Sokei-an and their teacher Sokatsu.

Ruth had still not met Sokatsu. "You will be visiting him, then? You must visit Sokatsu Roshi. He will be expecting you. Though he may not receive you."

In the old days, before the war, everywhere she went she found a great sense of purpose in the people's activities and action. Whether they moved quickly or slowly, there was a bold spirit. Now, even when there was important work to do—the whole country needed rebuilding, in many places there was still debris to clear—there was an undercurrent of purposelessness. Or not exactly that. It was despair. Resignation. Grief. Grim, joyless effort to accomplish some small portion of what was necessary, which was too vast to grapple with—not spirited, resolute enthusiasm in service of a grand vision, however destructive that grand vision had been.

It was confrontation with the reality of defeat. When the Japanese surrendered, hundreds of military officers, who would never submit to the shame of bowing down to the enemy, committed suicide. Hundreds more were put on trial and many executed for war crimes. The military, for centuries so integral to government and the national character, was abolished.

Nearly a million Japanese civilians had been reduced to ashes—in Tokyo alone the firebombing killed more than a hundred thousand people. The American bombings had severely damaged seventy major cities—what strange mercy had spared Kyoto? Ports, industries, roads—all were seriously damaged. What did the occupation forces expect to plant in this soil? Japanese media was subject to rigid censorship by the Americans. Did they fear the army would reawaken to attack again? It hardly seemed possible.

If the people had truly embraced the essence of Buddhism, rather than rejected or ignored or confined it to mere trappings, perhaps they would have been better prepared for this. Perhaps they would have taken a different course entirely. But the nationalistic fervor had been louder and had taken control of the national spirit. It had taken control of their minds. It had poisoned them against Buddhism, which they cast off as a foreign religion.

And now what remained of true Buddhism in the land and minds of the people was so much reduced, how could it be effective? Even before the war Sokei-an felt that Japan was not where Buddhism could prosper. It would be in North America—even if it took three hundred years, even if planting the seed of Buddhism there was like holding a lotus to a rock, expecting it to take root.

Ruth agreed with some of this. She saw that in Japan it might not even survive. And in America it was barely beginning. But it might be much quicker than Sokei-an imagined. And it needed Japan. There was no way Buddhism in America could develop without a true Japanese Zen master to carry it across, as Sokei-an had barely begun to carry it.

Passing the lamp—the light of Zen. Dharma transmission. Lineage. Finding a true successor. This is not a secondary concern. If there is no successor, the wisdom is lost. Once lost, it is very difficult to recover.

There is intrinsic wisdom simply in an observant human life. The attempt to arrive at it through books, stories, personal experiences of insight may eventually reveal something interesting, perhaps compelling, even apparently profound. Dr. Suzuki was beginning to promote a view that this is somehow sufficient—as if it could possibly grasp the subtleties of the true Zen experience. But without a true guide to provoke and verify—someone who has been there and knows the path and its pitfalls—there is no possibility of building or maintaining it. Without a true teacher, ultimately these sorts of efforts will amount to nothing. Rubble and dust.

During Sokei-an's final years, finding a successor became an obsession, occupying his profoundest yearning and much of his attention. He wrote to everybody in Japanese Rinzai Zen: "Please help identify someone who might be willing to come to America to take my place when I am gone. There are already a number of capable students here, but they are not ready, will not be ready before I am gone. Please send someone."

There was no one. Ruth was privy to these ruminations, helped keep records of the correspondence, heard about the particular characters and motives and peculiarities of the people Sokei-an contacted. No one was interested. America was a land of barbarians. Why should they waste their time?

After the war the attitudes became less determined, but not necessarily more favorable. People were starving, wounded, disturbed. There were food shortages—rice was rationed, meat and fish and butter were extremely scarce, bread was dark and

unpalatable, sugar and coffee were simply unavailable. Ruth
had her friends and helpers ship care packages. Electricity was
intermittent, fuel for vehicles and for cooking and heating was
severely limited, candles were practically nonexistent, kerosene
was crude and smoky, hardly better than fish oil.

What Ruth witnessed and experienced when she arrived solid-
ified her determination that they must find someone to bring to
America, and soon. It did seem possible, considering this current
state of affairs, that Rinzai Zen would not survive here. She was
deeply discouraged.

Goto Roshi did not express such doubts to Ruth—yes, it was
true that the current conditions limited the possibilities for the
present, but survival into the future was not in question. He
acknowledged the need for a teacher to travel to America, for
the sake of those serious students there who had made a start
and would find it difficult to come to Japan. Ruth had hoped
Goto himself would consider making the trip, if only for a year
or two. But he was too old; his health would not allow him to
travel. Of course he would help Ruth with her mission in any
way he could.

And he would be happy to accept her as a sanzen student.
As long as she was here, she should not miss this opportunity.
Sokei-an had written of her ability and progress—his words carried
the highest recommendation. She was working on translations—of
course Nanshinken Roshi had been correct to caution her that
it was not possible to translate any koan one had not mastered
personally in sanzen. Once she passed a given koan, Goto Roshi
would be quite willing to consult with her regarding its translation.

If she were to stay, she wondered if Goto Roshi might suggest
suitable lodgings nearby. It would simplify things.

"In fact, there is an old hermitage here on the grounds of

Daitoku-ji. From time to time the roshi has used it as a personal retreat. But for now, though we still have our temple grounds—at least Daito's domain, the Temple of Great Virtue, has not been much reduced from its former expanse—for now, as you see, we have few resident monks, not enough to maintain the many buildings and subtemples that constitute Daitoku-ji. You may find this particular hermitage that I speak of to your liking. Of course it will require some attention. But if you will consider staying here, we all may benefit from the arrangement."

So she found herself installed in Kyoto once again, taking up residence in a small house on the very grounds of Daitoku-ji, the preeminent Rinzai temple in Japan. Indeed, the fifty-six acres of temple grounds—a city within walls, containing twenty-four subtemples—seemed depopulated, if not nearly deserted. At least the main halls and paths were well maintained.

Unable to immediately fulfill her primary purpose, but available to revive her practice, it made sense to consider staying longer than she originally planned. Sokei-an had been gone four years already, and as her attention had become largely absorbed by organizational and literary matters, her progress had stalled.

Without a teacher to guide you, the words are empty nonsense. Nonsense may be valuable, but only if you know how to peel the skin away from your Zen eye. Which takes constant vigilance. She cast her mind back to Sokei-an's tales of his early years in America, performing zazen all night on a flat rock in a wild river in Oregon, solving a hundred koans on his own, with no one to confirm his insights, only to find when he returned to his teacher that he had all of them wrong. She accepted Goto's invitation.

Haru Yoshida—in New York known to all as Penny—was shipping books, coffee, and sugar to Ruth. This last she shared with

Goto Roshi, who would not admit outright to having a sweet tooth but whose delight seemed to extend beyond mere appreciation for the effort it took to get it to Japan.

It was Ruth's good fortune that she had met Haru, who had been in the relocation camp at Tule Lake, a nisei fluent in both languages. After the war Haru had gone to New York and found work at an art gallery. The gallery owner had cautioned her that so soon after the war, patrons would be uncomfortable with Japanese names, and thus Haru became Penny. Next to the gallery was the studio of a silkscreen artist who brought her along to a meeting at the First Zen Institute. Somehow it came up that Ruth needed a part-time secretary. Penny was interested, and Ruth hired her.

Though Ruth immediately recognized Penny's talents and devotion, it took a few weeks before she admitted that the "part-time" position was a test, and really she needed someone full time. So Penny became Ruth's personal assistant and began to take charge of the library at the institute, organizing and purchasing books for both the library and for Ruth. She would continue to work faithfully for Ruth and the institute for the remainder of Ruth's lifetime.

Ruth went north for an obligatory visit. Tomeko—Sokei-an's first wife, the prior Mrs. Sasaki—lived with Shihoko, the younger daughter, whom Sokei-an had never really known, and Shihoko's husband in a small town in the far north. Their house was not much more than a shack.

Tomeko was small and still quite pretty, nearing seventy. There was something about her that set Ruth on edge—not simply because of what Sokei-an had said about her. Something in her manner. She seemed to Ruth like a small dog who would bark fiercely at, and perhaps attack, a much larger animal—a bear, perhaps.

Shihoko, however, in addition to being very beautiful, was gracious and kind, with some of Sokei-an's easy humor. Ruth felt only warmth and friendliness from this radiant daughter, and she received only the same in response.

It was not so with Tome. She was polite but sharp and bitter. She had little to say, and nothing to ask, about Sokei-an. She hated America. She felt that Americans didn't know the first thing about generosity. She scowled at Ruth.

With Goto Roshi, Ruth felt fully at ease. His demeanor often brought to mind a kindly professor, though one with no apparent difficulty presiding over a large and eminent institution. In fact, he had been president of Hanazono University, otherwise known as Rinzai University, before settling into his role as abbot of Myoshin-ji and Daitoku-ji.

His moods in sanzen were more variable than Sokei-an's—who would dissolve into the intense light of dharmakaya, whose teaching was a direct expression of his full presence and the force of his being. Goto Roshi was more literary-minded, more intellectual than either Sokei-an or Nanshinken Roshi, who explicitly forbade reading beyond the text of a koan one was working on. If there was a certain beauty in a koan, Goto would reflect that in his handling of it and in himself. He would become many things in sanzen—as Sokei-an, while always only the one thing itself in sanzen, took on many shapes in teisho. In sanzen Goto would take on the radiant beauty of a particularly beautiful koan. It was a feeling of joyful appreciation of the splendor of the universe that could not be contained.

Goto had spent seventeen years in Korea, where he was known

among the Japanese there as an extraordinary preacher. When he arrived in Seoul, he encountered people who had no idea about religion, Zen or otherwise, and no hall that could be properly called a temple. By the end of his stay, he had built a magnificent temple there.

She realized she would have to do intensive language study. Her Japanese was improving, but she had never committed to perfecting it. And to work on the translations, she would need to master the language of the original koan texts—colloquial Chinese from the Tang and Song dynasties.

So much had ended. Sokei-an. And the war of course. Which was also the end of Japan—old Japan—not merely some idea of an old place but in fact the only Japan anyone, Japanese or otherwise, had ever known. That was over, obliterated. Only remnants and memories survived. Japan was still here of course, but different in a way no one quite understood. And no one knew what it would become.

Curiously, it was the beginning of a new life for Ruth.

Nanshinken Roshi had passed in 1935, not long after Ruth's return to the United States. She walked to Nanzen-ji to meet the new roshi and make an offering. It was already mid-December. There was a light mist in the air—in Kyoto the first snows rarely arrive before the New Year. She lamented the dire unavailability of tomatoes—or decent bread, for that matter—to make a proper tomato sandwich for the *butsudan*, which had been Nanshinken's specific request. Tomatoes were out of season; the lack of bread was another matter.

The feeling at Nanzen-ji was not what it had been. It was the same ancient place, but desolate. It was not that the place was in ruins, or even physically run down. The few monks in residence did what they could to keep it up. The current abbot, Shibayama Zenkei Roshi, had trained under Nanshinken Roshi for a dozen years, but after completing his Zen and receiving inka in 1926, he stepped away from temple life and went to teach at Hana-zono University, and at Otani University as a successor to D. T. Suzuki. With some knowledge of English and interest in the world beyond Japanese Buddhism—in his younger days he had studied Christianity, and mastered Esperanto, before hearing a talk by a Zen abbot that convinced him to take the vow to save his fellow beings—he interested Ruth a great deal, and eventually he would became a good friend and important ally.

He had come back to temple life only recently, invited to be roshi of Nanzen-ji in 1948, and had yet to attract a following. And in the atmosphere there was somehow a flatness. How could this be? Of course even this place was not immune, was infected by the appalling situation of the country, of the world. Everything depends. Beyond the emptiness of her initial Zen breakthrough, beyond the vast emptiness she had encountered in her subtly deepening journey, was a further emptiness. And it was not altogether inspiring. Is this what Sokei-an was getting at when he said he got Nothing?

She went to visit Awano Roshi at Manman-ji. Sokei-an had considered him, along with Goto Roshi, to be one of the best qualified potential candidates. He sent her to see Kajiura Itsugai Roshi at Shogen-ji, a mile from Suruga Bay near Mount Fuji, a day's train trip northeast of Kyoto. At this venerable Myoshin-ji branch temple, Zen Buddhism still seemed to be active and alive. There were forty monks who came to meet with Ruth and her translator, after their evening sanzen. When they learned of her expectations for Sokei-an's successor, a monk asked if she thought she would ever find such a person. She admitted it was exceedingly difficult, and might not be possible.

What were the precise qualifications for the teacher? He must have attained true satori, as well as completed his koan study, attained inka, and been granted permission to teach. He must have a personality and appearance appealing to American people. He should be a priest, not a *koji*, or layman, and have knowledge of Zen temple life and procedures. No family. Wide familiarity with Zen literature and some experience lecturing on it. A university education. Considerable knowledge of general Buddhism and Buddhist philosophy. Some English. And finally, if he were to come and make a permanent prospect, he would have to make up his mind to remain in America and die there in his work, not use his American experience as a springboard to further his ambitions in Japanese Zen. And he would have to come as a simple priest, expecting only the most simple of livelihoods to be provided and much hard work.

She walked at least an hour a day. In spite of everything, it felt good to be alive here. It felt good to walk. The winter air was crisp, and she felt strong. Determined, as always, she walked with renewed vigor.

There was another candidate to consider. Oda Sesso Roshi, Goto's sole disciple and Dharma heir, who had come to Goto at Myoshin-ji and then stayed with him the entire time in Korea, had been with him almost continually, and then received his inka and become a roshi in his own right—a subtle teacher of extraordinary insight, with a soft-spoken manner.

At Daitoku-ji, Oda served as Goto's deputy. In fact, because he had three years of sodo training, and Goto's sodo experience was less continuous, Oda was officially the sodo roshi. In reality, Goto was in charge, but he consulted with his disciple on every matter—they worked together in a partnership that was practically symbiotic.

Oda was only fifty and in perfect health. He spoke no English, but he met the other qualifications. Except that he was too good looking. Really, he had the physical beauty of a Hollywood leading man, which Ruth thought would be an insurmountable distraction for the women students. And therefore he was disqualified.

Ruth tried to visit Sokatsu Roshi. She went with a group of Japanese laymen from Engaku-ji, with some gifts, and he refused to see her because she was connected with Sokei-an, whom he had disowned. So she was sent away. Eichoku-san came to the door and sweetly made some excuses for Roshi. "I am so sorry. You have come all of this way. I am so sorry. Sokatsu Osho is not feeling well." It was basically what Ruth had been expecting.

Goto Roshi had entered temple life as a young boy, gone north to high school in Sendai, and decided he didn't want to be a monk. He had come to Sokatsu as a disciple only after taking off his koromo. At that time he was a philosophy student at Tokyo University.

When Sokatsu's group came back from America in 1910, Goto finished his Zen study and felt he would like to become a monk again. He returned to Myoshin-ji. Sokatsu, who only wanted non-monks, immediately disowned him.

Later when Sokei-an decided he wanted to become a priest in the line of Daitoku-ji, he wrote Sokatsu, who ordered him to come back to Japan immediately. Sokatsu lashed out at Sokei-an, telling him he was not fit to be a priest, and furthermore wasn't fit to be a roshi—he had never studied ikebana, he couldn't play *go*, his calligraphy was bad, and he didn't know tea ceremony. Sokatsu demanded five things of an accomplished Japanese roshi, and Sokei-an didn't have any of those. Sokatsu disowned him, just as he had disowned Goto Roshi.

Ruth went to visit Sokatsu's other surviving Dharma heir, Koun-an Eizan Roshi, Sokei-an's and Goto's younger Dharma brother. They had talked about him, and Ruth imagined he might be a candidate to succeed Sokei-an. But he had no English. More importantly, he was a lay roshi, had never been ordained, had never experienced the full temple training—his entire Zen life was lived under Sokatsu. He was in charge of the lay temple in Ichikawa that Sokatsu had founded after moving from Ryomo-an in Tokyo, as well as a professor of natural history. However worthy Eizan might be as a teacher, as a man—and Ruth considered him one of the finest she ever knew, and they became close friends—however exalted his Dharma lineage, for Americans it was important, as Sokei-an had determined, that the teacher be a priest.

Eizan was about Ruth's age. He first came to Sokatsu as a disciple at a young age, while still a university boy. As a youth, after some period of study when he was nineteen or twenty, he took three months off in the summer and went up to Matsushima in the north to do zazen in a cave by himself. During that period he made his real breakthrough into Zen.

After Eizan was married both he and his wife became interested in taking sanzen. They went to live in a house in the same compound with Sokatsu, and remained with him, first at Ryomo-an in Tokyo and then at the site in Ichikawa in Chiba Prefecture, even as Sokatsu managed to go through Eizan's fortune, just as he had Eichoku-san's.

What was Sokatsu spending his money on? For one thing he liked robes. And he liked to build, and he liked to collect antiques. He was an excellent painter and calligrapher, and he liked to have his things elaborately printed and published. There was always something. Despite this, Eizan and his wife were the most devoted students.

Shortly before the war, Sokatsu celebrated his seventieth birthday, and at the *dojo* in Ichikawa they had a huge party for him. On this occasion he announced he would be retiring. He said he had given five thousand people sanzen in the course of his teaching life, and nine of them had completed their Zen study. He had given his full Dharma transmission to four of them and made them roshis, and they were his heirs. That was the story of his work.

After that he went to Hyogo Prefecture to live with one of his students. Sokatsu left Eizan Roshi in charge of the place at Ichikawa.

Eizan was practically a priest. He dressed in robes. He had spent his entire life in Zen. But he had never been a priest. In fact he was the only real lay teacher—someone with complete mastery of Zen, full Dharma transmission, and inka—Ruth would ever find in Japan.

But then for some reason as soon as the war was over Sokatsu arbitrarily announced he had dissolved Ryomokyo-kai, and Eizan was no longer in charge of it. Eizan was disowned. Sokatsu wrote to Goto Roshi to renew their association. In the letter he said, "You are the only heir I have."

The day Eizan told Ruth about this, on another visit, after they had become close friends, his face became distorted with pain. He told of going to Sokatsu, saying, "This—why? Why, Roshi?" He said to Ruth, "*Why?*—that is the koan my teacher left me with."

Eizan had so many friends and personal students that as soon as Sokatsu dissolved Ryomokyo-kai, they formed a new society, Ningenzen (Human Being Zen) and put Eizan in charge of it. A large majority of the former members of the dispersed Ryomokyo-kai stayed or came back. Eizan never left. The students built more buildings and provided for him.

Ruth's friend Isshu Miura, who had been head monk during her stay at Nanzen-ji, was now Miura Roshi, abbot of Koon-ji in Hachio-ji, a Nanzen-ji subtemple in the mountains about forty miles west of Tokyo. When he had first seen Ruth at the Rohatsu osesshin in 1933, Miura had been skeptical—he expected her to wither, collapse from exhaustion, and slink away, defeated. Instead he witnessed her fortitude and discipline, and revised his estimation. In the end it had been he who thanked her for providing renewed inspiration to the monks.

With Nanshinken's passing in 1935, Miura had led fourteen other monks to Koon-ji—Nanshinken Roshi had already sent his Dharma heir Nakamura Taiyu Roshi there to restore the country temple, which had fallen into serious disrepair—to fix the buildings and reopen the sodo. The temple had few supporters, food was scarce, the roofs leaked rain and snow, and the gardens had become a wilderness. Miura stayed under these rough circumstances for two years, completing his Zen training and receiving inka as Nakamura Taiyu's Dharma heir. In 1937 he was appointed roshi of Kogen-ji, a mountain temple deep in Hyogo Prefecture west of Kyoto, and then in 1940 was sent to Erin-ji, a grand temple with famous gardens and many treasures in the Yamanashi mountains west of Tokyo.

When Miura Roshi arrived at Erin-ji, it was still operating essentially as it had since feudal times, and the life of the priest in charge still resembled that of a feudal lord. There were monks in the sodo to instruct, lands to administer, great ceremonies to conduct, distinguished visitors to entertain.

When the war came, everything changed. Monks from the sodo were drafted into the army, troops were quartered in the vast reception rooms, bombed-out civilians were evacuated to take shelter in the halls. Beyond this, young soldiers were sent for short periods of instruction in zazen before leaving for the front. The military commanders, many of whom came from samurai families that had historically supported the great Rinzai temples, considered zazen to be appropriate training for soldiers facing death.

After the war, the changes were no less drastic. The novices and monks were gone. The lands were gone, the wealth of donors who had kept Erin-ji in feudal splendor was gone. In any case, when Nakamura Roshi resigned as sodo roshi of Koon-ji in 1946 and retired to his home temple in western Japan, he asked his Dharma heir to take his place. So for three years Miura Roshi commuted between Erin-ji and Koon-ji. Finally, in 1949, he was appointed kancho of Koon-ji as well as its roshi. He left the fading glory of Erin-ji to make his home again in the country sodo where he had gone through his own final Zen training.

When Ruth went to visit Miura Roshi, Koon-ji was still far from flourishing. Though the rain and snow no longer leaked through the roofs, the winter wind continued to blow through wide cracks in the walls of the Founder's Hall where the three monks and a few lay students practiced their zazen. But the temple and grounds were spotless, the gardens well-tended and swept daily—the roshi's particular preoccupation—and of course the butsudan was immaculate.

A young monk met her at the gate and led her into the reception hall. He disappeared and returned with tea. After a time, he led her to the *hojo*, pausing on the veranda for her to take in a view of Mount Fuji to the south, exquisitely framed by the sculpted branches of bare plum trees, which in the spring would bloom into clouds of pink blossoms. She felt the brisk wind and turned with the monk, who led her to the back of the temple, where they climbed the hundred-odd steps of a covered passageway up the hill to the roshi's little house at the top, just as the students must climb for their morning and evening sanzen.

In spite of the requisite formalities, Miura Roshi greeted her with friendliness and expressed that, as ever, he admired her efforts in attempting to extend the Buddhadharma beyond the Eastern Sea.

She mentioned her purpose in coming to Japan, that, yes, it had to do precisely with those efforts. Without quite inviting Miura Roshi to consider taking the position, she outlined the expectations, as she had with all of the roshis she visited.

He spoke no English, but that would not be the biggest hindrance. Ruth sensed a reluctance in his personality, an indefiniteness—the opposite of Sokei-an—that could make it difficult for American students. Still, she would not rule out the possibility. If he were not the first choice, he was certainly qualified. Except for his ambivalence about America and Americans.

They spoke also about the state of the country and the prospects for Zen. He agreed that conditions after the war were dismal, but like Goto, he was not concerned that Buddhism would die out in Japan. "Buddhism was nearly dead in Japan before Hakuin revived it. There will be another Hakuin." Ruth did not challenge him but found the suggestion unconvincing. And there was something else that felt bothersome: An abdication of responsibility. It will be someone else. Someone will come and fix it. A savior. Ruth did not believe in saviors. She believed in personal action to make corrections. *Sampajanna*, alert, clear wisdom: seeing what is needed immediately as it is needed and acting unselfishly to accomplish it.

The New Year was approaching. Over the last two days in December, Ruth, along with everyone else, stopped at the market where peasant women parked their heaped-up carts to sell braided and fringed ropes of straw, the large oranges called *dai-dai*—a name that also means "long life"—and branches of pine, bamboo, and the earliest-blooming plum. Ruth, along with everyone else, brought these symbols of good fortune and congratulation to decorate the gateway of her house. She had been here three months, and with this act she felt like she lived here and belonged here.

In the tokonoma—the formal seasonal display niche in the house—she made an arrangement of the fruits of forest, field, and sea—a spray each of fern and of laurel, a white pounded-rice cake, a branch of dried persimmons, a large dai-dai, bands of gray seaweed, and a lobster, all on a stand of fragrant white *hinoki* wood.

The day before the New Year, everything was to be put in perfect order—making certain all the year-end bills were paid, preparing things to be eaten cold or warmed up, since it was customary to refrain from cooking during the first three days of the year, yet essential to have delicacies of the season to provide for visitors. Ruth, like everyone, cleaned her house from top to bottom, took her bath, had her hair freshly done at the beauty shop, and laid out her best clothing for the next day. Then, late in the evening, she, like everyone, took all the charcoal embers from her brazier and covered them with ashes in the garden. Thus anything that had accumulated dust and dirt during the past year would be removed, making way for renewal in the coming year.

When all other preparations were complete, they started on their pilgrimage up to Yasaka-jinja in Gion. Everyone went—

old men, old women, husbands, wives, lovers, students, serving maids, children, babies. At the booths lining the approaches to the shrine they bought hemp ropes, then slowly followed in the crowd to the great iron braziers of flaming pine bundles presided over by white-robed Shinto priests wearing high black-lacquer hats. The priest would seize a blazing bundle and light the end of her rope, and then the next person's, and the next. In a constant stream more than a half-million people presented their hemp ropes to be lighted, to burn until the approach of dawn.

With a full moon making huge black shadows of the ancient pines surrounding the shrine, and glistening silhouettes of the heavy tiled roofs of buildings and gateways, they walked through the compound on to the massive, imposing *sanmon* gate of Chion-in temple on Higashiyama, the eastern mountain of Kyoto. Up the three hundred steep stone steps, across the moonlight-flooded courtyard before the main temple building, again up uncertain steps hewn out of the mountainside, and through the forest to the tower holding the great bell of the headquarters of Jodo Shinshu Buddhism, the largest bell in Japan.

On the edge of the forest to the side of the bell tower, over boiling cauldrons propped on blazing bonfires, bent and wrinkled *obasans* and *ojisans*, like so many forest gnomes and witches, ladled out bowls of steaming sweet-bean soup to shivering watchers. Just before midnight, great candles on iron stands were put in place in the four corners of the earthen floor of the tower. They illumined the eager, pushing crowd and brought into sudden relief a huge and strange dark-faced figure completely wrapped in orange robes—a visiting monk from Ceylon, as Ruth knew. But just so must Bodhidharma have looked among the crowds at some ancient festival in China.

Before the simple Buddhist altar set beneath the bell itself, the kancho and attendant priests—arrayed in purple robes and golden kesas—recited sutras and burned incense until it rose in clouds. The gnarled old head bell-ringer, in front of the twenty-five assistant bell-ringers needed to sway the enormous log used to strike the bell, stood immovable, grasping the rope, watching for the signal that the year was done. A priest's hand dropped, the hour struck, with a resounding boom that went rolling over the entire city of Kyoto and far out to the fields and villages beyond.

Again the great bell was struck, and again, and again, one hundred and eight times. On the one hundred and eighth stroke, the great bell of the next temple north on Higashiyama sounded, and after that the next and then the next, until all the hills that surround the city echoed and re-echoed with the booming of the bells.

Late into the night the temple bells were still booming. And all through the city people still streamed toward the shrine and out into the city streets carrying their fresh fire.

A new year. A new beginning.

COMING AND GOING AND STAYING
New York–Kyoto, 1950–1953

In four months Ruth had visited eighteen roshis. When she traveled to New York in February 1950 without any of them accompanying her, she carried a letter from Goto Roshi asking the institute to be patient. They would have a teacher. For now, their zazen practice would benefit from Ruth's direction, as she was quite an experienced student in zazen.

The other concern: "Are you staying? Are you going back? How long are you here for? How long will you be staying in Japan this time?"

It was difficult to express how she felt at home in Japan, and that for the moment her work would keep her there, while still America was her home. Though in fact whenever she spoke of it this way, the sound in her ears rang slightly hollow. America was the land of her birth, yes, as Japan was the land of Sokei-an's birth. His life and work had brought him here, as hers was pulling her there. It was not entirely up to her.

And at the moment, as difficult as things were in Japan, there was a small opening, an opportunity to fully enter the life that truly called to her and, through persistence and devotion, to establish the conditions that might bear fruit some day. If the new master gardener had not yet arrived, the small plot at least must continue to be cultivated—the seeds had been planted, were beginning to germinate, and she would direct what water she could to their growth, so that they not wither—indeed, so that they would one day flourish.

Walter Nowick, a twenty-four-year-old concert pianist and veteran of the Pacific War, had been coming to the First Zen Institute since 1948; it was he who now organized and led sesshin for the students.

As soon as Walter had arrived at the institute, Ruth had recognized him as a serious and dedicated young man. He had grown up on a potato farm on Long Island and knew all about hard work. As a young child, he had displayed a precocious talent for music: he had perfect pitch, and before long it was apparent that he possessed a genuine gift. By fourteen, he was accepted into the preparatory division of the Julliard School of Music, where he continued until he was old enough to enlist in the army.

His company was deployed to Okinawa in the final weeks of the Pacific War, to participate in what would amount to cleanup operations, once the Japanese surrendered. The misery he witnessed there, and afterward on Honshu, the main island, troubled him deeply. Where was the sense in this? He had been trained to attack the enemy, but he found no enemies among the people he encountered. On Honshu his company took part in distributing emergency food and medicine; the desperate people who bowed in gratitude he never saw again. He would never know if they lived or died. Did his actions make a difference? What actions of his would relieve such suffering? He began studying Japanese. Though his company would be discharged in a few months, he would find a way to return to this beautiful and broken land.

Back in New York, he resumed training at Julliard. At his

teacher's house one afternoon, he noticed a book entitled *Cat's Yawn* and asked her about it. His teacher was a member of the First Zen Institute. She brought him to a meeting the same week and introduced him to Ruth and Mary. From that point, he did not miss a meeting and soon became a pillar of the group. After a year of disciplined zazen, he was ready for koan study. But there was no one to offer sanzen. Ruth was going to Japan, and she would bring back a teacher.

When Ruth returned without a teacher, she spoke to Walter privately.

"Are you prepared to leave behind your life in America and travel to Japan?"

"I have nothing holding me here."

"For a perhaps indefinite period, but certainly not less than a year or two?"

"Yes. I would like nothing more."

"And you are prepared for many difficulties, perhaps of an unforeseeable nature?"

"I am aware of the current conditions. I feel a great affinity for Japan and the Japanese people."

"What you have already seen may not be comparable to what you may experience in entering Zen training."

"I am accustomed to strong discipline. I believe I am ready."

"I have already spoken to Goto Roshi on your behalf. He is prepared to accept you as a sanzen student based on my recommendation. This is highly unusual, for a Zen master to do so without a face-to-face meeting."

"I understand."

"We should begin making arrangements immediately. The current military restrictions will be an impediment, but we will see to it that you receive the necessary clearance."

Attendance at the First Zen Institute had never really dropped off after Sokei-an's death: it had already been diminished by the war and his internment, but the senior students had continued sitting with him through these troubles and his declining health, and they remained as committed as ever. Now, five years after his passing, interest in Zen Buddhism and attendance at the institute were increasing. There were twenty regular members—five times the number of monks currently at Daitoku-ji.

Ruth's return sparked a new surge of activity. She began giving weekly talks about her recent experiences in Japan, with listeners enthralled by her descriptions of the places and people associated with Japanese Zen.

She did not spare the difficulties: she had no interest in romanticizing or promoting too rosy a view, and in fact a common refrain was reference to the current dire situation of Japanese Zen. Nevertheless, she spoke with deep admiration for the teachers and their accomplishments, and she only lamented that there was too little interest among the Japanese youth, too few capable students who might ensure the survival of Zen Buddhism in Japan. It was America where the next stage of development must occur.

In preparation for his trip, in addition to a rigorous zazen schedule, Walter was studying Chinese and Japanese and reading Buddhist texts. In March, Ruth had written a letter confirming that Walter would be gratefully accepting Goto Roshi's magnanimous invitation to formally take him as a sanzen student, and now in mid-June she wrote to Goto again and to Oda with details regarding Walter's arrival. Among her other remarks in the letter to Goto was a suggestion that Walter study tea ceremony and calligraphy: in spite of his ability and accomplishments as a pianist, working with heavy farm implements from an early age had somewhat coarsened the nervous and muscular sensitivity of his fingers, and he lacked the delicate control of his hands those arts demanded and could instill.

The paperwork took months. The military clearance to enter Japan remained in doubt until the beginning of June, when Walter finally was able to book passage on the SS *President Cleveland* for a July 7 arrival at Yokohama. Ikeda-san and a younger English-speaking guide, Tsuji-san, would meet him on arrival, and Tsuji-san would accompany him by train to Kyoto the following day. The initial plan was to stay at Daitoku-ji for six months.

As on her trip to Japan the previous fall and return to America in February, when Ruth returned to Japan in August 1950, she flew, on Pan American, by way of San Francisco and Honolulu. This time she was accompanied by her assistant Haru Yoshida, Penny. Ruth was also taking her invalid brother, David, accompanied by a nurse, as far as Honolulu, where he would reside in a rest home.

In San Francisco, she visited Alan Watts and his new wife, Dorothy DeWitt, who had been Joan and Anne's babysitter. Watts had joined a number of other philosophers and religious thinkers at the newly formed American Academy of Asian Studies, where he was giving well-attended lectures on his version of Zen, blended with notions derived from psychoanalysis, Hindu Vedanta, and whatever else struck him as relevant. He received Ruth like an old friend; he had dedicated his most recent book to her. He brought her to the academy, where he held forth with a group of colleagues and students, and invited her to present a talk. She declined for the moment but accepted in principle. Perhaps she would be able to lend a small corrective to his wide-ranging and unfortunately misleading ideas about Zen.

Alan Watts, circa 1956. Courtesy of Joan Watts.

He was still entirely too charming, too effortlessly convincing to his enraptured audiences that Zen—in his telling it was no longer Zen Buddhism, having conveniently lost that distinction; it was simply "Zen," no longer quite a religion—was both mysterious and spontaneously available. The notion of effort never seemed to emerge from his lips. On the topic of satori he had much to say, none of it based in actual experience. Yet this was what got people interested. And now it seemed he was beginning to suggest that study in Japan, if possible, would be helpful for anyone who truly wanted to discover the essence of Zen. Not necessarily submitting to the rigors of a Rinzai roshi, but—what? Somehow absorb a presumed Zen essence by simply wandering around and inhaling the air?

And who would they call on when they did arrive? Ruth envisioned droves of drivel-infested ninnies knocking on her gate, not having the slightest inkling of protocol or reverence. The thought gave her a shiver; her spine stiffened. She supposed she was the specific exemplar of Square Zen according to Alan's rubric—the squarest of the square. So be it. These people would arrive and have to be persuaded that actual Zen Buddhism—as ever, and still practiced—was altogether in this Square category, and the rest was romantic fluff and wishful thinking.

On arrival in Kyoto, Ruth found that Kato-san, who had been her housekeeper twenty years earlier, had cleaned the little house at Daitoku-ji and installed furniture that had been left at Ruth's former house on the Kamo River.

When Goto Roshi had offered her the small house, Ruth had immediately accepted, and she quickly set about planning the necessary repairs. The house had fallen into a sorry state over the years. It had been built for a previous Daitoku-ji roshi about thirty years earlier, as a retirement inryo, but he had used it for only two years before abandoning it to the elements; he died soon after.

There was nowhere to store the heavy winter beddings during summer. She would need a *kura*, a small storehouse. The scarcity of food in stores was still a problem. She needed a vegetable garden. She asked Goto Roshi if these additions would be possible. The house, which belonged to the sodo outright, was offered to Ruth rent-free, as a gesture of appreciation for her work. For a garden and land to build a storehouse, Goto would consult Oda Roshi.

Apparently there was some complication, which was not made clear to her. Yes, it would be possible for her to use the land as she requested, but for a small monthly payment of ¥1,000. No one explained why this was necessary, but she accepted the terms and went to work to grow as much of her own produce as she and her helper could.

The house needed a name. Goto said, "Why not call it Ryosen-an, after the old temple that used to be there?" Ryosen-an means "Dragon Spring Hermitage," which struck Ruth—who had been given the Dharma name Eryu, "Dragon Wisdom"—as perfect.

Ruth arose at four thirty for an hour of zazen, a small breakfast, and the hour walk to Goto Roshi's inryo for sanzen.

As head of Daitoku-ji, Goto found the constant formality demanded on its venerable premises tiresome, and so he had taken up residence elsewhere, at a small hermitage called Daishu-in, a side temple of Ryoan-ji, at the base of Kinugasayama a couple of miles west. Here the humble appointments were more to his taste, and he could live as a simple monk. The entire temple of Daishu-in consisted of a guest room; a room for the image of Manjushri, Bodhisattva of Wisdom, and the tablets of the *dankas*, the families that supported the temple; a four-and-a-half-mat tea room that he used as a study and sanzen room, where he spent most of his time; and two small dressing rooms.

The purpose of her own training, she now recognized, was to prepare the way for others. Had it ever been otherwise? Even seventeen years ago, her insights at Nanzen-ji carried with them the understanding that this experience must be shared, must be carried outward into the world, for the benefit of all beings. It had only become more and more clear that this meant carrying it forward, for the next generation, for the future and survival of human civilization.

In any case, as she progressed in koan study, the demands of her individual practice remained more or less constant: Active mind, present awareness. Supple mind. Persistence. Transcendence of selfish desire. Abandonment of concepts of subjectivity and objectivity. With more experience, the solutions did come more readily.

Walter was settling into life in Kyoto. He had begun sanzen and was continuing studies of Japanese and Chinese, as well as teaching English.

Alongside him at Daishu-in was a young man a few months older than Walter, a disciple of Goto Roshi's named Soko Morinaga, who had, at age nineteen and immediately after losing both parents, been drafted to serve in the Japanese army, along with all of his high school classmates. Surviving the war, he had returned to finish high school but found himself utterly at a loss for what to do with his life: all the certainties he had grown up believing now proved to be false. His ability to believe in anything had been destroyed. When he found his way to Daishu-in, after explaining why he had come, Goto Roshi challenged him: "You must believe in your teacher. If you can believe in me, I will accept you as a student. If not, you are wasting your time." He stayed.

There was another young monk, a couple of years older, named Sen Masaoki. He had also served in the Japanese military—in the naval air force—though unlike Morinaga, his participation had been voluntary and enthusiastic. After the war, he completed his degree in economics from Doshisha University and then took vows under Goto Roshi. He was the fifteenth-generation heir of the Urasenke house of tea masters descended from Sen no Rikyu, credited with originating the *wabi-cha* ceremony in the sixteenth century.

To Walter, he seemed aloof, and in spite of having entered Zen training—he had taken the Four Vows, and like all monks repeated them daily, vowing to save *all* beings—he treated Walter, a mere

American, as somehow less qualified, intrinsically less capable of progressing on this journey. It was all completely unspoken—the opposite of the boisterous and coarse ribbing of Walter's company mates in the army, which was anything but subtle.

In any case, Masaoki seemed too certain and accepting of things as they appeared. After all, he would become head of a clan and tradition that had survived many generations, through much turmoil. In some ways this was reassuring to Walter, even perhaps a source of envy; but it also brought doubts into his mind. Where was the willingness to abandon any attachment to a stable, predictable future? Where was the doubt that Walter understood as a fundamental starting point? In contrast, with Morinaga, he felt a brotherly bond that seemed to arise as much from a shared recognition of uncertainty as from their similar ages and parallel experiences of the war.

And he, Walter, was progressing. Goto Roshi acknowledged it, each increment, each solution. And his Japanese was improving. Another year, he felt, and he would be fluent.

This time when Ruth went to visit Sokatsu Roshi, she brought Walter. This time, Sokatsu received them, delighted to meet his Dharma grandson.

After Sokatsu retired, he first went to stay in Hyogo Prefecture, west of Kyoto, with a disciple who was an apothecary, along with Eichoku-san, his faithful lifelong companion.

After the war was over, a big airplane site at Higata, Chiba Prefecture, sixty miles north of Tokyo, was taken out of the hands of the army and returned to the Japanese people, sold to peasants. It was ideal land for growing sweet potatoes. A number of new villages sprouted up like little Wild West towns, made out of rough slabs of wood thrown together quickly, with streets that were dusty in the dry season and muddy as soon as it rained. The apothecary decided it would be a good place to go, so he moved up from Hyogo and built a little drug shop. Behind the shop he built a place for himself, with rooms for Sokatsu added onto it. Sokatsu moved up there with all his possessions and Eichoku-san.

Ruth and Walter were shown into a small room built out of the cheapest kind of lumber. And there sat Sokatsu, on a fine-looking cushion, with all of his robes and his *rakusa*. He sat as straight as is possible for anyone to sit. He was then close to eighty. The room they had come through, before entering Sokatsu's room, was packed to the ceiling with boxes of antiques, and in his room there was barely space for him to sit, for Ruth and Walter to kneel, and for Eichoku-san to get in the door. Lacquer boxes, *budos*, statues, and rolled-up paintings were piled up to the ceiling, and in the midst of this sat the old man. The only thing Ruth could think of was an old lion whose teeth had fallen out and who had no more claws—but there he was, king of the forest. This man who had been Sokei-an's and Goto's teacher was a giant from an age of giants. He was the greatest roshi she would ever see.

Walter bowed very sweetly and Ruth introduced him to Sokatsu as "your grandson." Sokatsu accepted that, sweetly and proudly. Then he called for Eichoku-san, who came in bowing like a *ninji*. Everything was done as if this were the great temple.

The day was warm, so they had the windows and shoji open. Across the street from the apothecary's shop was a processing plant for making alcohol out of sweet potatoes, the first raw alcohol. The wind came into the room, and the rank smell of sweet potatoes being decomposed and made into alcohol on a hot day came with it to tickle their noses—and there the old lion sat, proud as anything.

Ruth hired Kanaseki Hisao, a fluent English speaker who taught American literature at Doshisha University, to act as her secretary and translation assistant. Penny had returned to New York in April 1951 and proceeded to ship project supplies such as file cards, paper, and books, as well as clothes and food items—coffee and sugar were still in short supply.

Ruth in turn had Kanaseki-san help her ship zabutons and zafus to the First Zen Institute in New York. She also arranged for the building of storage chests and other Japanese furniture, to be shipped to the institute.

On Goto Roshi's altar was a *koro*, an incense burner, that she had always admired, which he had brought back from Korea. She arranged with a famous Kyoto potter to make replicas, which she had boxed in Japanese white cedar and tied with a special woven ribbon. These became treasured gifts for new members of the institute when they entered the sangha.

In 1951 Ruth wrote an article for a Buddhist magazine, *Bukkyogaku-Kenkyu* (Studies in Buddhism), on "Why Zen Buddhism Appeals to American People," the text of a talk she had given at the Ryo-koku University in Kyoto.

For a new magazine started in January of 1952 called *The Young East*, Ruth wrote "An American Appreciation," a review of the life of D. T. Suzuki. She wrote, "He has been one of the master-builders of the bridge over which Buddhist thought is slowly traveling from East to West. His influence in this movement is beyond being measured or assessed."

By March 1952 Ruth had finished translating Heinrich Dumoulin's *The Development of Chinese Zen After the Sixth Patriarch in the Light of Mumonkan* from German. Dumoulin was a Jesuit priest, scholar, and professor of history and philosophy at Sophia University in Tokyo, who had lived in Japan since the 1930s—one of the very few Christians whose encounter with Buddhism she felt was wholly respectful and not an attempt to convert but truly to promote mutual understanding.

She consulted with Goto Roshi over translations of koans, and sent drafts to Mary Farkas. The book became the second published by the First Zen Institute, in 1953.

It was becoming clear to Ruth that her life and work would keep her in Japan more or less permanently, making occasional trips back and forth to the United States and to Europe. Kato-san, Ruth's housekeeper and assistant from twenty years earlier, was still around and remained a friend, but she no longer had the energy to continue with such work. After giving several young women unsuccessful trial runs, Ruth hired Washino Akiko as her personal assistant. Washino, who had studied ikebana with a relative of Haru Yoshida, became the ideal housekeeper and traveling companion for the rest of Ruth's life.

In May 1952, Ruth wrote to the students at the New York institute:

> The people and the institutions of this country are suffering sorely, not only from the late war and its effects, but as the result of causes which lie deep in their earlier political and social structure. Faced with the vast confusion of the present-day world they find no solid ground upon which to stand. Intellectually and emotionally, socially and politically, they are at the mercy of constantly veering winds. And they have contented for so long with the shell of religion that they now seem

totally unable to marshal the courage and fortitude with which to penetrate to the true source of spiritual life. The very few who still have eyes to see, though bowed with shame and sorrow before the spectacle, are rendered impotent by the bonds of tradition which they do not seem to have the strength to break.

I had thought that I had been stripped of every notion or illusion, that I had experienced the depths of MU. But now I know that I still cherished many hopes and beliefs, including that in a religious organization and a method. Those have now been taken away from me. And it was right that it should be so. Everything must be taken away, everything including faith. One must first become "dependent upon nothing," as Rinzai says. But curiously enough, when nothing is left, everything is present. As Sokei-an said in one of his talks—at the end of my twenty years of Zen study I had nothing, but that nothing is very wonderful.

Circumstances are always kind to us. They never fail to present us with exactly the problem we need most to learn to solve. So let us take this period when we seem bereft of everything as the occasion for more ardently seeking the experience of that "Nothing."

Presentation copies of *The Development of Chinese Zen* had gone out, and it was receiving favorable reviews. But it did not become a financial success, and Ruth, even with her seemingly unlimited financial resources, began to be concerned.

She went up to see Sokatsu again in the cold winter of early 1953. The town was like an Alaska mining town, streets nothing but mud, little shacks all along the road. The wind and snow blowing off that plain were so bitter, and the dust flying, awful. She spent the afternoon with Sokatsu and Eichoku-san, drinking tea, looking at his artwork.

In spite of being wracked with arthritis, he sat erect and immoveable on his zabuton as before, in the tiny room surrounded by his paintings, bronzes, sculptures, pieces of pottery—relics of his great days. He had been a famous calligrapher and a fine painter, a good potter and also a lacquer-worker—an all-around fine artist, as have been many Japanese priests. He would have Eichoku-san take down a scroll and unroll it. They would examine it, perhaps he would say a word about it, perhaps Ruth or Kanaseki-san, who accompanied her this time, would ask a question. Then he would nod almost imperceptibly to Eichoku-san, and she would gather it up, roll it again, and replace it with another.

When Ruth got ready to go, Sokatsu insisted on coming with her to the railroad station. It was a desolate little outpost station about a half-mile from their home. Ruth and Kanaseki-san protested. He was eighty-three at this time. They said, "You can't go. It's too cold, and look at all the dust flying. It's four o'clock in the afternoon, it'll be dark soon. You can't go out on a day like this." But they couldn't talk him out of it. He was going to see Ruth to the train.

So Eichoku-san brought a great big coat that covered his koromo, and for a cap he had an old discarded army aviator's fur cap with flaps made out of moth-eaten squirrel. Around his neck was a single skinny and bedraggled red fox skin, such as farmers would kill and cure at home and wear in winter. He put on this old hat and picked up his big bamboo staff, and they started down the road, bitter wind blowing and dirt flying in their faces.

The railroad station was a single-track place with a picket fence to keep the dogs and cats and cows from getting on the rails. They got there about five minutes before the train came in. They said goodbye many times, then the train came and they had to go across to get on. When the train drew out, there was the old man standing all alone, tears streaming down his face, in his old squirrel aviator's cap, waving like a child.

The tears running down his face. That's the last time she ever saw him.

ENTERING SANCTUARY
Kyoto, 1953–1956

S he was staying. That much was clear. The translation projects were increasing—they would be finished one day, but as
soon as they were begun, they expanded. And one led to the next.
Her Chinese was improving, but she would need much more help
to do any sort of justice to the task. She would find it.

In October 1953, Ruth's friend Lindley Hubbell, a widely published and award-winning poet, arrived to help catalog books for
her library and lend support for her literary activities. By his late
teens, Hubbell had already learned several languages—a multi-
lingual aunt taught him German, French, and Italian, and private
tutors, when he quit high school before completing his second
year, taught him Greek, Latin, and Provençal. He had a lifelong
devotion to Shakespeare—he had memorized all of the plays by
age ten, and he never let a day pass without reading some. In
spite of never having attended a university, since the end of the
war he had been teaching drama—Shakespeare, Greek tragedies,
Ibsen—and modern poetry at a high school for the arts in Hartford, Connecticut.

Hubbell arrived in Japan by ship. At the Kyoto train station he
bowed deeply to Ruth and Kanaseki-san and said, "*Kechina yaro*

de gozansu"—"I am a humble and worthless fellow." Kanaseki was startled: this was the greeting used by *yakuza*, Japanese gangsters, on a first meeting. Where did this unremarkable-looking American, who had never been in Japan, come up with such a way of speaking? His delivery—guttural and half-scowling—was flawless.

Ruth, who knew Lindley well, smiled and said, "It's wonderful to see you." She could not help thinking of Sokei-an, who clearly had a role in this mischievous locution. Lindley, with his gift for language and flair for the theatrical, must have seduced his Zen teacher into instructing him in the rougher idioms.

He had been a student of Sokei-an's since the early 1930s. It was Lindley Hubbell who had signed the sponsorship form that helped secure Sokei-an's release from internment, and he had been with Ruth and Sokei-an at the celebratory dinner at Longchamps that turned desperate when Sokei-an had to be rushed to the hospital.

Before taking the teaching position in Hartford, Hubbell had spent twenty years as a librarian in the Map Division of the New York Public Library—interspersed with a year in Italy, half a year in Puerto Rico, and sundry other excursions. It had been his lifelong desire to come to Japan. Once he arrived, he fell in love with the country and never left.

Though he had taken sanzen with Sokei-an, his interests were aesthetic rather than religious. He became obsessed with Noh drama, attending every performance he could get to—more than eight hundred, eventually—not allowing any interruptions or distractions during the five hours of ritualized flute, drum, chant, dance, rapturously absorbed.

Ruth was a witness to his deepening settlement in his true home. They collaborated on translations from time to time—the May 1954 issue of *Zen Notes*, for example, included an English translation of some *Zenrin* poems. He enjoyed meeting Goto Roshi and many of Ruth's other Zen associates, but he had no interest in entering Zen practice himself. Instead he became a devotee of Shinto, which to him expressed the profoundest beauty imaginable.

Ruth saw that the longer she stayed in Japan, the less inclined she was to return to the United States for more than brief visits. This was where her work was. And as the years passed, she realized her social connections were deepening as well—which in Japan, more even than in America or Europe, were the basis of every dimension of life. So whatever wonderful qualifications her friend Lindley Hubbell had for teaching Shakespeare and English literature, it was because Ruth introduced him to the president of Doshisha University, a friend of hers, that Lindley was offered a professorship there.

There were inquiries from students about coming to Kyoto. A young scholar and poet named Gary Snyder had joined the First Zen Institute, writing to her asking about possibilities and conditions for studying with a Rinzai master in Japan.

Another young scholar, a Columbia doctoral student named Philip Yampolsky, had just arrived in Kyoto on a Fulbright scholarship. He was already fluent in Japanese. Right after finishing his bachelor's at Columbia in 1942 he had enlisted in the navy, which sent him to the Navy Language School in Boulder, Colorado, for training in an elite group of translators. And then he shipped out to the Pacific, where he fought at Iwo Jima and was awarded a Bronze Star for meritorious service as a translator.

He had been studying Chinese as well as Japanese and was deeply immersed in Zen and Ch'an literature. His dissertation, which propelled him to Kyoto, was on Huineng, the Sixth Zen Patriarch—central to Sokei-an's life and teaching as well. He would be a perfect fit for Ruth's projects. She hired him part-time and introduced him to Goto Roshi. Yampolsky, as a scholar, recognized the necessity of experiencing Zen practice from the inside. Goto Roshi was too ill to take him as a student, so he went to Oda Roshi, who did accept him.

Along with Yampolsky, Ruth found other scholars to form the core of her translation research team. Professor Iriya Yoshitaka, a scholar of Tang- and Song-era China at Kyoto University, with his deep knowledge of the texts, became the senior member and director of the group, with Yanagida Seizan, also a professor at Kyoto University, as a younger partner.

Burton Watson had first come to Japan on shore leave from the navy—he had enlisted at age seventeen in 1943 and worked on repair vessels in the South Pacific. After the war he had begun Japanese and Chinese studies as an undergrad at Columbia, and he returned to Kyoto in 1951 to work on his doctoral research. His interests and expertise tended toward the historical more than the religious; it was in the seminar-like work sessions with Iriya that he began a lifelong engagement with Buddhist literature, though he never personally entered Zen practice.

In the autumn of 1954, Ruth's brother, David, died, and Ruth went to Honolulu to take care of his affairs and then flew his ashes to be buried with their mother in Illinois.

David had never really recovered since he'd been beaten in 1945, around the time Sokei-an was dying. Already prone to depression, he had become morose. Living in Hawaii had helped his spirits somewhat, but there was no cure, no recovery.

Ruth had stopped in Honolulu to visit him and speak with his doctors in 1953, en route to New York. During that trip, with Eleanor's family moving West to Colorado, David in Hawaii, and Warren dead fifteen years already, and knowing she would stay in Japan, Ruth realized there was really no need to hang on to Swan House in Hinsdale or the apartments in New York. She faced the difficult task of sifting through twenty-odd years of belongings, deciding what to store and what to dispose of.

On the return trip through San Francisco, she visited her granddaughters Joan and Anne. Joan, at fifteen, talked about coming to stay with her in Japan. Ruth supposed that might be good for her.

Isshu Miura was interested. Yes, he thought he would like to go to the United States and meet the students of the First Zen Institute. And become their teacher. He would have to learn some English. And his temple, Koon-ji—he would have to work it out with them as well. The first trip would be to get acquainted, and then he would need a few months in Japan, perhaps a year or two, to improve his English and tie things up.

Ruth cautioned him that he must make no adjustments, apart from language, for cultural differences. "We need you to bring all of your Zen, just as you have always practiced. Not to imagine that you—or anyone—can know ahead of time which aspects will be necessary for Americans and which will be irrelevant. We need all of it. Later, when Buddhism is firmly established in America, we Americans will determine what American Buddhism will become. But the First Zen Institute of America is established according to orthodox transmission of Japanese Rinzai Zen, and the teachings must be delivered accordingly."

Miura, trained by Nanshinken Roshi, the strictest of the traditional Zen masters of his generation, agreed. He had no desire to

make exceptions for Americans because of their cultural inexperi-
ence. If they were truly ready, they would have to come the distance.

Ruth immediately wrote to Mary Farkas and George Fowler of
this development, and they began making arrangements for Miura
to take an introductory trip to America.

Walter had great respect for Miura Roshi as a teacher. But when
he, Walter, had stayed at Koon-ji, he found the other monks there
to be unpleasant and unwelcoming. Walter was well accustomed
to discipline and intense training. But the three disciples of Miura
Roshi at the temple seemed conspiratorial, arbitrary, actively
engaged in making Walter's life difficult, attempting to sabotage
his practice. What was their commitment to?

Walter returned to Kyoto after a couple of weeks, relieved
to find the health of his ailing teacher, Goto Roshi, momentar-
ily improved, and grateful for the immense gift of deep insight
expressed with the compassion of a stern but good-humored
Buddha—which only inspired Walter to practice more fervently.

In a 1953 letter to Ruth expressing intentions to study Zen in
Japan, Gary Snyder had written, "It has been my wish to see the
Zen tradition—as something concrete and alive—in relation to its
supporting culture."

Ruth responded with a description of the pitfalls as well as the
possibilities:

> Japan is today in an extremely disturbed condition, eco-
> nomically and "spiritually." The old patterns of life in
> every field have been thoroughly shaken up by the war,
> the Occupation, and the increasing dependence of Japan
> upon the western world. The temples of the Zen sect

have suffered seriously from this general disturbance. Economically, they are at low ebb due to their lands being taken away, in large part, and to the inability and disinterest of their adherents to support them.

The economic situation has changed the caliber of monk who is living and studying in the zendo. The number of monks in training has decreased to an alarming degree. For instance, at Daitoku-ji where there would normally have been about 30 monks, there are at present 4, and this is typical for all Japan.

The American student, coming into a present-day Japanese zendo, is more than likely to be highly disillusioned by what he finds there. An attempt is made to continue the traditional zendo life but it is far from successful.

Though Japanese people have been studying English for many years, there are very few Zen monks who can speak even a word of English. There is only one Zen Master who can speak English, and he is probably too old and frail to take new koan students. There are some admirable men among living Zen Masters but the student would have to know Japanese or at least have some facility with it in order to study.

All this boils down to this. A young man with an assured income of fifty dollars a month, who is willing to come to Japan and spend a minimum of three years there, who will for one year devote himself to the study of Japanese language and to acquainting himself with Japanese culture and to learning to practice zazen, then to spend two years under a Zen teacher—living in or out of a Zen monastery—may reasonably well expect to pass his first koan at the end of that time.

He must be prepared to endure extreme heat and extreme cold, providing himself with adequate clothing for both. He must also be prepared to adapt himself physically and mentally to a culture which, though charming and containing many real values, is alien to himself and at times difficult to understand, and he must, last of all, be prepared to have swept away every illusion he has ever held about Buddhism and about Zen. For such a person it is not impossible to study Zen in Japan.

For the twenty-fifth anniversary of the First Zen Institute, Goto Roshi sent a painting of Daio Kokushi, the teacher of Daito Kokushi, Daitoku-ji's founder, along with a poem of Kido Osho, who had been Daio's teacher: "Having knocked at the gate and meticulously polished himself a second time, he traverses the pathless place. I, the old monk Kido, make this prophesy: The children of the eastern seas will increase day by day." To this Goto Roshi added his own prophesy, which, translated, said "It is the expressed hope of Goto Roshi that the torch of Zen, handed to those in the still more easterly lands of America and Europe, may continue to burn brightly, until it forms one continuous encircling light, dispelling the darkness of ignorance and bringing awakening to men in all lands." Ruth carried the scroll from her teacher as she and Miura Roshi traveled to America in April 1955.

Ruth introduced Miura to his expectant American students at the institute in New York. Those who had already committed themselves to Zen practice sealed their commitment in a formal induction ceremony and then began their koan study with Miura Roshi. During six weeks at the institute in New York, Miura gave a series of lectures, beginning with the Four Vows, and otherwise focused on kensho and koan practice in Rinzai Zen. Ruth had been translating Miura's talks, with some help from Kanascki, and now helped deliver the English versions. Ruth and Miura began discussing the value of gathering the lectures into a book. Eventually these would form the basis of *Zen Dust* and *The Zen Koan*.

On the return trip from New York, Ruth took Miura and Washino on a brief tour of the American Southwest. They flew by jet to Denver, then on a small two-engine propeller plane to Santa Fe, where Eleanor and Carlton Gamer were waiting on the desert airstrip. They were the only passengers stepping off; their bags were tossed down unceremoniously. After a few minutes the plane took off again for Texas, leaving them in the cool, clear air under a brilliantly star-strewn sky.

The dinner that greeted Miura Roshi was unlike any he had encountered: a mammoth steak, overhanging its plate, garnished with corn tortillas. The food monks and priests prepare for themselves in their temples is vegetarian, but on almsrounds and other occasions their practice is to accept and eat whatever is offered— which often includes meat. But this meal was entirely beyond what most Japanese people, let alone a Buddhist priest, had ever seen or chewed on. Except for Sokei-an. But differences in personality and preference should not be looked at as differences in quality or suitability. Ruth said nothing about this, of course.

In San Francisco, Miura Roshi gave one of his talks on kensho at the Soto Zen temple, where a group of nisei and non-Japanese students had been meeting weekly for zazen; and Ruth gave her talk "Zen: A Religion" at the American Academy of Asian Studies, where Alan Watts was now dean. One young woman commented afterward, "Well, I suppose it is about time I stopped being a Zen dilettante and took up the study of Zen seriously."

Gary Snyder came to meet her at the hotel. He was working on coming to Kyoto that fall. The paperwork was mostly in order, but there were some delays with his passport. During the Depression his father had been an activist in the Unemployed League and a member of the Industrial Workers of the World; Gary, as a student at Reed College, had developed leftist political associations, and for a summer job working as a merchant seaman, he had joined the Marine Cooks and Stewards Union, which was considered communist.

But Ruth encouraged him to persist until they gave him his clearance. As far as entering Japan, that would be taken care of: she would be his sponsor, and if that proved to be insufficient, Miura Roshi would sign the necessary papers. And the institute would be providing him with a scholarship as well as a guarantee of funds, which would be important, considering that Snyder had no money of his own except what he had been able to earn working summers as a seaman dishwasher or a logger or a fire lookout. For travel to Japan, he would ship out on another freighter, as a dishwasher in the galley.

Between them was a gulf of not only generations but class and politics. Gary was a child of the Depression, which had hardly touched Ruth's wealth. His father had moved the family from San Francisco to Seattle, spent nine years out of work, got by splitting cedar shakes, raising a handful of dairy cows, fixing or building something when there was something to be fixed or built. But what Gary and Ruth had in common made the differences irrelevant. He was a passionate intellectual, a scholar, with a gift for languages. His dedication to the pursuit of true Zen practice was as her own.

This was the purpose of her invitation and the inspiration for her sponsorship: To further the vitality of the Buddhadharma in the world, it is of highest importance to support the humble aspirant—who may become the next Buddha. Without supporting the true student, the Buddhadharma would die out. And that would be a grave tragedy for the world.

His political affiliations? Not an issue.

Joseph Campbell—whom Ruth knew of as the translator and editor of Heinrich Zimmer's *Myths and Symbols in Indian Art and Civilization*, and as a friend of Sokei-an's early benefactor Ananda Coomaraswamy and more recently of Alan Watts, who had sent Campbell to look up Ruth in Kyoto—was on his way back from six months in India with his wife, Jean Erdman Campbell. They had been in Kyoto since April 1955, and they were still there when Ruth returned from America with Miura Roshi at the end of June.

Campbell had fallen in love with Kyoto. He talked at length of the difficulties and contradictions of travel in India—how it was a severe test of one's patience simply to get from one place to another, let alone to find more than a handful of educated, philosophically minded people who could converse intelligently about the incredible riches of India's ancient civilization.

Ruth recognized in Campbell a romantic encountering disillusionment. But, especially after India, he was completely enamored of Kyoto and charmed by Lindley Hubbell, who waxed poetic over Noh and Shinto, and by Goto Roshi, who gave them the run of Ryoan-ji, which Campbell found blissful in spite of the garden being in bad shape the afternoon they visited and the main hall taken over by manufacturers of kimono fabrics as a temporary showroom to provide extra revenue for the temple.

Toward the end of the Campbells' visit, Ruth and Walter took them for a picnic on Mount Hiei, where Walter had been teaching English to a young Tendai priest he had gone walking with the previous summer. Kimura, the priest, brought them to the most important temples on the mountain—many had only recently reopened after repairs—leading them into great dark shrines in back of the open shrines, where the secret Tendai ceremonies are conducted. For the picnic, Kimura-san brought them high up on the mountain, near some deserted tombstones. The view over Lake Biwa, shimmering in the afternoon light, was stunning.

Ruth enjoyed Campbell's company a great deal. Like some others she had known—Alan came to mind—he had a way with words, charm, charisma. He overflowed with enthusiasm, and it was contagious—for Kyoto, for stories, for his great realization of the commonality of the stories of all cultures. She did not feel a need to dispute him—it was not false. But she was suspicious of this sort of universalizing. As she saw it, what was common to all people was just that: common—and not always in the best sense. The means of Rinzai Zen were not widely shared: they were the unique expression of three hundred generations of dedicated practitioners who had developed methods to take a person beyond the ordinary, beyond the common. There was a place it was simply not possible to reach by any other means.

Campbell talked about how in Zen stories of enlightenment the pattern of the hero's journey could be clearly seen—and, well, yes, the difficult passage through the gateless gate can appear heroic. Though from inside the experience, that notion becomes less meaningful. These stories were themselves instruments of awakening, but they were useless as such to anyone not already dedicated in the particular method. Even more so the koans—they just seem like nonsense to anyone not using them actively in sanzen training, with a teacher capable of ascertaining a student's insight. The way of looking at stories that Campbell suggested might be comforting or even illuminating in some way, but it was unlikely to free anyone from self-delusion.

Ruth was getting up at four thirty every morning for sanzen. It was a delight to rise in the early morning, the most beautiful part of the hot summer days, to see the hot pink of the sky above Mount Hiei gradually turn to pale apricot, the moon sinking over the trees of the monastery across the way, to hear the doves cooing sleepily in her next-door neighbor's cot and the early morning bells of several nearby temples.

There was a constant flow of visitors, and Ruth took pride in receiving them graciously. Her dinners and parties were legendary. She had personally trained a pair of young women from the countryside to do the traditional American cooking she loved and presented to the enthusiastic guests she had for dinner several nights a week. She poured martinis. She loved conversation, and after work hours she enjoyed joining in free-flowing debate. She could hold her own with anyone.

For two years, almost to the day, Goto Roshi had been struggling with a severe and stubborn case of jaundice, with many complications. Several times he had been close to death. But he always said, "A real Zen man knows when he is going to die, and I am not going to die this time." He had recovered almost completely, in time to celebrate his seventy-seventh birthday.

He had been looking forward to this particular birthday with great anticipation, for now he would be able to use a special signature for his calligraphy: "Seventy-seven-year-old Goto Zuigan." In China and Japan, dates with double numbers are considered auspicious—weddings are often held on the eleventh or twenty-second of a month, for example—and in old age, seventy-seven, the double seven, is the most auspicious.

Every year a group of his lay students would hold a celebration for his birthday, but because of Goto's illness, the previous two years had been skipped. Thus the party for his seventy-seventh was particularly joyous, with more than forty guests gathered to ceremonially drink thick tea and eat small cakes. Among Goto's lay group were doctors, librarians, teachers, university professors—with not a single representative of the younger generations. And not a single one of those present among the Japanese guests had ever undertaken sanzen. They considered it almost impossibly difficult—a fact that greatly enhanced their admiration for Ruth and Walter.

Goto Roshi announced his retirement as kancho of Daitoku-ji, and his Dharma heir Oda Sesso Roshi was elected to replace him. Goto would continue training his current students, and he would act as sodo roshi during practice periods at Myoshin-ji. Oda Kancho would officiate at the ceremony honoring the founder of Daitoku-ji on November 22. Ruth would be traveling to Tokyo to meet Mary Farkas, who was arriving on the eighteenth, and together they would be back in Kyoto in time for this most important temple occasion of the year.

The Japan that Mary entered was experiencing the beginnings of a resurgence. Ten years after the war, the occupation forces had stepped aside, much had been rebuilt, much new was developing. There were signs of a renewed prosperity emerging. To Mary, arriving for the first time, the people all seemed bursting with vigor, intent on a multitude of activities, juicy and glowing with life—"succulent looking and full of the sap of flowing vitality."

The day before the Founder's ceremony, Ruth and Mary, along with Kanaseki-san, made their way to the temple to pay respects to Oda Roshi, who received them graciously. Mary was impressed with his elegance. After she managed a few polite phrases in Japanese, he complimented her pronunciation, adding that since all Japanese people spoke their language with a local flavor, only foreigners could speak Japanese with a pure pronunciation. He hoped it would be the same with Zen—that they would be better able to express it in its pure, objective form, without any Japanese subjectivity to flavor or distort its essential quality.

The morning of the Founder's Day ceremony, Goto Roshi came to visit Ryosen-an to see Ruth's newly completed study. This was significant, considering that for the previous two years his health had prevented him from venturing out. And it was an honor to be paid a visit by the newly retired kancho on the very day of his temple's momentous occasion.

Speaking only Japanese, he asked Mary how she was finding Kyoto. She replied, "It is like a dream. I cannot believe it yet." He spoke a phrase in Japanese, and then explained in English, "A state in which one does not know whether to stand or sit."

She took the opportunity to express the great gratitude of the Zen Institute members for the interest Goto Roshi had taken in their group, mentioning that it was exactly fifty years since he had come to America with Sokei-an and that now, with Miura Roshi coming—with Goto Roshi's help—they had completed the first step in the actual transmission of Zen to America. They deeply appreciated his part in this, and they wanted him to know how immense that part had been. They felt that his sending of the scroll with his calligraphy and the portrait of Daio Kokushi—the treasure of their modest temple—along with sending Miura Roshi, as he could not come himself, was the completion of his mission begun fifty years ago.

"Nothing in Zen might ever be thought of as completed. But it could perhaps be said that one step has been taken."

Mary continued, saying that meeting with Miura Roshi had instantly and spontaneously forged a bond of deep attachment between him and the students, which gave them great hope for the future. Goto seemed pleased to hear this: "Without a strong bond between teacher and disciples, regardless of the teacher's brilliance, nothing can be accomplished."

They took their places just inside the columns of the hondo, the great hall of Daitoku-ji, in a place of honor directly behind one of the featured participants, the esteemed tea master Sen Mugensai, the father of Goto Roshi's disciple Sen Masaoki and reigning *iemoto* of the Urasenke family. Some of his followers had come only to see him perform, which he did with the precise choreography of a master dancer, as a solo flutist played penetratingly in another corner.

Before the central image of Daito Kokushi, Oda Roshi intoned a chant in his honor, offering cake and then the tea, which was brought up by an old man with a long white beard who had traveled a considerable distance specifically to perform this honor.

The offering complete, a line of standing black-robed monks in the northwest corner, facing the center, chanted to the rhythmic beating of a wooden clapper, repeating the chant three times, as a dozen elaborately robed priests walked in interweaving concentric circles in front of the central shrine, all with intense concentration and great dignity. When they concluded, a large hanging bell was struck repeatedly, resounding through the hall.

Miura came to Kyoto the following day, and Ruth and Mary accompanied him to visit Goto Roshi. They spoke about Goto's health and gossiped about temple affairs, which the roshis agreed were, as usual, in an appalling state. They spoke rapidly in Japanese, Ruth trying to keep Mary up with what they said. Mary observed that both men regarded her with the greatest affection and esteem, and they did not hesitate to show it.

The discussion turned toward America, with Goto Roshi counseling and encouraging Miura Roshi about his imminent return, with reference to Mary's report on the gratitude of the First Zen Institute members for Miura's presence.

Rohatsu was upon them. Ruth brought Mary to the Daitoku-ji sodo to meet the head monk for instruction on zendo etiquette. She would be admitted to evening sessions, as Ruth had been on her first stay in Japan a quarter century earlier.

February 11. Miura Roshi came at noon, Mary completed some film business in Tokyo, and Walter came in time for a final dinner all together. Then Ruth and Washino brought the three to the airport and bid them farewell, before returning to the city after midnight.

They were gone. She was staying. The next day Ruth and Washino returned to Kyoto by train, both sleeping most of the way. Ruth contemplated the eighty-one letters that had accumulated in the three months of Mary's visit, needing to be answered.

The members of the institute were delighted to have Miura Roshi back again, this time with Walter translating. On February 15, the twenty-sixth anniversary of the institute, Miura Roshi again sat in the master's place. He presented a bronze sanzen bell that had been given to him by his teacher Seigo Hogaku.

Miura stayed again for two months. Then he returned to Japan, to stay mostly in Kyoto and turn his attention more completely to studying English and preparing to move to America permanently. He would only visit Koon-ji for a few days each month, intending to wrap up his obligations there gradually over the next year or two.

Gary Snyder arrived in Japan in May 1956. At first he stayed at Rinko-in, as Miura's cook and attendant and English teacher, studying Japanese, joining Ruth's translation team as secretary and assistant, meeting the others in her wide circles, practicing zazen intensively, even though he would not begin koan study for months at least. He immediately secured Ruth's respect—which, once earned, never departed—with his capacity for zazen.

He had plenty of patience. He had the fortitude to stand being told he had it wrong every day for a year and a half until one day he had it right and could move on to the second koan. And after that, the answers did come more quickly.

Phil Yampolsky became a guide for Kyoto life and culture for Gary, introducing him to Kyoto streets and sake bars. Snyder, who had studied anthropology at Reed College, was impressed to find out that Phil—named Philip Boas Yampolsky—was indeed the grandson of the great anthropologist Franz Boas. And Gary was also entertained by Phil's preference for speaking in the low street dialect of Kyoto—even in sanzen with Oda Roshi, who scolded him for sounding rude and admonished him to please use standard Japanese.

There were too many people arriving to accommodate. There were too many books. It was not possible in Ruth's small hermitage house to do the work she needed to do. She needed a place for the research team to work on the translation projects, a place to keep the now thousands of note cards. A place for both work and small-group zazen. Not in her house.

Ruth went to Goto and Oda and asked them for permission to build a library, and in 1956, they granted her request. Wakita-san broke ground in July.

The library would eventually hold over a thousand books and journals in Japanese, Chinese, French, German, English, and Sanskrit, on Buddhism, literature, philosophy, Japanese culture, and Eastern religions. It was to become the Kyoto headquarters of the First Zen Institute; Ruth began the arrangements to incorporate a Japanese religious corporation—the First Zen Institute of America in Japan.

Joan Watts and Ruth (with Washino).
Courtesy of Joan Watts.

Ruth's granddaughter Joan Watts came to stay for a year. Ruth arranged for a friend of Washino's to teach her Japanese, for a master *sumi-e* artist to give her painting lessons, and for her friend Kobori Sohaku, a Daitoku-ji priest, to teach her tea ceremony. Together they would visit temples and historic sites, craftspeople and artists. Perhaps Joan would be bored without her American friends and the young life she was accustomed to. But she was an artistic and adventurous girl, and Ruth expected she would make the best of it.

Huston Smith and his wife, Kendra, stayed for eight weeks in the summer of 1956. Both of them joined the zazen group, and Huston took sanzen with Goto Roshi. He had been born in China—the son of Christian missionaries and devout in the faith of his family—and lived there until 1935, when, at sixteen, he went to America to formally study the religions of the world at the University of Chicago. What he found at the great academy was something other than religious understanding: his professors, the whole academic world it seemed, treated religion as no more than something to read and write books about—not something to engage in as the inherited repository of living wisdom. It was discouraging, but he persisted, never letting this dismissive attitude get in the way of his deepest intuition—that religion can, indeed must, offer the deepest possible experience in a human life, and must be the basis of sanity, peace, and humane relations between all people; and that this fullest expression of life is not confined to one particular religious path but in fact is shared by every great religion.

Smith came to Buddhism in the 1950s, after ten years of Hindu Vedanta meditation, first through the writings of Alan Watts and then through meeting D. T. Suzuki—by interviewing him on public television, part of a series in which Smith would question well-known figures such as Eleanor Roosevelt about which way the world was heading. Suzuki made satori seem like an available possibility and inspired and encouraged him to visit Japan.

He brought his response. As Smith was halfway through explaining his solution, Goto Roshi shouted, "You have the philosopher disease!" and continued, more softly, "There's nothing wrong with philosophy. But philosophy works only with reason, and only to the extent it is based on experience. Your reasoning is fine, but your experience is limited. Enlarge your experience!" The sanzen bell rang: *Out!*

During the summer osesshin, Smith was permitted three hours of sleep every night. Never enough. By the end of the week, trying to push through the koan-gate in this deranged state of sleep deprivation, he snapped. He stormed into the sanzen room. As he entered, he checked himself and bowed, forehead to the mat. His eyes locked with Goto's in a seething glare.

Roshi barked, "How's it going?"

"Terrible!"

"You think you are going to get sick, don't you?" It was a taunt.

"Yes, I'm getting sick!" His throat was closing up. It was hard to breathe. "Because of you!"

Roshi's face relaxed. Matter-of-factly, he said, "What is sickness? What is health? Put aside both and go forward."

The despair evaporated. He could breathe again. What, after all, did it mean to be human? A state of total peace, completely unexpected, enveloped the room.

Osesshin ended. Ruth had the Smiths over for a festive farewell meal. By now she had warmed to Kendra, who at first had found her completely aloof: it was hard for Ruth to know what to do with people who were not there to immerse themselves in Zen.

Huston went to say farewell to Goto Roshi. His teacher welcomed him at the doorway of his tiny inryo, dressed casually, and introduced him to Okamoto-san, who cooked for him. He also gave him a peek at the television where he liked to watch sumo wrestling and another at the empty beer bottles by the back door—remnants from watching sumo.

"Koans can be a useful exercise, but they are not Zen. And sitting in meditation—that is not Zen. You will be flying home tomorrow. Do not overlook how many people will help you get home—everyone."

Goto put his palms together in gassho and bowed toward the gate agents, pilot and copilot, flight attendants, cooks, janitors. He pointed to the beam that supported the corner of the house and bowed to it. He pointed to the ceiling that kept the house dry, and bowed to it.

Then he bowed to Huston. "Make your whole life unceasing gratitude. What is Zen? Simple, so simple. Infinite gratitude toward all things past; infinite service to all things present; infinite responsibility to all things future. Have a safe journey home. I am glad you came."

EVERY ROCK IS SURELY KANNON
Kyoto, 1956–1958

Many visitors arrived—professors of Chinese, psychology, history, religion, science; newspaper and radio and television journalists; bankers, doctors, psychiatrists, Christian missionaries, artists, students of religion, travelers, curiosity seekers. Many of them wanted zazen practice, even if only in Kyoto for a few days.

A group of Protestant missionaries approached Ruth to lay out a plan for their study of Zen. Ruth refused to have anything to do with it and told them she thought their wish to go snooping into sodos and zendos for the purpose of observing training and monastic life, so they might better understand how to proselytize against it all, was decidedly impudent. But after every roshi and other Zen organization refused them, Ruth finally softened and read to them from her pamphlet *Zen: A Religion* and made them sit on zabutons.

In the damp fall of 1956, Ruth had a heavy chest cold mixed with asthma and seemed to have no physical or mental energy. It turned into bronchitis. In the midst of this season of fatigue and coughing fits, Joan had her eighteenth birthday, and Ruth had to do something big, since it was a landmark occasion and since Joan had never had a really big party given for her. Ruth arranged a debutante ball of sorts at the swankiest restaurant in town, with all the young men she could find—not so many, but of a more respectable sort than some Joan had met in Alan's circles in San Francisco—and closed the night with French champagne.

Gary and Walter sat the Rohatsu osesshin at Daitoku-ji in December 1956, along with fourteen other kojis and monks—there were now several new monks entering the temple—with Oda Roshi overseeing. Walter went up to Daishu-in twice a day for sanzen with Goto Roshi, while Gary remained in the zendo the entire week, except for when he had to leave to get an infection in his hand lanced—it had started as a scratch and become swollen and painful, but he returned directly to sitting.

In a Tendai temple called Sanjusangen-do, in Higashiyama just east of the Kamo River, is a thirty-three-*ken* main hall that houses a thousand and one Kannon statues: a thousand identical five-foot standing images in five rows of fifty on each side, guarding the central image, an eleven-foot-tall golden seated Thousand-Armed Kannon, the bodhisattva of compassion, all symbolizing the total manifested universe in which every existence is Kannon herself.

Looking at the library building, at the rocky pool, and at the garden gradually coming into being, Ruth was overcome with this recognition: that each and every workman, tree, plant, and rock is surely Kannon, graciously dispensing some one of the expressions of her mercy, truly carrying out Buddha's wondrous work of transformation for the benefit of sentient beings of the future. "I wonder if they know who they are?"

The library was finished. In March 1957 they held a simple opening ceremony, with Miura Roshi officiating. It was a beautiful building, well-suited to the work that was its primary purpose. But it immediately became apparent that moving furniture out of the way for a group to sit zazen was impractical and not conducive to the desirable attitude for meditation. So Ruth began plans to build a separate zendo, to house sixteen people.

Opening of the Ryosen-an Library, 1957. Philip Yampolsky, Gary Snyder, Donatienne Lebovich, Ruth, Miura Isshu Roshi, Vanessa Coward, Manzoji Yoko, Walter Nowick, and Seizan Yanagida. Courtesy of the First Zen Institute of America.

"But what is going on with Miura Roshi? He is happy to offer his observations about the building projects and sit for the opening ceremony. And he has been perfectly reasonable to work with on *Zen Dust*—though his work on that is more or less complete by now. But when I ask about his plans, he is silent. The members in New York are prepared to receive him. They gave their formal invitation, but for months, no word. With me he speaks only Japanese—and little at that. Has he even been practicing English? Gary, you've eaten with him twice a day for the whole year. Does he say anything?"

"Very little. And mostly in Japanese. Occasionally he throws in an English word. I gather his ability is more advanced than he lets on. But in any case, all of it is about what I would expect from a roshi."

"And he made you wait a year before agreeing to give you sanzen."

"You yourself had warned me this would be the protocol."

"Even after the year, he seems reluctant."

"If that is the right word."

"And within sanzen?"

"He is all that any student could ask for. But I will begin working with Oda Roshi soon."

"When Miura goes to Koon-ji for his monthly visit, he seems animated."

"He does not seem to be wrapping up his business there."

"And yet he did submit his acceptance to the institute—after we pressured him for months to give us a decision. Though I suspect it was only because of Kanaseki going to America that Roshi did finally write the letter. This has been going on for months."

"His heart is not in it."

"Walter seems to think it was something that happened on the last trip. Though I suspect it's even deeper than that. You know that trip was not an easy one for Walter."

"So he said. But he's too discrete to reveal any details."

The remnants of Ryosen-an contained no hint of its glorious past. Though always a subtemple, Ryosen-an, founded five hundred years ago, had itself once controlled many temples in the country around Tokyo. Daitoku-ji priests receive ordination according to the lineage of their masters, typically affiliated with a particular subtemple. Though the temple itself had been completely destroyed at the beginning of the Meiji era and its treasures transferred to other temples, the Ryosen-an line continued. This, it turned out, was Sokei-an's lineage. He was a Daitoku-ji priest of the Ryosen-an line.

It takes a single day to raise and join the heavy timber frame of a small temple building. Wakita-san, the master carpenter, had spent the previous two months in his shop overseeing the careful work of forming and fitting massive timbers with intricate, interlocking joints that would be disassembled, conveyed to the building site, and reassembled—in a single day—with locking pins, entirely without nails. The inner and outer walls of the zendo would be constructed mainly of sliding panels; the finish work would take several weeks.

It had been raining continuously for ten days. This did not seem particularly auspicious. But on the afternoon of April 25, the rain stopped and, even though the sky was still heavy and brooding, Wakita-san's men brought the timbers. The next morning the sky remained thick with dark clouds. But with no actual rain, the carpenters got to work. By four thirty, they were locking the last timber into place—a specially curved log of Japanese cedar, slightly planed down. As the first guests were beginning to arrive for the dedication ceremony, the sun burst forth.

Oda Kancho officiated, assisted by Miura Roshi and Kobori Sohaku. They had set up a temporary altar on the bare earth beneath the rooftree. On it were a vase of flowers, a bundle of fresh vegetables, one dish of salt and one of uncooked rice, a lighted candle, and an incense burner. The kancho chanted a sutra calling upon the sixteen gods of Indian origin who protect Buddhism to drive all evil influences away and protect the building throughout the future; at the same time the other priests chanted other sutras to a similar purpose.

All the members of the institute living in Kyoto were present, along with friends, forming a small crowd of two dozen people. Of course all of the builders were there—honoring them was a central purpose of the ceremony.

As soon as the formalities concluded, the workmen gathered around a table they had set up in the garden, to receive offerings: for each, a box of fish and vegetables and a box of rice, hot sake served in tea cups, and a special white envelope tied with red string containing money, the amount depending on the recipient's type of work. They continued drinking sake into the night, singing and telling jokes, as the other guests, after admiring the new maple garden, signing the guest book, drinking coffee, and eating French pastries, took their leave.

In January 1957 Kanaseki Hisao, going to New York to study and teach at Columbia, had carried with him Isshu Miura's letter of acceptance to the First Zen Institute. And then in May, Miura suddenly resigned, with no explanation. The institute members sent a letter of dismay and regret, hoping he might reconsider his decision. Mary Farkas sent a personal letter expressing that she still considered him her teacher.

Joan was getting married. She had met a young U.S. soldier posted in Kobe. The wedding would be in August 1957—three months shy of Joan's nineteenth birthday. A large, elaborate wedding,

*Bridesmaids at Joan's wedding in Japan, 1957. Anne Watts
is in the front row, second from left; Ruth is at the right.
Courtesy of Joan Watts.*

which Ruth launched into planning—in spite of too many projects
and too little energy, enlisting her trusty assistant Haru Yoshida
in New York to purchase wedding and bridesmaids gowns and to
take care of innumerable small details.

The new zendo, formally dedicated on July 15, was named Suiget-
su-do: "Water-Moon Hall."

Joan's wedding was held at St. Francis Xavier Cathedral in Kyoto,
one of the oldest churches in Japan, built in 1890—the groom was
Catholic—with a grand reception at the Miyako Hotel. Eleanor
came from Colorado Springs and Anne from England. After the
wedding, they stayed in Kyoto another six weeks.

"Is there no way around it? I'd been hoping to avoid this."

"There is no other possibility. Ryosen-an will be a *matsu-ji*. Sokei-an is posthumously named Founder of the Restored Ryosen-an, and you will be made *jushoku*, temple priest. The lands must be used exclusively for temple purposes and must be administered by a resident priest. That is the simplest way to put it."

"Then we must have it written with conditions. That matters of succession be left to my decision and not the whim of the Daitoku-ji hierarchy. And finances must remain under my complete control. Ryosen-an must remain completely free from any domination, control, or interference from the Honzan or any other Daitoku-ji temples. You must have some idea how complicated this will be—I came here imagining a life of simplicity."

"There is no question of your qualification."

"I am the only person qualified. I have done the work. There is no one else. Sokei-an himself had no idea regarding such matters. He had no interest in living in Japan or having anything to do really with temple matters. He was a koji, a layman, at heart, even though he had the ordination. His entire training was as a koji. Only after he had completed his Zen and saw how Americans needed an official priest, only then did he join the temple apparatus."

"In any case, it is a great honor."

"That it indeed is. And make no mistake, I accept it and embrace it fully. I have nothing but the deepest esteem and affection for my teachers and friends here. But it is slightly preposterous. Practically unimaginable. I did not want to make this a matsu-ji and had no intention of being the first foreigner, let alone foreign woman, to become the priest of a Rinzai Zen temple. If I had known at the beginning what the irrevocable rules of Daitoku-ji were, I should probably never have stayed here beyond the first six months."

"And yet . . . The forces have been set in motion."

"By ignorance, which no one took the least trouble to dispel. It is only through the friendliness of certain of the priests that we can make it come out right in the end: to preserve for our New York institute the indefinite right to continue using the buildings we have put up, to control our own finances, to have complete freedom of action."

"The buildings will be property of the matsu-ji—owned by Ryosen-an, under Daitoku-ji. All furnishings, books, and removable objects will remain assets of the institute. That is the best we can do."

Daito Kokushi—his posthumous name, which means "National Teacher of the Great Lamp"—after he had completed his training and received Dharma transmission as a Zen master from his teacher Daio Kokushi and returned from China, lived as a beggar in a robe made of reeds under a bridge in Kyoto for thirty years before revealing himself.

The emperor, who had heard of Daito's great mastery, somehow learned that this recluse beggar-teacher loved melons. So he sent soldiers out to find him with a whole cartful of the fruit. To each beggar the soldiers met, they offered a melon, with the demand, "Take this melon without using your hands." They did not know what answer to expect, but the emperor had told them they would recognize the correct response when they heard it.

When they came to Daito, saying, "Take this melon without using your hands," the beggar-monk immediately replied, "Give it to me without using your hands." The soldiers pounced and brought him to court, where the emperor received his instruction and had him establish Daitoku-ji, first as a modest monastery, and then in 1326 as an imperial temple.

On May 17, 1958, the thirteenth anniversary of Sokei-an's death, the Restored Ryosen-an was formally inaugurated as a matsu-ji, a subtemple of Daitoku-ji. In the same ceremony, Sokei-an was posthumously installed as the Founder of the Restored Ryosen-an, and Ruth Fuller Sasaki was ordained as jushoku, temple priest of Ryosen-an, and given the name Jokei.

Ryosen-an library, zendo, and grounds.
Courtesy of the estate of Ruth Fuller Sasaki.

A few weeks before this, the tedious process of registering the new temple with the prefectural government had been completed— it had taken months to prepare the many documents with their countless official seals. Then, in a simple, intimate ceremony, Ruth had taken *tokudo*, the formal "passing over" from secular life into religious life. She took monastic vows from Oda Sesso Kancho—normally the supplicant's head is shaved, but her case was considered exceptional.

She was led into the hondo, where she bowed and burned incense before the life-sized wood figure of Daio Kokushi, deep within the main shrine of the hondo. The carved figure sits, as he must have in his lifetime, full of power, with glass eyes glaring in the light of the candles, his real stick uplifted, ready to strike. To stand face-to-face with him in that shadowy place was startling. She felt a shiver. Ruth saw herself in this innermost place—and at the same time caught a fleeting glimpse of Sokei-an as a child, imagining himself a little mouse, sneaking into the innermost chamber of his father's Shinto shrine to see the god contained within. But this was not a trick. And not a god: she was face-to-face with the fierce teacher of generations upon generations of teachers—her teachers. She felt herself bathed in inexpressible generosity from her ancestors and gratitude toward them. She pressed her forehead to the ground.

The next several weeks were given over to preparations: the guest list, the gifts to be given, the food, what Ruth was to wear, each intricately choreographed detail of the ceremonies themselves—every detail was carefully recorded by the chief secretary of the Honzan in his handsome calligraphy, which became Ruth's guide-book for all of it. Her constant personal mentor through the maze was Kobori Sohaku, whose excellent English reinspired Ruth's gratitude to the late Beatrice Lane Suzuki, who had been Kobori-san's English teacher.

Before the invitations could be sent, Ruth had to visit each of the kanchos and roshis to personally invite them to the ceremony. In the same way, each of the written invitations had to be carefully addressed in accordance with the rank or relationship of the person invited. Later, the gifts had to be wrapped and inscribed according to the same protocols. Kobori-san, with a fine calligraphic hand, spent many days on this writing project alone.

Three days before the ceremonies, the rain began. It did not let up. The gardeners worked regardless, two of them draped outlandishly in white vinyl tablecloths of the sort used locally in restaurants. Just before midnight on May 16, the clouds let loose with another torrent—but when Ruth awoke at 4:00 a.m. on the seventeenth, the air was as cool and clear as crystal.

At five o'clock all the helpers arrived. They laid long stripes of matting on the black tiled floors of the zendo and the covered passageways connecting the buildings. The gardeners raked the gravel paths for the last time and watered the stone walks for the arriving guests. Over the front entrance they hung the big purple silk curtain-like *maku* bearing the crest of the Sasaki family in white—the original Ryosen-an crest had been forgotten, so this became the crest of the Restored Ryosen-an. Inside the front entrance, under the brocade cushions in the reception room, and on top of the *tans* on both sides of the zendo, they laid the red felt carpets always used on festive occasions. Near the entrance they placed shelves to hold getas and shoes of the guests, and in the little house near the front gate—normally used for parking bicycles and scooters—they set up tables for the two priests who would receive and record the gifts brought by the guests.

The lay and foreign guests began arriving at eight o'clock and were all in their places before nine. Exactly ten minutes before nine, the priests, who had first assembled at the Honzan, came in a procession according to their rank. For Goto Roshi a special seat of honor had been prepared close to the Manjushri altar. Oda Kancho took his place before this altar, the chief secretary stood by his side, and the Daitoku-ji priests stood in two lines along the *tans* facing the center of the zendo. Ruth stood directly in front of Goto Roshi, wearing her long plum-colored dress and a rakusa that Goto Roshi had presented to her.

*Ruth and priests assembled in the zendo for her ordination
ceremony. Courtesy of the estate of Ruth Fuller Sasaki.*

The service opened with the chief secretary announcing the
opening of Ryosen-an, stating the appreciation of Daitoku-ji for
Ruth's work, and welcoming her into the Daitoku-ji priesthood.

*Priests from all over Japan enter the Ryosen-an grounds
for the ordination of Ruth into the priesthood.
Courtesy of the estate of Ruth Fuller Sasaki.*

Then he presented her the koromo. She immediately left the
zendo, put the koromo over her dress, and returned to stand at the
bottom of the line of Daitoku-ji priests. Meanwhile, Oda Kancho
had burned incense before Manjushri and bowed formally three
times, kneeling and putting his forehead to the floor. The priests
chanted sutras, and at the conclusion the kancho read an *eko* to
Manjushri, which extolled the virtues of intrinsic wisdom and
offered a petition that the Buddhadharma might spread throughout the world, intrinsic wisdom be awakened in the adherents of
the new temple, and all beings attain salvation.

Then the kancho walked to the altar beneath the portrait of
the original founder of Ryosen-an. Early that morning a tray
of specially prepared food had been placed upon it, along with
bowls containing whipped green tea and hot water, as well as

fruit, cakes, and flowers. Similar offerings were placed at Manjushri's altar. Oda Kancho burned incense and bowed as before,
then lifted the tray of food and held it in the smoke of the incense,
as a purification. The assembled priests again chanted sutras, their
voices resounding in the zendo.

Thus concluded the first part of the ceremony. Everyone filed
out of the zendo in their respective order, again the priests through
the front entrance, the lay guests through the rear. They walked
the gardens, rested in the house, chatting or quietly appreciating
the day, and gradually drifted over to the Daitoku-ji Honzan.

At exactly ten o'clock, with everyone assembled in the main
hall, the second part of the ceremony began. The Daitoku-ji
priests were seated in the large area in front of the main altar;
the high-ranking clerical guests were to the east of it, and the lay
guests to the west. Directly in front of the altar to Daito Kokushi
was a small brocade-covered table; Oda Kancho stood behind it,
and Goto Roshi stood to the left with his attendant.

Ruth moved forward to the table, where Oda Kancho spoke a
few words of greeting and presented her with the kesa. She bowed
to him and to Goto Roshi, and walked out. In another room she
put on the kesa, then returned to sit in the lowest place in the ranks
of the Daitoku-ji priests, remaining there while they walked in an
intricate pattern before the main altar reciting sutras in memory of
Sokei-an, whose tablet stood in the center of the altar just under
the image of Shakyamuni Buddha. The kancho then read an eko
in homage to Sokei-an; he had already burned incense and bowed.
Afterward, Goto Roshi came forward and paid his respects to
Sokei-an's tablet. Ruth followed, and then all the clerical guests,
the Daitoku-ji priests, and the lay guests in turn.

While the others were paying their respects to Sokei-an, Ruth
went alone to the altar of the founder of Daitoku-ji, bowed three

times with forehead touching the ground, and entered the deep recess of the altar, where only disciples in Daito Kokushi's line may enter. As previously, she bowed and burned incense before the life-size figure seated in its depths.

When she emerged, all had taken their places for the meal. Monks and novices began bringing in the red lacquer table-trays with red lacquer dishes used in temple meals. The room was resplendent with its gold-painted screens and black-and-white sliding panels, its famous paintings high on the walls, and the priests sitting in their purple robes and gold brocaded rakusas, with the red lacquer trays on stands in front of them. Along the side stretched the age-darkened timbers of the deep veranda, and beyond, the white sand, rocks, and trees of the temple's famous gardens, with the misty blue outlines of the distant mountains beyond.

Still wearing the black koromo and heavy brown silk kesa, and carrying a rosary of coral and amber and a fan with red lacquer sticks, Ruth went to each of the three groups of guests in turn, accompanied by the leading priest of the Ryosen-an line and the priest of Hoshun-in. The Ryosen-an priest spoke for her, expressing her profound thanks for their attendance, while she knelt, her closed fan before her and her head on the tatami. The host of such a ceremony, as Ruth was that day, always bows thus before the guests, with someone else giving voice to such expressions of gratitude.

As always for such an event, the meal concluded with whipped tea and pink-and-white cakes. Gifts were then distributed. Finally, little white wooden boxes, wrapping paper, string, and white cotton *furoshikis* were handed around so the guests could wrap the extra food to take away with them—as usual, much more food had intentionally been served than could possibly be consumed.

By one o'clock, Ruth had shed her formal attire and was drinking plain tea with some of her fellow priests in the back room, commenting on the occasion.

When Ruth finally returned to Ryosen-an, she found the tokonoma in the reception room piled high with boxes, along with a carefully written list of the gifts and their donors.

Later in the afternoon, Kobori-san came over, and they began wrapping and inscribing the gifts that must be presented within two days: to her two teachers Goto Roshi and Oda Kancho, to the chief secretary, to the Daitoku-ji priests who had helped with the preparations, to the priests of the Ryosen-an line who had come down from Tokyo, to several other Daitoku-ji priests who had done some special service to Ruth, to the kanchos and roshis of the other Rinzai temples. Most of the gifts were money, but to the last group she gave a rare kind of incense used only by eminent priests.

The next morning, Ruth stood with Washino at the gate of the chief secretary's temple. He was out sweeping his garden. Ruth heard later that day that early the previous morning, before the ceremony, he and Oda Kancho had themselves swept the main walk between the Honzan and Ryosen-an. She considered that the greatest possible indication of their respect.

After breakfast on the nineteenth, the last of the Tokyo priests, who had been staying at Ryosen-an, said their farewells. By that evening, the formal calls had all been made and the final gifts all presented. Now it was time to get back to usual, everyday living—except for the callers that would continue coming and the endless stream of letters that must be answered. And with the Japanese press reporting on the event and an article in *Time* magazine, it seemed that the flow of curiosity seekers might never cease.

Ruth on her ordination into the priesthood.
The photo appeared in Time *magazine on May 26, 1958.*
Courtesy of the estate of Ruth Fuller Sasaki.

Her priestly duties were light: voting in elections at the Daitoku-ji Honzan, attending one ceremony a month, and being present at certain major religious occasions. Her koan study was nearing completion, and once the ceremonies quieted down, she continued going to Daishu-in five mornings a week for sanzen with Goto Roshi, on the *Mumonkan* koans.

In the fall of 1958, Ruth took a trip with Washino to Copenhagen, Zurich, Geneva, Paris, and London to take care of publication business, and then to the United States to see friends and family. She was always tired. At first she assumed it was simply aging and the demands of the previous year, but this fatigue was beyond the usual. She had no stamina to do what she needed to, even to get up. She visited her old doctor and found she had very low thyroid.

In Chicago she visited her granddaughter Joan, who now had a baby, Ruth's great-grandson—named David after her late brother—and then went on to Colorado Springs to spend the holidays with Eleanor and family. Afterward she went back to New York, where she had rented a small apartment at the Gramercy Park Hotel—the institute was taking over her other apartment—to dispose of everything she had stored in a warehouse. She spent weeks sorting and sending items to Eleanor, Anne, and Joan.

It had all taken too long. She had been away too long. She was exhausted. When she and Washino arrived back in Kyoto after six months away, all the household and all the library staff stood outside to greet them. She felt some trepidation as she walked through the first gate. There was the gnarled old pine just as she had left it—looking more vigorous if anything. The camellia near the stone lantern had held on to a mass of its vivid coral blossoms to greet her.

At the front entrance to the house they took off their shoes. Ruth's feet forgot to slip into the felt slippers, partly in her eagerness to see the house again, partly because they had lost the habit. In the hall were the long, low bookshelves with their rows of blue-boxed sutras. In the dining room tokonoma hung Goto Roshi's "Dreams" that Ruth especially loved; in that same room's shrine, which sheltered an antique Korean Buddha that Goto had given her years ago, were flowers and tea and incense—as usual. The two cats came meandering in.

Ruth's room was just as she had left it. Flowers on the desk and Eleanor's picture under them. Her books all in order in the case to the right, her typewriter on the low table to the left with a new ribbon in it. In the tokonoma, the great map of China showing the sites of Zen temples in the Tang and Song eras, and flowers again; on the raised *biwadana* shelf, Sokei-an's photograph with fresh incense before it. On the south veranda her canary was singing.

Then to the kitchen, spotless as always and bustling. Green branches and tea as usual in the tiny shrine to the kitchen god and in the shrines of those spirits who preside over the face-washing room and the toilet as well.

Now she must quickly wash her hands and go to the *ozashiki* reception room, from which she had thus far been carefully excluded. There a big table had been set. In the center, lying on a bed of red camellias, was a huge boiled *tai*—a kind of red snapper, symbol of congratulation at all Japanese feasts—and around it all sorts of other good things to eat and drink. All the Ryosen-an family had assembled, including Gary, who had himself returned just the week before from America. It was only much later that the merrymaking subsided and all the guests but Walter said good-night. Then he and Ruth and Washino sat down for all the gossip about everything that had taken place during their absence, both in Japan and in America.

Far too soon the bath was ready. In a Japanese household one is never excused from the daily evening bath, and soon after dinner the master of the household is made clearly aware that the bath is waiting—for the master must bathe first, then each member of the household successively according to his or her order of prece-dence. Ruth, being head of the household, was therefore expected for the first bath. This night, in honor of her return, the water had been made unusually hot. Not only was the water scalding, the iron tub itself was still red hot. As she got into the tub for the customary soaking after scrubbing and rinsing, the water was so hot she could not tell whether it was burning hot or freezing cold. Where could she sit so that her skin was not against iron? She was soon out, looking like a boiled shrimp, and into the cold face-washing—no heated bathrooms in Japanese houses.

Her bed was ready—a thin futon spread on the mat-covered

floor, with thick quilts filled with the floss from the cocoons of wild silkworms, lighter and warmer even than goose down. Inside reposed her favorite companion, the Japanese metal hot water bottle—it warms one's bed all night in winter and keeps the sheets dry during the spring and summer damp. Again everything was as usual. The reading lantern by her side, the book she would read for a few minutes, her glasses. When she was settled among the bolsters in her warm padded coat—it was the end of March, still quite cold—her little family, headed by Washino-san, came in to bow and say goodnight as they always did. Everything was just as usual. But in the morning, not quite the same. Her bones ached. The fancy box springs and mattresses of America had temporarily spoiled her, and the chairs as well.

After breakfast and a quick look at the garden to ascertain that the weeping cherry had not yet come into bloom and that the goldfish in the pool were fat and healthy after the winter, Washino-san and Ruth were knocking at the gate of Daishu-in to bring their greetings to Goto Roshi. Later in the day, wearing her robe and kesa, Ruth went to the Honzan to burn incense before the founder of Daitoku-ji. The following morning she bowed before the image of Daio Kokushi at the monastery and paid her respects to Oda Kansho. Next, she went to her neighboring temple of Hoshun-in to burn incense before the statue of the original founder of Ryosen-an, kept in the pagoda of Hoshun-in until they might have their own Founder's Hall. Then again to the Honzan to call on the chief secretary. Only after these official calls had been completed could Ruth settle down to the routine of daily life.

TRANSLATIONS
Kyoto, 1958–1967

Translation is never simply a matter of one-to-one relationships, any more than anything else is. What is the purpose of translation? It is this: to somehow carry a particular experience directly from one mind to another. But where is the cart that can truly deliver such precarious goods? To carry a thought, an idea, a teaching, from one mind to another is an intricate undertaking. Every misunderstanding compounds misunderstanding. How, then, is it possible to bring forth understanding?

"The Way that can be spoken is not the true Way. And yet speaking is necessary. Saying is not blowing breath. Saying says something."

Sokei-an taught by *becoming* the experience and conveying it through his illuminated presence. Dharmakaya, the absolute state. It cannot be captured in a text. And yet—with the person absent, there must be a way. Not to capture it or contain it, but to produce it again. The known means for effectively producing it have been encoded in the process of Zen training and transmission for a thousand generations. It may not be the only available means, but as it has been developed and preserved, it would be a great loss to the world if it were abandoned. In any case, the words, the texts, are such an integral part of the practice—the signpost of understanding—they must be made available.

Ruth said, "I want a peaceful stretch of time in which to write and translate. With the zendo complete, there is nothing of any consequence more to do here."

The literary work was completely absorbing. Not the same sort of absorption as meditation, which could reach unfathomable depths. But a fully satisfying absorption nonetheless. It took her completely outside of herself. It demanded a different sort of effort. Time passed effortlessly—and eventually the project would be finished. Yes, there was an explicit goal for the literary efforts. That was a difference. And people working together toward the same goal, which was not always smooth, but so far had been fruitful.

Meditation might have a goal of sorts—the Four Vows were explicit aspirations at least. An ultimate goal: I vow to enlighten all beings. But it was completely immaterial. In meditation, a momentary goal—beyond the ever-present aspiration to improve in effort and concentration—typically amounts to delusion, and typically in layers concealing further layers of delusion. Shed all delusions—what is left? The willful urge to experience will hinder your ability to experience. You must somehow go beyond willfulness, without giving up effort.

The goal of meditation—in any case sitting in the zendo was wonderful—the big quiet room, the dim light, the faint smell of coarse incense, the cold fresh air, the sounds of the night coming from a distance. Passing voices, the throb of the Nichiren drum, the notes of a flute, the Chinese noodle man's whistle—all seep in, all absorb any sense of a separate self.

Ryosen-an zendo. Courtesy of the estate of Ruth Fuller Sasaki.

She was working, still, on *Zen Dust*, based on Miura Roshi's talks at the First Zen Institute in New York in 1955. The main text was ready. But there were more notes, which were necessary, and had to be correct, and had to include the Chinese as well as the Japanese of course, and then it made sense to include the context, the biographical and historical details about the masters whose words were being referenced—that was important. And as she worked on it she was completing her own koan study, which, in the later stages, relied heavily on jakugo—the capping phrases that indicated understanding beyond merely answering correctly, reflecting the correct mind-state of the student. For her personal practice Ruth had already translated the five thousand jakugo verses compiled in the *Zenrin-kushu*. Miura Roshi agreed that a selection of these should be included in the book that would become *Zen Dust* and chose two hundred from her translations.

Alongside this project was a dictionary of Zen Buddhist terms.

There simply was nothing useful in existence, so they had to make
their own. There were four sets of index cards—Chinese characters, Chinese and Japanese roman-letter transliterations, Sanskrit,
and English. There were more than three thousand cards in each
set, starting with the work Sokei-an had begun on the *Record of
Rinzai*, which they had been working on in those uneasy weeks in
Arkansas, and before and since in New York, and now without
Sokei-an. As soon as she returned from the United States in the
early spring of 1959, Ruth organized a group to study the Chinese text alongside Sokei-an's English translation. They had been
meeting for four hours once a week, with Iriya as director, and
Yanagida, Burton Watson, Phil Yampolsky, Gary Snyder, Walter
Nowick, and Ruth. Now the other members of the group were
focusing on that text, as Ruth completed her work on *Zen Dust*.

The translation group at work in the Ryosen-an library.
Courtesy of the estate of Ruth Fuller Sasaki.

Ruth was aware that her employees at times considered her attitude excessively demanding—she was accused of being autocratic. But she knew that only with strong discipline would it be possible to complete this immense task, and cutting corners would only diminish the value of their efforts. It was true that these scholars—and they were brilliant, all of them, perhaps none more so than Professor Iriya, whose vast and deep knowledge of the Tang and Song colloquial language was unparalleled—knew the Chinese better than she ever would. And the younger professor, Yanagida Seizan—who had spent time during the war at Tokai-an, the Myoshin-ji subtemple where Goto Zuigan Roshi was priest at the time, and did koan study with him—was a master of Chinese Zen history and bibliography. Under the auspices of the First Zen Institute, with Walter's help he was compiling an index of the names of all the priests mentioned in the major Chinese collections of Zen biographies, amounting to around five thousand persons and several thousand more entries—many of those included were known and referred to by multiple names.

But Ruth's knowledge was sufficient to use the material in her koan training, which was something she had that none of the others did. Yampolsky took sanzen but had only just entered it, Yanagida's koan study had been a matter of scholarly interest and proximity to an esteemed teacher, and Watson's interest in Zen was purely intellectual. She was in a position to identify where a koan could not be rephrased for presumed clarity, if that would eliminate a crucial key to its solution. Goto Roshi remained the final authority in these matters.

To adequately translate these works, beyond a basic knowledge of Buddhism and of Chinese Buddhist literature outside of Zen, direct knowledge of Zen from within was necessary—not merely a literary, bibliographic, historical knowledge, though that of course was also essential—but knowledge based in the actual practice. Direct knowledge.

And since Zen texts are written as much in the colloquial language of the period as they are in Classical Chinese, knowledge of those idioms is indispensable. And of course a thorough knowledge of English—how could any sense be accurately conveyed if the translator is not an absolute master of the destination language?

To find all these talents embodied in one person would be a virtual impossibility. So Ruth gathered her interdisciplinary team, with people who possessed the needed specialized knowledge, who might contribute their particular abilities toward a joint translation.

The process worked, mostly, though not without contention.

Miura Isshu Roshi changed his mind again. He decided that he would go to the United States after all to be the teacher for the First Zen Institute. Perhaps he had simply needed more time to wrap things up in Japan. In February 1959 he went to New York.

Ruth had nearly completed her koan study and been ordained as a temple priest. But she did not want to become a roshi or a Japanese citizen. She never shaved her head, never relinquished her pearl earrings. She wore the garments of a Rinzai priest according to the occasion. But she remained American in her heart and mind, had no interest in giving that up—in fact, it would have been contrary to her purpose, would have aroused suspicions of mere self-interest rather than supporting her true program of delivering the gift of genuine Rinzai Zen Buddhism to Americans, as an American.

Her friend Lindley Hubbell became Japanese. He loved Japan

and all things Japanese. It suited his theatrical nature. From the start he adopted Japanese customs and quickly became a master of the language. In 1960 he took the oath to become a Japanese citizen, adopting the Japanese name Hayashi Shuseki, "Autumn Stone in the Woods." From the time he first came to Japan, for the rest of his life, he never left.

She loved Lindley, but he was consumed with an all-encompassing, passionate romanticism, which she considered an obstacle to real understanding. She did not consider him a model for younger Americans. In her own efforts toward the many Western students who were arriving in Kyoto, she focused rather on dispelling any romantic notions. She especially did not want to waste her time with the casually curious—particularly those inspired by the outrageously sloppy and misinformed portrayal of Zen in Jack Kerouac's *Dharma Bums*, which had come out in 1958 and had quickly become popular among a crowd of young and undisciplined boys who imagined that Zen was easy, there was nothing to it.

Maybe the author of that rubbish had heard something about Buddhism from his friend Gary Snyder—whose understanding was as accurate as any American's of his generation—but the Buddhism Kerouac presented was, as she told Snyder, the most garbled and mistaken she had read in many a day: "I expect you to consider these the words of a square old woman, but when you have lived as long as I you will see that present day 'Dharma bums' are just the same type of boys that appear in every generation, each time with a new name and a new line, but intrinsically just the same 'bums.'"

There were too many people coming who wanted to study. Enough of them were serious and deserved a decent place to stay. She could

not house them at Ryosen-an, and her friend Ogata-san only had
room at Chotoku-in for one or two at any given time. Ruth asked
for and received permission to remodel and refurbish a Daitoku-ji
dormitory building called Zuiun-ken (House of the Auspicious
Cloud), which could house up to six students at a time.

Walter Nowick was becoming distant. He could be prickly—he
had somewhat outgrown his youthful enthusiasm, though never
his seriousness, about Zen practice. His musical career had taken
off, both as a performer and as a teacher. He was traveling around
giving performances, coaching and conducting choral groups and
soloists as well as teaching piano and vocal students around the
country. He was often away. When he was in Kyoto, he would
lead zazen at the Ryosen-an zendo. Until he resigned.

In December 1959, he told Ruth he would be stepping down
as vice president of the First Zen Institute of America in Japan. In
fact, he was resigning from the institute altogether. He needed to
devote himself entirely to his own Zen training with Goto Roshi.
Ruth accepted his resignation, and his explanation, though not
without a noticeable chill.

The real blow came when Goto Roshi severed relations with her.
She was not expecting this. Why? Had she offended him? She
could not imagine. Her sanzen had slowed down, but that was
no reason to cut her off. She was more and more focused on
the translation projects, but that had been her clear purpose here
from the beginning. More students were coming, and she had set
up Zuiun-ken, and he and Oda Roshi had given permission to go
ahead with that. What happened? She was devastated.

Goto had summoned Walter, Phil Yampolsky, and Gary Snyder
to offer an explanation of sorts. He needed to relieve himself of all

responsibilities apart from his teaching. He was resigning from the board of the First Zen Institute.

Perhaps Goto felt she had overstepped. Originally he had wanted Ruth to return to America and Europe as some sort of Zen missionary. She had resisted. She did not feel suited to that sort of work. Perhaps he took this as insubordination. But she never overstepped in any way visible to herself, whether in the translation work or in her personal relations. Unless there was someone who was displeased with her authority and working to undermine her. Walter? She had trusted him implicitly. Now he had removed himself from Ryosen-an and the institute and was constantly at Goto Roshi's side. Could it be?

The sanzen relationship was unique and irreplaceable. Finding the right teacher was not unique in the sense of a marriage, where there are two people only—although lord knows a marriage could lack intimacy, or could become a war zone or a prison. But the sanzen relationship was a deep form of intimacy. Deeper than practically any sort of intimacy between lovers—though with Sokei-an of course it was that as well, which one might suppose would complicate the sanzen but in fact did not, was intertwined and inextricable but completely apart as well, a complete world unto itself.

There are multiple doorways into the deepest self. It is possible for a teacher to have many students, but for each student a true teacher presents the face that this particular student needs to see. Was this the face she needed to see? Sokei-an broke through her defenses, her rigidity, in ways no one else had or could. Goto Roshi—by the time she went to him, she had already softened in so many ways, though not everyone saw that. By the time she went to Goto she had honed herself, had become her truest self.

No, that was not quite right either—she had always been her true self, that was never the difficulty, although every step forward made the truth truer. The self is largely fictional. She had demonstrated her awareness of that fact. She had deepened her understanding of the preciousness and precariousness of a moment. Life was never certain. Impermanence permeates everything. And now this. Well, he was still living. But she could not reach him.

When Sokei-an and Goto Zuigan referred to each other as Dharma brothers, this was not a fiction. They had both experienced the intimacy with their teacher as a father with his sons. And they expressed their own versions of this intimacy toward their students. The intimacy of sanzen was different than any other relationship. It was completely different. It was absolutely precious. Now it was gone. Where did it go? She could not grasp it.

Even after so many years of practice, there were times when the sting of rejection was not secondary—when it was the very basis of the confrontation with delusion. Sokatsu throwing Sokei-an's statue out the window. She got that—intellectually, which was where she had always turned for refuge. But this, Goto, her dear teacher? She had been making progress. Was he being seduced by rumors? She knew they talked among themselves, behind her back, the Americans in her library. They were being sloppy with their work; they accused her of being too rigid. That's not exactly how they put it, not directly to her face. But the work had to be done right! There was simply no use doing it incompletely—and allowing errors to enter the translations. That would be worse than abandoning the project entirely.

But why would Goto Roshi be influenced by such talk? Sanzen must be completely separate. It should not be at all subject to rumors or politics. Of course, within sanzen Goto had never strayed from its pure purpose. But now he had cut her off, with no explanation.

Once she had slightly recovered from the shock, she went to visit her friend Koun-an Eizan Roshi at Ningenzen in Chiba. Sokatsu had cut him off and formally disbanded Ryomo-an. Why? This was the koan Eizan's teacher left him with, Eizan had said to her. This rejection. Just as Sokatsu had rejected Goto and Sokei-an.

At a certain point, if a teacher rejects every last one of his successors, after they have already proven themselves independently, he subverts his own legitimacy. Insight has been verified and certified, the transmission has been transmitted—can it really be revoked?

Ruth was not a roshi, would not become a roshi. But she was still capable of carrying the teaching forward. She could not grasp a value in this rejection. How could it be a purposeful teaching? Perhaps that was her insurmountable barrier, which she needed to get beyond.

Ruth visited Lindley Hubbell. He had a gift for lightening her mood. But ultimately he could not grasp the cause of her misery— he had no direct personal experience of the depth of a true teacher-disciple relationship. He could not penetrate her loneliness.

She continued sending gifts to Goto at the expected occasions, not knowing if he would ever acknowledge them—or her—again. After sinking for a few weeks into dark and dismal depths such as she had rarely experienced, she emerged—sad, mourning, perhaps with less vigor than before, but still with purpose. There was work to be done.

Toward the end of 1959 Gary Snyder returned after some months away, followed in late February 1960 by his girlfriend Joanne

Kyger. He had met or known her in San Francisco and invited her to come to Japan to live with him. Of course they would have to be married if they were to be together under the auspices of Ryosen-an and the First Zen Institute. Ruth and Gary talked to Oda Roshi, and he agreed to conduct a simple wedding ceremony—something of an innovation, as Japanese weddings are traditionally the jurisdiction of Shinto priests, while Buddhists are responsible for funerals. But it could be done, and it was, the day after Joanne arrived from the two-week ocean crossing and train from Yokohama.

Joanne was young and pretty, and she reminded Ruth somewhat of her own granddaughter Joan—spirited and adventurous, willing to take a chance on a new opportunity. Whether she was well-prepared for it was another matter. She had done some zazen, but not so much that she knew what she was doing. It was not clear that she knew what she wanted to be doing, and it took a while for her to settle in and simply get used to being there.

Meanwhile Gary was sitting as solidly as ever, leaving every morning at five thirty for sanzen, out all day teaching English or working in the library, and sitting with the Ryosen-an group at the zendo every evening—and then staying at the sodo and up all night for the osesshin weeks. That couldn't have made it any easier for a displaced American with no Japanese, at least at first when she didn't know anybody. Ruth had them over for dinner every week or two at first. At least having familiar American food on occasion would help ease the transition, even if otherwise Joanne had a hard time feeling comfortable around their host.

After a three-day fishing and diving trip to some small islands off the coast west of Kobe, Gary and Joanne returned to find Ruth by the Ryosen-an gate with a letter in her hand, crying. Phil was comforting her. They learned that her good friend Dr. George Kennedy, a Yale professor of Chinese who had just left Kyoto—after several months in which he had conducted an inspired weekly seminar with Ruth, Phil, Gary, and Iriya, and worked with Ruth on translating the *Sayings of Layman P'ang*—had died on the ship home, of a heart attack.

Visitors and letters arrived daily, requiring more and more of Ruth's attention. She had a secretary helping with correspondence, but visitors required her personal attention. It was always a challenge for Ruth to be patient with people who were not there to study Zen.

> The majority of them are faddists or just curious, and Zen is not for them. In the Western world Zen seems to be going through the cult phase. Zen is not a cult. The problem with Western people is that they want something easy. Zen is a lifetime work of self-discipline and study. Its practice destroys the individual self. The ego is, as it were, dissolved into a great ego—so great that you take your place in it as each cell in your body takes its place or performs as it is called upon to do. The result is oneness with nature and the universe.

Alan Watts seemed to be the source of a good deal of this misinformation. "We have so much to do to straighten out people who have read his books or heard him lecture on Zen. His presentation is so glib and so enticing that they are sure we are the ones here who don't know what Zen is. Why he remains such a glamour boy I can't imagine. But he certainly does."

Ruth decided that, in the current climate of confusion about what exactly is Zen anyway, it would be useful to present the material from some of the talks she had given and from her letters published in *Zen Notes* as small books or pamphlets, for the purpose of clarifying Japanese Rinzai Zen as concisely and directly as possible. The first of these were offered as a boxed set of three small books, elegantly printed and bound: *Zen: A Religion*; *Zen: A Method for Religious Awakening*; and *Rinzai Zen Study for Foreigners in Japan*.

The pamphlet *The First Zen Institute of America in Japan* described the purpose of the work of Ryosen-an, including the library and the zendo, with sixteen pages of photographs. It also listed the enormous holdings of the library, which included English copies of works still in manuscript. The two final pamphlets were *Ryosen-an Zendo Practice*, which outlined the rules and customs of Ryosen-an, and *Wooden Fish*, an introduction to sutra chanting with a number of sutras in roman-character Japanese and English translations, compiled by Gary Snyder with Gutetsu Kanetsuki.

The members of the library team argued against taking more time out from their major projects to produce these practical manuals. But they were a great success and had somewhat of the desired effect. Gradually, the wave of curiosity seekers and faddists seemed to subside, and those who came were prepared to stay at least the requested two-month minimum.

In the spring of 1961 the Americans in the *Rinzai Roku* study group—Phil Yampolsky, Burton Watson, and Gary Snyder—confronted Ruth's seeming lack of progress on the *Zen Dust* footnotes and suggested she was not equal to the task. They needed her input on the *Rinzai*—when would she be available? She told them, in that case, she would put *Zen Dust* aside and immediately devote herself to working with them on the *Rinzai*.

Phil had become difficult, at times outright defiant: he refused to transliterate the Chinese and Japanese text of the *Rinzai Roku* into roman characters, on the grounds that he thought it should not go in the book; he was supposed to prepare a bibliography for the *Rinzai* along with Yanagida and had done nothing for it. Yanagida had written the introduction and footnotes, and now Watson was supposedly translating it. Ruth, with her full attention now on this project, checked the beginning of the translation against Yanagida's Japanese original, which she could read with effort, and found the versions did not agree. Watson acknowledged that Yanagida's Japanese was difficult to translate and consented to rework it. But the second version was not much better. By now, June 1961, he was upset that Ruth had called him on his sloppiness—and Phil was furious that Ruth would question his friend's ability.

Around this time, Yanagida came to Ruth, saying he was very worried—he had been looking at the translation of the later part of the introduction and the footnotes, in spite of his limited English, and found that the translation was strange. Equally troubling, it seemed that the footnote material had been only partially translated. Apparently Watson had left out whatever he thought was too much trouble.

In the middle of July, Yanagida again came to Ruth, greatly distressed, to share something Phil had said to him: Phil was intimating that Ruth should get out of the way and leave the scholarly work to the scholars, that she wasn't qualified—and if she wouldn't get out of the way, then he was prepared to produce his own version of the book. Had he possibly already begun to do this? Ruth was livid.

The next morning Ruth contacted two board members, a law-yer and a businessman, and asked them to be present when she questioned Phil in front of the entire staff. When confronted, he acknowledged the gist of the statements. She asked about his notes. Where were they? What did they include? "Have you already begun to prepare this alternate version?"

He said he had been thinking about doing it but had not begun to. He went and got his notes and gave them to her, along with an explanation. Somewhat deflated—she more or less expected he had already begun what he had threatened—she apologized. But she could not abide by his threats and insults and intransigence. It was too much. She was hereby dismissing him. He would have full pay through the rest of the year, but he was no longer welcome to work here.

Burton Watson, who would be leaving for America in two weeks in any case, immediately resigned in protest. Gary Snyder, though not deeply involved in the project, resigned in solidarity with his friends. Over the next week, Ruth had several confer-ences with Yanagida and Iriya and the board members. Ruth was firm in her decision to dismiss Phil, who genuinely wanted to stay. Snyder and Watson tried to persuade her to rethink her position: it was a misunderstanding—unfortunate, but not malicious. She refused. Emotionally bruised, she felt it would not be possible to continue working with him.

It was all connected. This had been building for a while—she had been slow to recognize it at first, in her overlong absence in America the previous winter, in the sadness about losing her teacher. But gradually it became clear. It had started with Walter's resignation—perhaps before, as far as he was concerned, though at the time she made little of the possibility that the bad feelings might spread like a fungus, like the lung infections that plagued her every winter.

Previously the feeling in the group had been cordial—even more than cordial: inspired, excited, devoted, dedicated, respectful. Ruth had known Phil Yampolsky for eight years and had worked closely with him much of that time. She had trusted him implicitly. If at times he had bristled at her demands, it was within an agreeable atmosphere of shared endeavor. Until Walter turned away and, apparently, pulled Phil into his designs.

There were rumors. Ruth heard stories—maybe they were true—that Walter was conspiring to replace her. He had worked his way fully into the confidence of Goto Roshi, who had then cut Ruth off. The plan, apparently, was to have Ruth retire from Ryosen-an and appoint Walter as its priest instead. And she should retire from her library work as well, leaving Phil in charge of the projects. She was getting too old, was incompetent.

In truth, though she was physically weakened by her thyroid problem and recurrent bronchitis, the real issue was the emotional trauma of Goto's rejection. It was true, in the weeks following that blow, she had been a complete wreck and, she could admit, difficult to work with. But she was never incapacitated. And once the initial wound had begun to scab and scar over, she was as capable, as completely qualified, as ever. The work still needed doing, and it was hers to do.

Along with his formal resignation from the institute, Gary wrote a friendly letter to Ruth thanking her for all her kindnesses and support, and for the support of the institute. He and Joanne were planning to go to India soon anyway, so his departure was only a couple of months early. Ruth considered his decision quixotic, but she understood his loyalty to his friends. After India she would invite him over again, and they would remain friends.

For Gary's part, of course her support had been immense and invaluable. On a day-to-day basis, he had found her challenging to work for, but she was good company after hours, in the wide-ranging dinner conversations with luminaries—religious figures, government ministers, artists, scholars—from all points west and east.

Since Joanne had been here, there was less of this—they had a busy social life with friends of their own generation, and Joanne never felt fully at ease around Sasaki-san. Too many rigid Victorian assumptions, too much judgment. If you weren't already confirmed in your devotion to zazen and disciplined in your practice, she treated you as a lesser being. True, she had occasionally shown Joanne a genuine concern, even a sweet tenderness. Sometimes she seemed so sad and lonely. But then she would clamp up again, resorting to joyless formality. And her self-pride could be grating.

The Japanese members of the group had been too reverent of the impressive credentials of the Americans, with their Columbia degrees. Iriya did not feel it was his place to do more than a cursory check of their work, to make sure it was generally on track— and in any case he only had one day a week to work with the group. Yanagida had not felt not confident enough in his English to expect he could identify errors.

Ruth, on the brink of nervous collapse, was relieved that the vacation month was beginning and she would have a chance to recuperate and restore her energy.

By the end of the year her enthusiasm and hopefulness had gradually returned, so that she was feeling like her old self again. "But at my age it takes time, perhaps more than I shall ever live to have to recover fully," she wrote to Mary Farkas.

Ruth learned from Sokei-an's daughter Shihoko—still a Christian minister, now living in Wakayama Prefecture not far south of Kyoto with her husband and two children—that her mother Tome Sasaki, the first Mrs. Sasaki, had been killed in an automobile accident.

In March 1962 Ruth had to make an unanticipated trip to New York to take care of some serious dental work. For the first time she was able to make the trip by jet plane from Tokyo to San Francisco—still with a layover in Honolulu, but with hardly more than ten hours in the air total. In San Francisco she saw her younger granddaughter, Anne, and met Anne's fiancé, Joel. She flew to Colorado Springs to see Eleanor and family, and then to Chicago en route to Indianapolis where she visited Joan, who now had two children—David, who had just turned three, and Elizabeth, now nearly two, meeting her great-grandmother for the first time. She felt a special attachment to these two because of the year Joan had spent with Ruth in Kyoto, where she had met and married her husband.

The First Zen Institute of America had moved into new quarters, an old four-story brownstone with a small garden at the rear, at 113 East Thirtieth Street, just east of Park Avenue.

There were difficulties with Miura Roshi. He was an intensely private person, not given to interacting with strangers or to excessive demands being made of him. Any demand beyond sanzen for his students, zazen for the Zazenkai (Meditation Society) in the meditation hall four nights a week, a teisho on a *Mumonkan* koan for this group once a month, and leading the sutra-chanting service for the Wednesday meetings in the institute shrine room was excessive. He did not give talks at the public meetings. He did not want to come to the telephone to talk directly with anyone he did not know—Japanese or American. He did not like to meet with anyone individually that he did not know well. The institute was getting a reputation for being unwelcoming. The gregarious ferment of Sokei-an's day was a hazy memory to those who had sat with him. This current teacher—he seemed not fully comfortable in his position.

That summer back in Japan was oppressively hot. The completion of work on *Zen Dust* was finally in sight. So she imagined.

The zendo group had matured—the group of students was serious and committed, most of them there for at least a year. Since Walter's resignation, Kobori Sohaku had been serving as *jikijitsu*, the head monk in charge of zazen. The atmosphere was just right. One evening a week, Ruth would give a one-hour talk; Kobori-san also gave a talk once a week.

In the fall of 1962 Eleanor came to Kyoto with Carlton and their fourteen-year-old son, Michael. It was Carlton's and Michael's first trip to Japan. Both had been preparing by studying Japanese for months.

On Ruth's seventieth birthday, October 31, Ruth's granddaughter Anne—who had married her fiancé the previous spring—gave birth to a baby girl. Ruth was pleased with the timing.

She was looking forward to finishing her book projects. "I am writing steadily with the printer at my heels and hope in the next month or two to finally finish *Zen Dust*. This started out to be a book of about 125 pages, but has now grown to be some 325 pages, if not more. Every day is full of interest, and except that I get tired by evening, I feel as young and my head seems as good as it ever was. How grateful I am!" By the time it was finally completed, however, the book was nearly six hundred pages.

In 1963 Ruth fell and broke her left arm, impairing her ability to sit at the typewriter. But her spirits continued to be strong. Some of the people in her life who had been involved in her difficulties were making gestures of friendship and reconciliation. Walter Nowick sent regards to her through Gary Snyder. Gary and Joanne came to dinner for the first time since Gary's resignation and their travels in India and Southeast Asia, and they spent an amiable evening describing their experiences. And for the first time in nearly five years, Ruth began to imagine that whatever had caused Goto Roshi to reject her might be repairable.

A few weeks later Gary and Joanne came for dinner again, bringing their friend Allen Ginsberg, who had been with them in India and was staying with them at their rustic hermitage on Mount Hiei. Gary had given Ruth a copy of *Howl*, which she had read; they spent almost the entire evening discussing it.

Poetry and Zen had been intertwined from the beginning—the immensely poetic Tang and Song material the library group had been working with could be mistaken for poetry—though Ruth was always careful to maintain that neither quite depended on the other.

Ginsberg was enthusiastic—by Ruth's reckoning, in a slightly misplaced way—about religious awakening, with no apparent taste or aptitude for the rigors of Zen. He wanted to shake up the world with ecstatic poetry. Perhaps if he could learn to settle his mind. In India it seemed his purpose had been *bhakti* yoga, to lose himself in blissful devotion to some swami who chants mantras of love. Whether he found such a swami was not entirely apparent. But he spoke more favorably of India than Gary or Joanne did. He felt he could truly be himself there.

Miura Roshi resigned from the institute in 1963. He moved to an apartment on West Seventy-Second Street and continued to see some individual students privately—those he had formed positive relationships with and whose progress he felt he could still support. Both Mary and Ruth were puzzled—why would he stay in New York and yet remove himself from the institute?

But he had been trained entirely in traditional Japanese temples and monasteries, which were always run by men, and he was never comfortable serving in an organization run by a woman. As a roshi, he must be in charge of his teaching and not be subject to the management of a director—who was his student. He needed to be independent. He remained in New York because his students were in New York.

When Alan Watts came to Kyoto with a tour group he was leading, he stopped by first on his own to visit with Ruth:

> If I hadn't expected him, or if I had passed him on the street, I should hardly have recognized him. It is a long time since I last saw him, before Joan's marriage. So I was not prepared for the middle-aged man with a plumpish stomach and rounded jowls and the tired or dissipated eyes. A rather mixed group of middle-aged or older people came along, fifteen of them, with one or two younger people among them. He introduced them as Mr. So-and-so, Mrs. So-and-so, Miss So-and-so, Mary Jane Watts, Dr. So-and-so. I

had heard that he married the person with whom he had been traveling around for some years. But since he said of her only what I have mentioned, I said nothing more. She merged into the group, and only once or twice asked a simple question. She is certainly an unprepossessing person, strong and rather tough, I should say.

They all went to see the library and the meditation hall, where one of the students gave them a long talk on the practices here. I did not enter into this. Then they came back and we had tea and they asked questions about Japanese life and houses, and then they went off. The word "Zen" wasn't mentioned in my presence. The next day Alan sent me some beautiful roses and birthday greetings. Everything went pleasantly and easily, just as if we had never had any personal relations. No one in the family was mentioned.

I understand that Alan is going decidedly "Square" where Zen is concerned. He is stressing the hard practice which Mr. Sasaki gave him! as one of his major qualifications for being a Zen man. But, poor thing, it must be hard to have to earn your living by your wits and your tongue.

As inexplicably as Goto Zuigan Roshi had broken off relations with Ruth, he restored her to his favor. She had never ceased sending gifts for the New Year and his birthday; at the beginning of 1964, he sent her a card thanking her for the New Year's gift, as if there had been no gap. He invited her to return to sanzen. She felt like a gaping hole in her life had been repaired.

Word reached Ruth of activities in San Francisco. Shunryu Suzuki had been there since 1959, and the Soto Zen group he had established was active and expanding. There were individuals who had been interested in Rinzai practice, including some who had visited Kyoto, but found it too arduous, hierarchical, dependent on Japanese—not what they expected. She saw Alan's hand in these expectations. Perhaps with this mild and sweet-tempered teacher they were finding something more to their liking. Soto, the "silent illumination" school, was all about simplicity. The practice in San Francisco was simply zazen.

Perhaps this would be more in step with the prevailing climate; it was, after all, the more popular form in Japan as well, where Rinzai practice was considered too arduous for regular humans. That was all fine as far as it went—Ruth had no interest in popularizing Rinzai Zen, which had always been for the few. Attempts to popularize would erode it beyond recognition. Her mission, as ever, was to see that it continued in its fullest expression.

But there were other matters that concerned her. Watts had at some point been introduced to LSD, and he apparently felt favorably about its potential as a shortcut to religious awakening. There were reports of students at the San Francisco Zen Center coming to sit zazen high on LSD. Ruth was appalled. There were no shortcuts.

In the fall of 1964, Ruth contemplated moving back to the United States. The Japanese climate and style of house was bad for her rheumatism, which in the cold, damp weather became severe to the point of nearly incapacitating her. *What is sickness? What is health?*

A lifetime of meditation had cultivated a somewhat detached perspective on comfort and discomfort—after all, what was Rinzai

Zen training if not an extended journey through realms of intense challenge, both physical and mental? Not exactly indifference—it was not as if you no longer felt something. But after feeling something intensely and being bothered by it and enduring it, and then feeling it but not being bothered by it, and then merely noting the feeling as sensation, the pain does diminish. It becomes completely nonpersonal. With no person experiencing the pain as suffering, it becomes merely sensation. Heat or cold, noise or quietude—you are aware of them but they make no difference. You welcome them as opportunities to test your progress. Not that they should be sought out and made the usual conditions to endure—and certainly in the beginning they pose unnecessary difficulties. But the experienced practitioner of zazen makes use of them, as she does of every situation that presents itself—the long hours of practice and few hours of sleep during sesshins, the cold of Rohatsu and the heat of the late-July sesshin—opportunities and privileges, not arbitrary hardship or callous severity.

Ruth was seeing the limits of what her health and age would allow her to do. She decided to give up her lease of Zuiun-ken, the dormitory, and gave notice that it would be closing. She also decided to limit the schedule of the zendo and not accept any new students. With *Zen Dust* finally, at last, reaching completion, the library team had returned to the *Rinzai Roku*, and Ruth to *Ho Koji Goroku: The Recorded Sayings of Layman P'ang* as well. She thought it would take another year or two to complete the *Rinzai*, which needed to be done here. But perhaps after that she would return to America.

They had sent the final lines of the index for *Zen Dust* to the printer. In 1965 a shorter version of the book, titled *The Zen Koan*—without the voluminous notes and appendices—was published in Japan first, directly by the First Zen Institute, and then by Harcourt in New York. The hardcover full edition would arrive shortly. It was the first scholarly examination in any language of the historical development and traditional method of koan study in Zen Buddhism, with an introductory history of Rinzai Zen written by Ruth, followed by the translated talks of Isshu Miura. Part 3 presented translations of two hundred jakugo phrases, and part 4 a collection of zenga drawings by Hakuin Ekaku done in 1686, followed by the massive notes and bibliography, which included extensive biographical and historical details. They planned to print fifteen hundred copies of *Zen Dust* and a thousand copies of *The Zen Koan*. After problems and delays with the printing, it finally found its way into the world; the initial print run sold out quickly.

Ruth and Washino took a trip to Europe and the United States to meet with the printers and publishers. The day after they returned, in April 1965, Goto Zuigan Roshi died. Every other activity was suspended for the weeks of ceremonies in his honor.

Ruth had never quite completed her koan training. After the break and repair with Goto, she returned to sanzen, but he was frail, and she had reached a place in herself where it no longer seemed personally important. The important thing was simply that kind human relations were restored. That was what mattered. It had never been her purpose to become a teacher. In any case, she had gone far enough, nearly to the end, far enough to perform the task of accurately translating as many koans as she needed to include in the books. Other people would continue and extend the work she had started. Would they do it as well as she? At a certain point, it was beyond her control. She had done her part—and would keep going, as long as she was still alive.

With Goto Roshi gone, Walter Nowick moved back to Maine. Before he left Kyoto, he came for a long visit with Ruth. They acknowledged each other. There was peace between them. There was mutual respect. They were friends again.

In July 1966 Ruth's first Zen teacher, Daisetz Teitaro Suzuki, died at the age of ninety-five. He had continued working nearly to the end of his life.

Ruth and Washino-san decided to sleep in the Kokusai Hotel during the winter months in order to have warmer rooms and a warmer place to bathe—hoping to avoid the long sieges of bronchitis that had become a chronic problem during the winter.

In April 1966 Ruth and Washino went to Europe to visit with many people who had come to Ryosen-an over the years and also to talk with printers. While there, Ruth caught pneumonia and had to skip the London part of the trip. They returned to Japan in September.

She collapsed in her bath. It had all caught up with her. The deep fatigue from her work and her travels. Exhaustion. It was too hot, that first bath when she came home after a trip—this was home— her household greeting her, welcoming her home. "Sasaki-san, the bath is ready."

It was too hot. The first bath was always too hot. She lowered herself in. It was so hot it felt like ice. She felt faint. She did not remember anything else.

It was probably a small stroke. Washino-san, who was standing nearby with a towel, called out and with help from one of the kitchen girls got Ruth out of the bath.

It took weeks for her to be able to do more than sit in the garden or lie down to rest.

A few days later, Oda Sesso Roshi died.

> I must say that I look forward with increasing longing
> to the day when my work here is completed. We are
> having a beautiful, though rather cold, autumn and are
> promised a warm winter. I hope it keeps reasonably
> warm until we leave here, as I don't want to go through
> an entire winter of the cold and damp that are normal
> here. I admit to longing for a comfortable bathroom
> with steam heat and running hot water, at least in the
> winter time.
>
> And I long for my friends.

In January 1967, Ruth wrote to her lifelong friend Blanche Matthias, "I'm much better, I'm happy to say, but still must budget my strength. I try to work on the new book for three or four hours a day." For the winter, she and Washino again moved to the hotel to sleep—days were spent at Ryosen-an, though inside the library it was often only forty-five degrees at 9:00 a.m.

In July 1967 Ruth went with Washino to San Francisco to see Blanche, and then to Colorado Springs to housesit for Eleanor and Carlton and look after their dogs while they were vacationing in Europe. Even in summer, in the dry air of Colorado, she was unable to shake her bronchitis. She was exhausted. She got some rest before going on to New York and Europe, and came back to Kyoto in the middle of October. "I have been saying I was tired to the marrow of my bones . . . but my mind remains too clear and active if anything."

She wrote to Blanche, "There are tears, rising from many different emotions, in my eyes as I say a last thank you for everything, yes everything!"

The bath was too hot.

On October 24, 1967, Ruth died suddenly of a heart attack. She and Washino had just returned to Ryosen-an. It was a week before her seventy-fifth birthday.

ZEN ASH, ZEN BONES
Kyoto, 1967

The rain came down in torrents. But Eleanor was expecting that. Kanaseki was there at the Osaka airport to meet her. He was a welcome sight. However much she was expecting him to be there, it was still a relief and comfort that it was him—the best of all of them, quietly competent and relaxed and funny. Not that this was a time for laughter. When they arrived in Kyoto, there were Washino-san and Tanemoto-san, two old women waiting up at this late hour, almost midnight, dismal and weepy—not unexpected. And two priests from the Daitoku-ji Honzan, and the whole zendo crew. That was unexpected.

It turned out they were keeping constant vigil, chanting sutras and burning incense around the clock in the library, where the body was lying in state. Her mother. Packed in dry ice to keep the body from decaying before the cremation ceremony could be held, awaiting Eleanor's arrival. There were flowers all around. She stayed up until four thirty talking to Washino.

It was pouring rain, a typhoon that would not let up. In the morning the house began to fill up with priests, First Zen Institute members, friends, and neighbors, coming in for breakfast—Washino had hired a caterer—drinking tea, chattering, laughing, visiting, the undertaker shepherding people around according to rank. Finally at 3:00 p.m., Eleanor was escorted into the library and seated in a chair near the coffin. Surrounding the coffin was an exquisite temporary altar constructed of fresh green bamboo; a recent photo, with a black bow on the frame, stood on the coffin, which was draped with Ruth's koromo. Dozens of priests, easily more than a hundred guests in all, were gathered under the awnings on the veranda, outside the fully opened wall panels, making the library room like a stage, with the battering rain half-drowning out the sound of the eulogy and chanting.

Shortly after, as Eleanor was in a corner of the library talking to one of the institute board members, someone came up and put the ihai in her hands and brought her back over to the coffin, which was now bare. Assistants were rushing around with scissors cutting off all the flower heads and shoving them into people's hands, for tossing into the coffin, now open. There was cotton batting all around the body, so only the face showed. It was ghastly.

After more waiting and tea drinking, the cars arrived, and Eleanor went with the three officiating priests, Gary Snyder, and a few others, following the hearse up the hill behind Kinkaku-ji to the crematorium. There the coffin was hoisted onto an altar in a big, open building, amid more chanting and incense. And then the undertakers took it across the way to the ovens. They hung a nameplate above Number 5, opened the door, and slid her in.

It took about an hour to burn the body to ash and bone. The guests and Ruth's family waited. They drank tea and smoked. Eleanor wanted to make sure the wedding ring was included with the urn bound for New York, where half of her mother's ashes would be buried next to Sokei-an.

The small group was led back to the furnace building and gathered around a long metal stretcher, upon which were the bones, now a dull gray, still slightly warm. The undertaker gave everyone a large pair of chopsticks.

"What are these for?"

"Sorting. Here, two white porcelain urns. Here's a tooth. A skull plate. A thigh bone—what surprisingly small bones she had for so large a woman! These are the finger bones."

Eleanor was horrified. She took up her chopsticks and lifted a bone into one of the urns. The undertaker provided ongoing commentary—"yes, a rib, and that one is the tibia"—completely matter-of-fact, as if this were a perfectly normal thing to be doing. After half an hour of picking and sorting, both urns were filled—except for a single bone, the neck bone, which had been set aside for Eleanor to perform the honors. She placed it carefully on a piece of cotton in one of the urns; at that point she added the ring, which she had been carrying.

The urns were packed with cotton in wooden boxes and wrapped in white cloth. Washino and Eleanor each carried one back to Ryosen-an, where there was another short service, chanting and incense, in the study, where the priests had reassembled the green bamboo altar and placed the two boxes in the tokonoma.

Washino was still weepy in the morning. They spent the whole morning dealing with accounts—bills and assets, estimated expenditures. The entire business, including all the ceremonies, was expensive. It was customary to give money gifts to all the priest guests. And all the staff had to be paid through November, another month. By then hopefully the disarray would be cleared. No one knew how much money there was. The household accounts were all under the Zen Institute, with Ruth as the signatory, and it was unclear at first how soon any funds would be released. Three different people at the bank didn't know what to do with some checks that Ruth had written to Furuta Kazuhiro, who had been helping with the translation work in the library. The bankers didn't know what to do—they said it was all too difficult; they would have to hold an emergency conference and would call back on Monday.

Washino's brother arrived, and then Kanaseki, and they discussed Washino's future. The will provided her with whatever household items she wanted and money to live comfortably. She wanted to leave Ryosen-an as soon as possible. It was too painful to stay. They had been constant companions, she and Ruth, for the past fifteen years. Practically married. Though of course it wasn't at all like that—she was an employee, a servant. But still.

They decided to give Ruth's koromo and some of Sokei-an's woodcarvings to the New York institute. Washino brought in some things that she thought should go to Sokei-an's grandson Mineru—she and Ruth had visited him in San Francisco. Just a few weeks ago, in fact.

An old priest with a long white beard, one of Ruth's best friends at Daitoku-ji, came by and hollered sutras for two solid hours and then stopped for a well-sugared, milky cup of coffee and spent an hour reminiscing. Miura Roshi sent his disciples from Tokyo to pay his respects and make the customary gifts of money, food, and flowers. Eleanor tried to convince Washino that this money was meant to help defray expenses; Washino said they would lose face if they used it for that and must donate it to the local neighborhood aid society.

Miura had stayed in New York. He was the only one who could properly conduct the burial services there. Would he be willing, after all the bad feelings? There was no one else.

Walter arrived. That was a relief. Immediately he was drawn into the discussions of what to do about the big funeral coming up in two weeks—the actual burial, which would be conducted by the

Honzan. Walter said, "Yes, the Honzan takes care of it, but we have to prepare the guest list."

Washino thought the Honzan was spending too much money—they thought, everybody thought, Sasaki-san was a rich woman. So of course they would expect the biggest possible funeral. It was too much. Washino was beside herself, in tears again.

Walter was worried. "Have you come across any personal notebooks?"

"My mother never kept a diary."

"Not exactly a diary. Koan notes. Everyone makes them. No one should be able to use someone else's koan notes. We have to find them and destroy them."

"There's a locked filing cabinet in the study. Maybe they're in there."

"Is there a key? We need to find it."

"If anyone can turn up a key around here, it would be Washino."

Mary Farkas approached Miura to conduct the burial services in New York. He refused. He wanted nothing to do with Mary or the First Zen Institute of America. So Mary wondered if Eleanor and some of the institute members in Japan could approach him. If that made no headway, Eleanor would see if the Daitoku-ji Honzan would take the matter up with Shibayama Roshi at Nanzen-ji—Miura's ultimate boss. Ruth's friends in the Honzan—especially Kobori Sohaku, and Fukutomi Roshi, kancho of Daitoku-ji since Oda Sesso died—said that if Miura did not perform the service for Sasaki-san, he would be a very ungrateful friend and a very bad priest, and would completely lose face in Buddhist circles in all of Japan. One just doesn't act that way. It would be grounds to take his temple away.

After a break in the storms, the rains let loose again. Walter came over, and he and Eleanor spent hours going through stacks of papers. They found all of Ruth's private koan notebooks, simply buried under piles of papers and other books. They burned the koan notes. They also found Sokei-an's private koan book, which they packed up to send to his Dharma brother Eizan Roshi, as was proper.

The big funeral was November 13. Everything was in place. Fuku-tomi Roshi gave the eulogy. There was chanting and incense and vegetarian food. They buried the urn.

Two days later, Eleanor boarded a plane for the United States. She carried a suitcase full of papers, a burial urn containing a wedding ring on top of ash and bone from half a human body, and her mother's pearl earrings.

Gravestones of Sokei-an and Ruth, Woodlawn Cemetery, New York. Courtesy of Janica Anderson.

AFTERWORD

In 1966, over three weeks in the late spring, Gary Snyder recorded nine hours of interviews with Ruth Fuller Sasaki, on a reel-to-reel tape recorder he had brought with him upon returning to Japan after a recent trip to the United States.

They spoke of Ruth's life in Buddhism, of her earliest stay in Kyoto at Nanzen-ji, of Nanshinken Roshi. They spoke of her meeting Sokei-an and their life together—his teaching, his time in New York, the early days of the First Zen Institute, the war, his internment and release, their marriage. They spoke of Sokei-an's teacher Sokatsu Shaku, of temple Zen and lay Zen, of Zen coming to America, of Americans coming to Japan.

> I think we foreigners come with too many illusions, too many dreams of what we imagine Zen masters to be. On the other hand, I don't think people here demand enough of such people.

These recordings of Gary Snyder interviewing Ruth are the starting point of this book, as well as one of the primary sources.

After seven years as a research assistant in the psychology department at Harvard, Janica spent ten years as an instructor at Esalen

Institute, where she knew Alan Watts, Joseph Campbell, and many other teachers who came through there. Through Alan, Janica got to know his daughter Joan Watts. Joan told Janica about her grandmother Ruth—who reminded Janica of her own grandmother, who graduated from Wellesley in 1899.

After leaving Esalen, Janica started an audio publishing and preservation company, which she called Big Sur Tapes, beginning with the audio archive of Esalen.

Steven had spent a year in Asia before going to Boulder, Colorado, to attend the Naropa Institute (now Naropa University) and complete an MFA in writing, then moved to San Francisco. He responded to a classified ad, and ended up working for Janica in her publishing company. As Janica now had the capacity to transfer old reel-to-reel tapes to cassette and digital audio tape, Joan Watts gave the set of tapes containing the Gary Snyder–Ruth Sasaki interviews to her. After transferring the recordings, Janica had them transcribed. Steven edited the transcriptions. Janica sent a set of the cassettes to Gary Snyder.

Joan encouraged Janica to do a book about her grandmother, as Ruth's contribution to Zen Buddhism was relatively unknown at that point. Janica found Ruth's voice and life enchanting, and through listening, became intrigued by Sokei-an as well. She became more and more focused on researching their lives, seeking out more material, traveling across the country to see the places in Ruth's life and interview many of the people connected to Ruth, to find letters, and to visit the First Zen Institute of America in New York. She compiled hundreds of pages of notes, letters, newsletters, and photos. She had Anne and Joan Watts to ask questions of.

Janica created a draft of the book, but needed a skilled writer to turn the material into a viable manuscript. She turned to Steven, who wholeheartedly entered the project in 2013 to help bring it to completion.

Acknowledgments

Janica Anderson: This book would not have been written without the encouragement and ongoing support of Joan Watts. I spent many hours at Joan's art studio near my home, talking with her about Ruth. Joan and her sister Anne's love and respect for their grandmother profoundly engaged my heart in this work. Gary Snyder's sensitive interview of Ruth also drew me into the story.

I had a delightful visit with Walter Nowick in Surry, Maine, where he had formed Moonspring Hermitage. He took us to the shrine of his former Zen master in the woods; during our visit, there were Russian opera singers in residence.

I had a fruitful visit in Pennsylvania with Haru Yoshida, Ruth's tireless New York secretary while Ruth lived in Japan. Carlton Gamer in Colorado Springs, Eleanor's second husband, gave me a great many personal details that Ruth had confided to Eleanor. And I got to meet their son Michael and his wife Anna in Lakewood, Colorado.

The staff of the Hinsdale Historical Society were helpful finding the home Ruth grew up in, and information on Swan House, which Warren and Ruth built. Ann Grube, the current owner of Swan House, graciously let me wander the beautiful home and grounds and gave me a copy of the architectural drawings of the house. The Yale University Library was helpful in allowing me access to Ruth's letters to her very close friend Blanche Matthias.

I am very grateful to Michael Hotz at the First Zen Institute of America in New York for opening his files of letters, newsletters, photos, and newspaper clippings and allowing me to copy whatever I felt I needed. I spent a few days there, and he has continued to be helpful over time. I was fortunate during that visit to be able to see the brownstone purchased by Ruth for the institute, as it was on the market for sale and vacant.

Closer to home, my visits with Huston and Kendra Smith were very helpful and illuminating. I found it particularly interesting to hear Kendra's perceptions on Ruth's attitudes about visitors to Ryosen-an who were the wives of male Zen students. Peter Coyote has given me a lot of encouragement, which I have been very grateful for. The support of my husband Ted Anderson and good friends Linda New and Jeri Jacobson have helped carry me through the stressful times. Doris Ober has provided useful advice.

I am very grateful that Steven Schwartz came to work for me when I oversaw my publishing company Big Sur Tapes, and I got to know of his excellent writing skills, so that when I had pulled all of my hundreds of notes into a first draft, I had him to call on. I am also grateful that Steven took the initiative to return to the source material to pull out more of the story, and to enrich the text by filtering it through the lens of his personal practice.

Steven Schwartz: Thanks to Janica for pulling me back into this project after so many years and reawakening my interest in the story of Ruth and Sokei-an, to Sheryl Elshout for reading early chapters and offering helpful comments, and especially to my wife, Julia Perlman, and son, Nathan, for putting up with the demands of the work.

We would both like to thank the staff at Wisdom—Josh Bartok, Andy Francis (who showed early enthusiasm for the project), and particularly Laura Cunningham, whose steady support has been there for both of us throughout the final writing process.

NOTES

9 *I consider that the core of Buddhism:* Ruth Fuller Sasaki, interview by Gary Snyder (recorded on six reel-to-reel tapes), tape 1, side A. February–March 1966. Used by permission of the Estate of Ruth Fuller Sasaki.

11 *Please do not worry:* Ruth Fuller Sasaki, interview, tape 1, side A.

15 *roshi had agreed:* Ruth Fuller Sasaki, letter for November 1962 *Zen Notes*, newsletter of the First Zen Institute of America, ed. Mary Farkas, dated October 8, 1962.

15 *you begin with this:* Ruth Fuller Sasaki, letter for November 1962 Zen Notes, dated October 8, 1962.

18 *she went every night:* Ruth Fuller Sasaki, interview, tape 1, side A.

25 *He never drank sake:* Ruth Fuller Sasaki, interview, tape 1, side B.

27 *the feeling was wonderful:* Ruth Fuller Sasaki, interview, tape 1, side B.

29 *what she said in her speech:* Ruth Fuller Sasaki, interview, tape 1, side B.

35 *The Buddha he was to carve:* Ruth Fuller Sasaki, interview, tape 1, side B.

39 *a set of wooden doors:* Ruth Fuller Sasaki, interview, tape 5, side B.

42 *the dynamite work:* Shigetsu Sasaki, *Holding the Lotus to the Rock: The Autobiography of Sokei-an, America's First Zen Master*, ed. Michael Holtz (New York: First Zen Institute of America, 2002), 102.

43 *its first hint of light:* Ruth Fuller Sasaki, interview, tape 5, side B.

45 *My country?:* Sasaki, *Holding the Lotus*, 103.

47 *seventy-five dollars a week:* Sasaki, *Holding the Lotus*, 91.

49 *There was a sailor:* Sasaki, *Holding the Lotus*, 94.

61 *the stuffy, constricting rooms of Hinsdale:* Eleanor Everett (Watts) Gamer, unpublished writings. Collection of Joan Watts.

64 *memorize the dreams:* Sasaki, *Holding the Lotus*, 28, 29.

64 *infinite time and infinite power:* Sasaki, *Holding the Lotus*, 26.

65 *I have not been there yet:* Sasaki, *Holding the Lotus*, 26–27.

67 *this bruised toe:* Sasaki, *Holding the Lotus*, 40.

67 *the constant dwelling place:* Isshu Miura and Ruth Fuller Sasaki, *The Zen Koan: Its History and Use in Rinzai Zen*, with reproductions of ten drawings by Hakuin Ekaku (San Diego, New York, and London: Harcourt Brace, 1965).

69 *keep your strength in your nature:* Sasaki, *Holding the Lotus*, 45.

71 *Amida Buddha:* Ruth Fuller Sasaki, interview, tape 5, side B.

72 *he was not alone:* Sasaki, *Holding the Lotus*, 38.

72 *and that was all:* Sasaki, *Holding the Lotus*, 33.

75 *conceal their circumstances:* Ruth Fuller Sasaki, interview, tape 2, side A.

76 *and Sokei-an:* A fourth disciple, Ichimu-an Ohazama Chikudo, also received Sokei-an's Dharma transmission but died before the war, before becoming a teacber.

76 *treated both of them poorly:* Ruth Fuller Sasaki, interview, tape 2, side A.

84 *Chicago, St. Louis, and Omaha:* Isabel Stirling, *Zen Pioneer: The Life and Works of Ruth Fuller Sasaki* (Emeryville, CA: Shoemaker & Hoard, 2006), 4.

86 *she quelled her protests and acquiesced:* Joan Watts, interview by Janica Anderson, July 10, 2012.

86 *Plymouth Congregational Church in Chicago: Chicago Daily Tribune,* April 7, 1917.

90 *to help conceive a child:* Ruth Fuller Sasaki, interview, tape 5, side A.

91 *to be raised in his household:* Ruth Fuller Sasaki, interview, tape 5, side A.

91 *after the birth:* Ruth Fuller Sasaki, interview, tape 5, side A.

91 *absolutely devoted to her:* Ruth Fuller Sasaki, interview, tape 5, side A.

92 *in the uncle's place:* Ruth Fuller Sasaki, interview, tape 5, side B.

93 *he is not your friend:* Sokei-an Sasaki, *Original Nature: Zen Comments on the Sixth Patriarch's Platform Sutra,* Kindle ed. (iUniverse, 2012).

93 *it embraces everything:* Sasaki, *Original Nature,* 58.

93 *A few people came to listen:* Sasaki, *Holding the Lotus,* 36.

94 *a stone may hear:* Sasaki, *Holding the Lotus,* 36.

95 *living with her:* Ruth Fuller Sasaki, interview, tape 5, side B.

95 *Everyone on earth is pure!:* Sasaki, *Holding the Lotus,* 30.

95 *to his uncle's house:* Sasaki, *Holding the Lotus,* 44.

96 *his own pot:* Sasaki, *Holding the Lotus,* 36–37.

97 *He pounded the floor and wailed:* Ruth Fuller Sasaki, interview, tape 5, side B.

99 *wisdom in action:* Sasaki, *Holding the Lotus,* 124.

102 *never spoke to him again:* Sasaki, *Holding the Lotus,* 249.

103 *with his inka:* Sasaki, *Original Nature,* xvi.

103 *Sokei-en was reinstated:* Sasaki, *Holding the Lotus,* 250.

104 *It is too terrible:* Samuel Lewis, "Sufi Vision and Initiation: Meetings with Remarkable Beings," quoted in Sasaki, *Holding the Lotus,* 248.

105 *the shortcoming of individualism:* Sasaki, *Holding the Lotus,* 212.

105 *the seal of the Buddha's teaching:* Sasaki, *Holding the Lotus,* 128.

105 *a precious thing:* Sasaki, *Holding the Lotus,* 215–16.

105 *That is all:* Sasaki, *Holding the Lotus,* 136.

108 *his bluff assertive exterior:* Archive of the First Zen Institute of America.

113 *in our next meeting:* Stirling, *Zen Pioneer,* 22.

114 *among the deaf and mute:* Sasaki, *Holding the Lotus,* 143.

119 *the tomato sandwiches that he loved:* Stirling, *Zen Pioneer,* 24.

120 *everyday activity: Zen Notes,* December 1967 and January 1968.

121 *retreat from the world:* Ruth Fuller Sasaki, letter for August 1960 *Zen Notes,* dated July 5, 1962.

124 *an attempt to be eccentric:* Ruth Fuller Sasaki, interview, tape 5, side B.

126 *their pencils stopped moving:* Mary Farkas in Sokei-an Shigetsu Sasaki, *The Zen Eye: A Collection of Zen Talks,* ed. Mary Farkas (Tokyo and New York: Weatherhill, 1993), ix–x.

127 *not by force but by practice:* Sasaki, *Original Nature,* 131.

127 *absorbed in Reality:* Sasaki, *Original Nature,* 134.

128 *for all to see:* Farkas in Sasaki, *Zen Eye,* ix–x.

129 *the first stage:* Sasaki, *Original Nature,* 135.

129 *what he was experiencing:* Ruth Fuller Sasaki, interview, tape 3, side A.

130 *but relaxed and alert:* Farkas in Sasaki, *Zen Eye,* ix–x.

131 *The plum tree is living:* Sasaki, *Original Nature,* 137.

138 *He did not risk it:* Alan Watts, *In My Own Way* (New York: Pantheon Books, 1972), 106.

141 *the Library of International Relations:* Carlton Gamer, handwritten chronology of Eleanor's life. Provided to Janica Anderson by Carlton Gamer.

142 *forget these things:* George Woodhouse, *The Artist at the Piano* (London: Novello, 1910), 5.

144 *getting out of it:* Watts, *In My Own Way,* 152–53.

144 *the rest of his life:* Watts, *In My Own Way,* 153.

145 *the Thames on fire:* Monica Furlong, *Zen Effects: The Life of Alan Watts* (Woodstock, VT: SkyLight Paths, 2001), 67.

148 *the blood had been drained:* Eleanor Everett (Watts) Gamer, unpublished writings and reminiscences. Collection of Joan Watts.

152 *would never leave her:* E. Gamer, unpublished writings.

158 *any vestige of delusion:* Ruth Fuller Sasaki, interview, tape 3, side A.

159 *director of the First Zen Institute:* Sasaki, *Holding the Lotus,* 257–58.

160 *arose and were quelled:* Mary Farkas eulogy for Ruth Fuller Sasaki, from *Zen Notes,* December 1967–January 1968.

162 *greatly impressed Alan:* Watts, *In My Own Way,* 137.

163 *my own pure mind:* Sasaki, *Zen Eye,* 164.

170 *for the first time:* Watts, *In My Own Way,* 167.

175 *outlandish dancing:* Watts, *In My Own Way,* 183.

176 *something for you:* Watts, *In My Own Way,* 148.

179 *would not be here today:* Sasaki, *Holding the Lotus,* 201.

179 *struggles, wars:* Commentary on *Sutra of Perfect Awakening,* given September 27, 1939, published in *Zen Notes* 56, no. 4 (fall 2009).

183 *to be a human being:* Ruth Fuller Sasaki, interview, tape 6, side A.

185 *aches my heart:* Sasaki, *Holding the Lotus,* 203.

188 *the whole group:* Sasaki, *Holding the Lotus,* 258.

188 *Alice in the Wonderland:* Sasaki, *Holding the Lotus,* 205.

194 *very kind to me:* Sasaki, *Holding the Lotus,* 208.

199 *Your father sends his regards:* A number of letters preserved in the archive of the First Zen Institute of America are typed carbon copies; therefore they bear no signature.

199 *what that camp was like:* Sasaki, *Holding the Lotus,* 210.

212 *Sokei-an accepted this offering:* Mary Farkas, quoted in Sasaki, *Original Nature,* xvii.

213 *The only way:* Edna Kenton notes, quoted in Sasaki, *Zen Eye,* xx.

214 *I vow to attain it:* Sasaki, *Original Nature,* 169.

215 *the seal of the Buddha's teaching:* Sasaki, *Holding the Lotus,* 128.

224 *in our time:* Sasaki, *Holding the Lotus,* 256.

224 *to be effective:* Sasaki, *Holding the Lotus,* 255.

238 *much hard work:* Ruth Fuller Sasaki unpublished letter, "Dear Fellow Students," January 23, 1950. Archive of the First Zen Instititute.

244 *evening sanzen: Zen Notes,* April 1955.

247 *their fresh fire: Zen Notes,* January 1954.

253 *demanded and could instill:* Ruth Fuller Sasaki to Goto Roshi, June 19, 1950.

253 *for six months:* Ruth Fuller Sasaki to Goto Roshi, June 19, 1950.

257 *He stayed:* Soko Morinaga, *Novice to Master: An Ongoing Lesson in the Extent of My Own Stupidity* (Boston: Wisdom Publications, 2002).

260 *measured or assessed: Young East* 1, no. 1 (1952): 11–16.

262 *of that "Nothing":* Ruth Fuller Sasaki to "Fellow Students," May 11, 1952. Archive of the First Zen Institute of America.

264 *she ever saw him:* Ruth Fuller Sasaki, interview, tape 2, side B; Ruth Fuller Sasaki letter to First Zen Institute, "Dear Everyone," July 19, 1954. Archive of the First Zen Institute of America.

265 *in Hartford, Connecticut:* "Lindley Williams Hubbell: A Memoir by Yoko Danno," *The Montserrat Review,* 1999. http://www.themontserratreview.com/bookreviews/LWilliamsHubbell.html (retrieved April 1, 2016).

270 *its supporting culture:* Gary Snyder to Ruth Fuller Sasaki, May 3, 1953. Archive of the First Zen Institute of America.

272 *Zen in Japan:* Ruth Fuller Sasaki to Gary Snyder, June 10, 1953. Archive of the First Zen Institute of America.

272 *to men in all lands:* Zen Notes, August 1955.

273 *the study of Zen seriously:* Ruth Fuller Sasaki, "Letter from Kyoto," *Zen Notes*, August 1955.

274 *as a dishwasher in the galley:* Ruth Fuller Sasaki to Gary Snyder, January 8, 1956.

277 *hold her own with anyone:* Stirling, *Zen Pioneer*, xii–xiii.

278 *admiration for Ruth and Walter:* Ruth Fuller Sasaki letter to First Zen Institute of America, "Dear Everyone," October 22, 1955.

278 *temple occasion of the year:* Ruth Fuller Sasaki letter to First Zen Institute of America, "Dear Everyone," November 11, 1955.

278 *of flowing vitality:* Mary Farkas, Kyoto diary, November 19, 1955.

279 *its essential quality:* Farkas, diary, November 22, 1955.

280 *nothing can be accomplished:* Farkas, diary, November 23, 1955.

280 *resounding through the hall:* Farkas, diary, November 22, 1955.

282 *use standard Japanese:* Gary Snyder, *Evergreen Review* 1, no. 3 (1957): 132.

284 *make the best of it:* Ruth Fuller Sasaki to Blanche Matthias, June 14, 1956.

285 *enlarge your experience:* Huston Smith, interview by Janica Anderson. This story is one retold many times by Huston Smith, in often very similar terms, with slight variations: for example in Bill Moyers's *The Wisdom of Faith with Huston Smith*, "Hinduism and Buddhism" (1996; transcript at http://billmoyers.com/content/wisdom-faith-hinduism-buddhism/, retrieved August 6, 2017); Huston Smith with Phil Cosineau, *And Live Rejoicing: Chapters from a Charmed Life* (Novato, CA: New World Library, 2012), 49–55; and Huston Smith and Jeffrey Paine, *The Huston Smith Reader* (Berkeley, CA: UC Press, 2012), 86–87.

285 *enveloped the room:* Smith and Paine, *Huston Smith Reader*, 86–87.

286 *immerse themselves in Zen:* Huston and Kendra Smith, interview by Janica Anderson.

286 *I am glad you came:* Smith and Paine, *Huston Smith Reader*, 86–87.

287 *sit on zabutons:* Ruth Fuller Sasaki to Mary Farkas, December 9, 1956.

288 *French champagne:* Ruth Fuller Sasaki to Blanche Matthias, December 20, 1956.

288 *returned directly to sitting:* Ruth Fuller Sasaki to Mary Farkas, December 9, 1956.

288 *know who they are:* Zen Notes, January 1957.

292 *took their leave:* Zen Notes, June 1957.

292 *with no explanation:* Ruth Fuller Sasaki to Gary Fowler, Sam Reiser, and Mary Farkas, June 10, 1957.

292 *considered him her teacher:* Mary Farkas to Miura Roshi, August 8, 1957.

293 *Water-Moon Hall:* Zen Notes, September 1957.

295 *the best we can do:* Ruth Fuller Sasaki reporting on "developments" from discussions with First Zen Institute attorney (unidentified) in Kyoto, and corresponding negotiations with Daitoku-ji Honzan, to members of the council (Farkas, Fowler, Reiser), April 2, 1958.

303 *might never cease:* Zen Notes, July 1958.

304 *on the Mumonkan koans:* Zen Notes, July 1959.

305 *to greet her:* Zen Notes, June 1959.

307 *of daily life:* Zen Notes, June 1959.

309 *Saying says something:* Chang Tzu, *Inner Chapters.* Trans. A. C. Graham (Cambridge, MA: Hackett Classics, 2001), 52.

310 *more to do here:* Ruth Fuller Sasaki to Haru Yoshida, February 1957.

310 *without giving up effort:* Zen Notes, April 1957.

310 *sense of a separate self:* Zen Notes, October 1957.

311 *from her translations:* Zen Notes, November 1957.

313 *Yanagida Seizan:* Called Yokoi Seizan prior to 1959, when he was adopted into his wife's family, after which time he has been known as Yanagida Seizan.

313 *multiple names:* Zen Notes, January 1958.

314 *a joint translation:* Ruth Fuller Sasaki, "Publications Committee Report" to First Zen Institute of America, 1957.

314 *New York:* Zen Notes, October 1958.

315 *just the same "bums":* Ruth Fuller Sasaki to Gary Snyder, November 13, 1958.

321 *nature and the universe:* Ruth Fuller Sasaki to Blanche Matthias, collection housed at Beinecke Rare Book and Manuscript Library, Yale University, October 30, 1960.

321 *he certainly does:* Ruth Fuller Sasaki to Blanche Mattias, October 30, 1960.

324 *working with him:* Ruth Fuller Sasaki to Mary Farkas, December 30, 1961.

326 *west and east:* Stirling, *Zen Pioneer*, xiii.

326 *could be grating:* Joanne Kyger, *Strange Big Moon* (Berkeley, CA: North Atlantic Books, 2000).

326 *Mary Farkas:* Ruth Fuller Sasaki to Mary Farkas, December 30, 1961.

327 *Park Avenue: Zen Notes*, July 1962.

328 *comfortable in his position:* Ruth Fuller Sasaki to First Zen Institute of America Council members, June 12, 1962.

328 *pleased with the timing:* Ruth Fuller Sasaki to Blanche Mattias, December 2, 1962.

329 *How grateful I am:* Ruth Fuller Sasaki to Blanche Mattias, December 2, 1962.

331 *and your tongue:* Ruth Fuller Sasaki to Blanche Mattias, November 3, 1963.

333 *or callous severity: Zen Notes*, September 1962.

336 *for my friends:* Ruth Fuller Sasaki to Blanche Mattias, October 31, 1965.

336 *three or four hours a day:* Ruth Fuller Sasaki to Blanche Matthias, January 1967.

336 *too clear and active if anything:* Ruth Fuller Sasaki to Blanche Matthias, September 24, 1967.

337 *yes everything:* Ruth Fuller Sasaki to Blanche Matthias, September 24, 1967.

339 *a welcome sight:* This section is based almost entirely on Eleanor Gamer's letters to Carlton Gamer, October–November 1967.

PUBLISHED WORKS

by Sokei-an and Ruth Fuller Sasaki

SOKEI-AN'S PUBLISHED WORKS

Amerika yawa (Night Talks about America). Tokyo: n.p., 1922.

Ananda and Mahakasyapa. New York: n.p., 1931.

Beikoku o horo shite (Vagabond in America). Tokyo: n.p., 1921.

Cat's Yawn. New York: First Zen Institute of America, 1940–1941.

Doru no nyoninzo (Portrait of the Dollar Woman). Tokyo: n.p., 1928.

Hentai magaiko (Thoughts on the Red-Light District). Tokyo: n.p., 1928.

Jonan bunka no kuni kara (From the Land Troubled by Women). Tokyo: n.p., 1927.

Kane to onna kara mita Beikoku oyobi Beikokujin (America and Americans Seen from the View of Money and Women). Tokyo: n.p., 1921.

Kyoshu (Homesickness [poetry collection]). Tokyo: n.p., 1918.

Original Nature: Zen Comments on the Sixth Patriarch's Platform Sutra. Mary Farkas, Robert Lopez, Peter Haskel, eds. Bloomington: iUniverse, 2012.

Three-Hundred-Mile Tiger: The Record of Lin-Chi. Mary Farkas, Robert Lopez, Peter Haskel, eds. Bloomington: iUniverse, 2013.

Zen Eye: A Collection of Zen Talks. Mary Farkas, ed. New York: Weatherhill, 1993.

Zen Pivots: Lectures on Buddhism and Zen. Mary Farkas and Robert Lopez, eds. New York: Weatherhill, 2000.

SOKEI-AN WAS ALSO A REGULAR CONTRIBUTOR TO:

Chuokoron, Tokyo

Hokubei Shippo, New York.

Great Northern Daily News, Seattle.

RUTH FULLER SASAKI'S PUBLISHED WORKS

The Development of Chinese Zen After the Sixth Patriarch in the Light of the Mumonkan, by Heinrich Dumoulin. As trans. New York: First Zen Institute of America, 1953.

A Man of Zen: The Recorded Sayings of the Layman P'ang: A Ninth-Century Zen Classic. As trans., with Yoshitaka Iriya and Dana R. Fraser. New York: Weatherhill, 1992.

Rinzai Zen Study for Foreigners in Japan. Kyoto: First Zen Institute of America in Japan, 1960.

Zen: A Method for Religious Awakening. Kyoto: First Zen Institute of America in Japan, 1959.

Zen: A Religion. New York: First Zen Institute of America, 1963.

Zen Dust: The History of the Koan and Koan Study in Rinzai (Linchi) Zen. As trans., with Miura Isshu. New York: Harcourt Brace & World, 1966. (Eight lectures by Miura Isshu, translated from Japanese with notes and appendices by Ruth Fuller Sasaki.)

The Zen Koan: Its History and Use in Rinzai Zen. With Isshu Miura. Kyoto: First Zen Institute of America, and New York: Harcourt Brace & World, 1965.

Sources for *Zen Odyssey*

Abe, Masao, ed. *A Zen Life: D. T. Suzuki Remembered.* Tokyo and New York: Weatherhill, 1986.

Chicago Daily Tribune society pages: February 15, 1915; February 10, 1917; April 7, 1917; April 15, 1917.

Everett, Edward Warren. *Far East for 90 Days: Narrative of a Trip to Japan and China in 1930.* Chicago: Central Manufacturing District Magazine, 1930.

Farkas, Mary. Personal writings. Archive of the First Zen Institute of America.

Farkas, Mary, ed. *Zen Notes.* Newsletter of the First Zen Institute of America, 1954–1964.

Fields, Rick. *How the Swans Came to the Lake.* 3rd ed. Boston: Shambhala Publications, 1992.

Furlong, Monica. *Zen Effects: The Life of Alan Watts.* Woodstock, VT: SkyLight Paths, 2001.

Gamer, Carlton. Interview by Janica Anderson. Colorado, July 2003, and other dates.

Gamer, Eleanor Everett (Watts). Unpublished writings and reminiscences. Personal collection of Joan Watts.

Gamer, Michael, and Anna Gamer. Interview by Janica Anderson. Colorado, July 2003.

Haru Yoshida. Interview by Janica Anderson. Pennsylvania, May 2003.

Hoover, Thomas. *The Zen Experience*. New York: Plume, 1980.

Hotz, Michael. Interview by Janica Anderson. New York, June 2003.

Kyger, Joanne. *Strange Big Moon*. Berkeley, CA: North Atlantic Books, 2000.

Miura, Isshu, and Ruth Fuller Sasaki. *The Zen Koan: Its History and Use in Rinzai Zen*, with reproductions of ten drawings by Hakuin Ekaku. San Diego, New York, London: Harcourt Brace & Company, 1965.

Morinaga, Soko. *Novice to Master: An Ongoing Lesson in the Extent of My Own Stupidity*. Boston: Wisdom Publications, 2002.

Nowick, Walter. Interview by Janica Anderson. Maine, June 2005.

Sasaki, Ruth Fuller. "Dear Everyone" letters, included in *Zen Notes*, 1954–1964.

Sasaki, Ruth Fuller. Letters. Personal collection of Joan Watts, and Archives of the First Zen Institute of America.

Sasaki, Ruth Fuller. Letters to Blanche Matthias. Beinecke Rare Book and Manuscript Library, Yale University.

Sasaki, Ruth Fuller. "Night on the Rigi," essay published in the *Lampadion*, Kenwood Institute yearbook, 1911.

Sasaki, Ruth Fuller. Nine-hour interview by Gary Snyder. Six reel-to-reel tapes. Recorded February–March 1966.

Sasaki, Shigetsu. *Holding the Lotus to the Rock: The Autobiography of Sokei-an, America's First Zen Master.* Edited by Michael Hotz. New York: First Zen Institute of America, 2002.

Sasaki, Sokei-an Shigetsu. *The Zen Eye: A Collection of Zen Talks.* Edited by Mary Farkas. Tokyo and New York: Weatherhill, 1993.

Sasaki, Sokei-an Shigetsu. *Zen Pivots: Lectures on Buddhism and Zen.* Edited by Mary Farkas and Robert Lopez. Tokyo and New York: Weatherhill, 1998.

Sasaki, Sokei-an, trans. *Original Nature: Zen Comments on the Sixth Patriarch's Platform Sutra.* Edited by Mary Farkas, Robert Lopez, and Peter Haskel. Kindle edition. iUniverse, 2012.

Smith, Huston, and Kendra Smith. Interview by Janica Anderson. California, August 2005.

Stirling, Isabel. *Zen Pioneer: The Life and Works of Ruth Fuller Sasaki.* Emeryville, CA: Shoemaker & Hoard, 2006.

Stuart, David. *Alan Watts.* New York: Stein & Day, 1992.

Suzuki, D. T. *Essays on Zen Buddhism.* London: Rider, 1927.

Watts, Alan. *In My Own Way.* New York: Pantheon Books, 1972.

Watts, Anne. Interviews by Janica Anderson. California, 2003–2016.

Watts, Joan. Interviews by Janica Anderson. Montana, 2000–2016.

Wind Bell 8, nos. 1–2 (fall 1969). Zen Center of San Francisco.

Glossary of Japanese Terms

BENTO. Lunch, with rice and vegetables (pickled or cooked), and usually fish or meat; also the special compartmentalized tray used to carry such a meal.

BUTSUDAN. Buddha altar.

DOJO. Training center, schoolhouse.

GASSHO. Bow, with palms together in front of chest, signifying gratitude, respect, acceptance.

GETA. Traditional wooden sandals, with an elevated wooden base and cloth thong.

HAIBUTSU KISHAKU. Literally "destroy Buddhism, kill Shakyamuni"—the wave of anti-Buddhist persecution and temple destruction in early Meiji Japan.

HOJO. The living quarters of the head priest at a Zen temple.

HONDO. The main hall of a Zen temple.

IEMOTO. The founder or head of a family-based traditional art, such as tea ceremony.

IHAI. Stone memorial tablet.

IKEBANA. Traditional Japanese flower arranging; one of the five traditional arts expected of a roshi, according to Sokatsu Shaku.

INKA. The final authorization of a Zen master to begin teaching.

INRYO. A roshi's private rooms.

JAKUGO. Capping phrases, verses traditionally selected from the *Zenrin-kushu* and delivered by the student upon definitively passing a koan, particularly in the advanced phases of koan practice.

KAMI. Japanese nature spirits/deities, often associated with a particular place or natural feature (such as a mountain); the basis of Shinto.

KANCHO. The abbot of a Zen temple; a roshi may serve as kancho, or the offices may be separate.

KENSHO. An enlightenment experience; seeing into one's own true nature; in Rinzai Zen, associated with successful mastery of a koan.

KESA. Zen priest's robes, made from patchwork, in continuity with the original garments worn by the Buddha and his followers, worn for zazen and ceremonial occasions as the outermost garment.

KOJI. A layperson engaged in Zen practice.

KOROMO. Traditional robes worn by ordained monks.

MATSU-JI. Branch temple.

NISEI. Second-generation Japanese American (American-born child of Japanese immigrants).

NYOI. Ceremonial baton held by a roshi.

OBASAN. Auntie (*obaasan* = grandmother).

OJISAN. Uncle (*ojiisan* = grandfather).

ONJI. Servant; personal cook.

OSESSHIN or SESSHIN. Intensive meditation retreat period, typically seven days, observed with strict protocols.

RAIHAI. Full prostration before the butsudan or roshi.

RAKUSA. Mini-kesa, a small cloth patchwork panel with a neck loop, worn by ordained priests in place of the full kesa on less formal occasions.

SAMU. Monastic work practice; manual labor performed as meditation.

SANZEN. Private interview between roshi and student, in which the student attempts to answer a koan.

SATORI. Literally "understanding"; experience of sudden enlightenment, considered an initial step; roughly synonymous with kensho, often used interchangeably.

SEIZA. Traditional Japanese kneeling posture.

SHAMISEN. Traditional Japanese stringed instrument.

SHOJI. Paper screens used to divide rooms.

SODO. Monks' hall; the temple building used for monastic training, where monks meditate, eat, and sleep.

SUMI-E. Ink painting.

TAN. Raised platform in a sodo or zendo, on which meditators sit for zazen.

TATAMI. Straw mats.

TEISHO. Teaching lecture, traditionally based on a text.

TENZO. Head cook in a monastery or temple.

TOKONOMA. Formal display area in a traditional Japanese house or temple.

YOZASHIKE. An outer, private room in a traditional Japanese house, with screen walls that may be removed to open the room fully.

ZABUTON. Wide cushion used for zazen, placed directly on the floor, tatami, or raised tan, with the zafu set on top.

ZAFU. Round, firm cushion used for zazen.

ZAZEN. Seated meditation.

ZENDO. Meditation hall.